THE DELTA DOGS

- - - o - - -

by

Major George A. Durgin

The Delta Dogs by George Durgin

Published by:
>
> GMD Distribution Co.
> 4464 La Quinta Place
> Oceanside, CA 92057-5055

ISBN   978-0-9815144-1-3
ISBN Paperback   978-0-9815144-2-1

Library of Congress Control Number: **2008900686**

Printer in the United States of America
First printing, 2009.
Second printing, 2010.
Third printing, 2012
Fourth printing, 2014
Fifth printing, 2016
Sixth printing, 2017

ACKNOWLEDGMENTS

The names, locations, and actions are as recorded during the 1969 Tet offensive in Vietnam with three exceptions. The names of Lieutenant Bird, Captain Walters and Lieutenant Colonel Elliott are fictitious names for obvious reasons.

I want to thank all the contributors and all the Delta Dogs. Those who contributed to this memoir are Bart Brevik, Chris Collins, Dan Brings, Joe Dodson, Larky Evans, Roger Faust, David Giles, George Henke, Ronnie Janes, Barbara Javor, Vera Jonath, Lola Kay, Don Prochaska, Merlin Puck, Nancy Ralston, Inez Strange, and Bill Terry.

The author as a Private First Class in Fort Bragg, North Carolina as a member of the 82nd Airborne Division.

PREFACE

In a world of billions of people, how much significance is there to the suffering or loss of one life? Probably none of importance. However, when the one life is that of a loved one, the life lost has a tragically profound affect. When the young heroes described in this book, whom I knew and fought along side, came home unscathed, wounded, or in a box, few Americans knew the details of their ordeal. I wrote *THE DELTA DOGS* from the journal I kept so the families and friends of these brave young men would know what they endured and the sacrifices these men made for their country.

It might have been difficult for the loved ones to understand what these men suffered, since they probably didn't share their traumatic experiences when they returned. It would have been hard for them to share, for only combat veterans understand the secret, seldom spoken language of loss that we infantrymen felt. I know. When I wrote these memoirs it was difficult for me to relive those challenging times.

Before writing this book, I had written several letters to family members of fallen Delta Company soldiers. However, over the last thirty-five years the families had moved, and I could not reach all of them. I hope that this historical memoir will somehow enable folks close to these men to finally understand how much they endured during their service as infantrymen in Vietnam.

This is the story of **THE DELTA DOGS** of Company D, Third Battalion, First Infantry, Eleventh Light Infantry Brigade, Twenty-Third American Division during a few months of their 1969 battlefield engagement in Vietnam during the 1969 Tet offensive.

While reading this book, to better understand the jargon and to get a feel for what we experienced, please refer to the Glossary in the back of the book for the slang and acronyms used.

> Major George A. Durgin
> United States Army, Retired

v

**Major George A. Durgin, US Army, Retired,
in the army tuxedo, called the Mess Uniform.**

Major Unit Locations

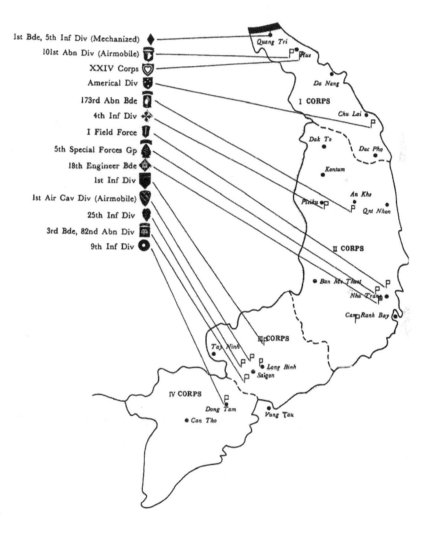

1st Bde, 5th Inf Div (Mechanized)
101st Abn Div (Airmobile)
XXIV Corps
Americal Div
173rd Abn Bde
4th Inf Div
I Field Force
5th Special Forces Gp
18th Engineer Bde
1st Inf Div
1st Air Cav Div (Airmobile)
25th Inf Div
3rd Bde, 82nd Abn Div
9th Inf Div

Quang Tri
Hue
Da Nang
I CORPS
Chu Lai
Dak To
Duc Pho
Kontum
An Khe
Pleiku
Qui Nhon
II CORPS
Ban Me Thuot
Nha Trang
Cam Ranh Bay
III CORPS
Tay Ninh
Long Binh
Saigon
IV CORPS
Dong Tam
Can Tho
Vung Tau

Large map of Duc Pho and the surrounding area.

Chapter One

Private First Class Roger Wilson
Private First Class Steven Hill
Specialist Fourth Class Marcos Rodriguez
Specialist Fourth Class Michael S. Jarmus
Specialist Fourth Class Robert Lombardo

"Whump, whump, whump," the sound of the helicopter blades was deafening. I jumped out with my rifle and my backpack, which was filled with everything I needed to survive for three days. The dust and dirt that swirled around in the dry rice paddy was even more annoying than the whirl of the spinning blades. As the chopper lifted back into the air, the temporary commander of my new infantry company came out from his defensive position to meet me in the hot, humid, dusty open field. I had just arrived in Hell. My clean, crisp, uniform was in stark contrast to the stained, dirty uniforms of the men I was joining. I felt like the football player who was substituted into the game for his first play during the last few minutes of a football game played on a muddy field.

First Lieutenant (Lt.) Bird was the unit's senior officer in the field. He had been commanding the infantry company for a couple days, ever since the previous company commander had been evacuated to the rear. Lt. Bird knew I'd be arriving this day to take command of Company D.

I had spent the morning meeting the company personnel in the rear base-camp. In the field I met the officers who commanded the three rifle platoons and the sergeant commanding the weapons platoon. I also met First Lieutenant Faust, the company Artillery Forward Observer. After quick introductions, I ordered the company to resume the search-

1

and-destroy mission they had been conducting before I arrived.

I had previously commanded a reconnaissance platoon, a cavalry troop, and a headquarters company. I must say, however, I didn't expect to command an infantry company when I was sent to Vietnam. In preparation for Vietnam service I completed jungle training in Panama, tactical jungle training in Chu Lai, Vietnam, and three days in the field with another infantry company near the village of Duc Pho. After all that preparation, I was assigned to command this infantry company.

The arrival of a new commanding officer changed nothing for the soldiers. The sweating, tired infantrymen of Company D continued to patrol the area they had been assigned. I trudged along with them in no-man's-land. We conducted the search-and-destroy mission in the rice paddies in the Quang Ngai Province of South Vietnam. The Americans called this area I-Corps, the zone farthest north and closest to the demilitarized zone (DMZ) that divided North and South Vietnam.

After an uneventful day and just before 1600 hours (four in the afternoon), the battalion frequency net radio blared, "Delta Six, this is Hotel Three, over."

I grabbed the handset from Mac, my radio telephone operator, and replied, "Hotel Three, this is Delta Six, over."

His call sign told me I was speaking with Major Vaughn, the battalion operations officer.

"This is Hotel Three. Return to Lima Zulu by Baker, X-ray, Romeo, Lima, over."

"Roger, out," I responded, acknowledging the order. Then, I quickly checked the daily Signal Operating Instructions (SOI) to decode the message. The radio communication was an order to return to our base-camp, Landing Zone (LZ) Bronco, by 1700 hours.

I turned to Joe, my company radio net operator and ordered, "Inform the platoons we are stopping for a break. After they establish security, have the platoon leaders join me."

While he was radioing the message to the platoons, I told Mac, "Tell Midge and Doc," two other men in my company command group, "we are going to take a break."

Mac acknowledged my order, "Roger that," and then he dropped his radio and pack to take a much needed break. Mac plopped down on the ground and relayed the good news to the other two men. Lt. Faust and I also dropped our backpacks and took a break in the shade while I studied my topographical map. I determined LZ Bronco's back gate was closer to our position than the main entrance to the base-camp.

The company had already maneuvered over 6,000 meters, or almost four miles, during the search-and-destroy mission. I knew we had to move fast to make it to the base-camp by the required time. Trekking through no-man's-land was a slow and dangerous excursion. Each step had to be checked for booby-traps and spike-filled-holes. We had to carefully survey the trail we were taking to be sure it was not an enemy kill-zone, a location which could be used to ambush us.

When the platoon leaders joined me, I told them of the order I had received. I asked if anyone knew how to get to LZ Bronco's back gate. I had only been in this battle zone for four days and only been in the field with my infantry company for two hours. I wasn't sure of the exact location of the back gate. We were southeast of the base-camp, and the main entrance was at the west end of Bronco. Since the base-camp was about the size of a small airport, with a diameter of 1,600 meters (about 1 mile), walking around to the main entrance would

3

have made us at least an hour late. I figured the back gate was the only way to make it on time.

No one in the company headquarters group and none of the platoon leaders knew where the location of the back entrance was. I asked the platoon leaders to check with their men when they rejoined them to see if anyone knew. After they returned to their units, they each reported that none knew the location. While I was being flown out to join the company, I had observed as much of the area as I could from the chopper. I thought I had a general idea of where the back gate to the base-camp was located.

Since I appeared to be the most knowledgeable of the terrain around LZ Bronco, I gave the platoon leaders the order-of-march. My company headquarters command group would lead the column, followed by the First, the Second, and then the Third Platoon. The Weapons Platoon would follow up in the rear. My company command group consisted of seven other soldiers, consisting of two radio telephone operators (RTO's), an Artillery Forward Observer (FO), the FO RTO, a medic, and two Vietnamese soldiers. One was a Vietnamese Kit Carson Scout, and the other a South Vietnamese Army Lieutenant. They were not with us that day.

The artillery RTO, Private First Class (Pfc.) Millard Anderson (Midge), whose radio was in the rear area waiting to be repaired, volunteered to act as the point man for our one hundred-five man tactical column. My battalion net RTO, Specialist Fourth Class (Spc.4) Wayne McBurnett (Mac), walked in front of me and behind Midge. I directed Mac which way to have Midge move as we maneuvered through An Lac (3) and An Lac (1) towards the back gate. The rest of the company followed the three of us.

- - - o - - -

4

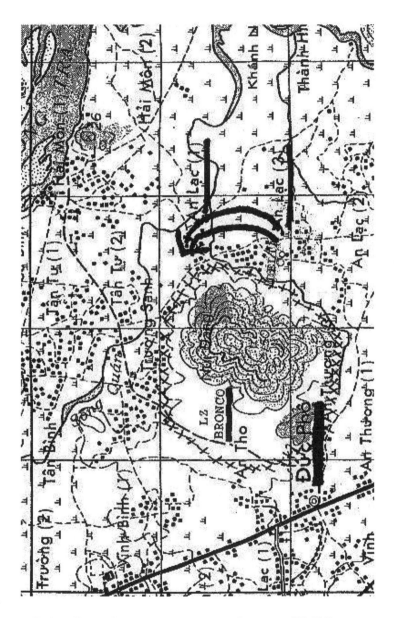

Delta Dogs in route to the back gate of LZ Bronco.

He wasn't fully grown yet, he wasn't old enough to drink yet, he hadn't bought his first car yet, he hadn't experienced being a father yet, yet he was leading one-hundred-four jungle warriors through no-man's land in Vietnam. Eighteen-year-old Midge Anderson had matured quickly after leaving high school. He was a teenager who was transplanted from his safe, comfortable hometown in Ohio to this Asian battlefield before he could even buy a beer. He had one thing going for him, his girlfriend, who was his high school sweetheart. She encouraged him to do his best and kept his morale up. I felt he had a lot to look forward to when he got home. In a short period of time, he learned well the military tasks that were forced upon him. He was serving valiantly and apparently fearlessly as he led us through the unfamiliar area to our base-camp. Although he was a kid, those of us following him knew what a heroic man he was to take the point position. As we trudged on, I wondered if his hometown mayor, city council, high school administrators, or if his neighbors and friends would ever know how courageous this boy was. I hoped that one day he would get the recognition he deserved for enduring so much for his countrymen.

I had the same thoughts for each of the platoon leaders. Lt. Wilson was twenty-one years old and Lt. Claybaugh was twenty-five years old. The Vietnam War was truly a young man's war. I wondered if anyone state-side could possibly understand and appreciate what these fine young men were enduring for their fellow citizens.

- - - o - - -

In Vietnam, a village was given a number after their name when additional subsections developed around the original village. An Lac (3) was the second subsection to develop along side <u>An Lac (1)</u>. The village <u>An Lac (2)</u> was the first subsection. Although they were identified on the map, most of the villages had been abandoned. Based on the condition of the deserted dwellings, it looked as if the inhabitants had moved into safer hamlets some time ago.

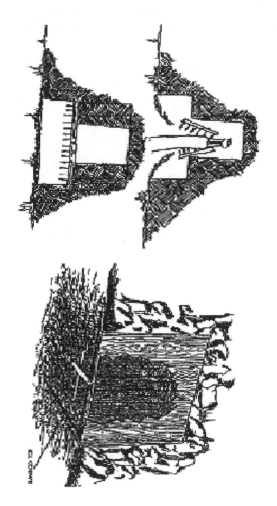

Spike filled holes.

My men moved cautiously over the dry rice paddies and past the destroyed wooden storage bins and thatched-roofs of the deserted farmer's hootches. Since one of the main hazards in the I-Corps war zone was booby-traps, the movement was slow. The men looked for wires across the path, leaves that could have hidden antipersonnel land mines, and covered spike-holes. The spike-holes were usually covered with a thin layer of dirt and leaves. The pits were full of sharpened spikes that were pointing upward. The bamboo or metal spikes were covered with human waste and other hazardous substances to cause serious infections after falling into the pits. We also moved a little slower as a result of each man carrying nearly a hundred pounds of equipment. We all carried three days worth of meals, ammunition, water, as well as ponchos, steel helmets, and everything else that was needed for day-to-day living and fighting. Our packs were so heavy we didn't wear flak jackets. They were just too heavy and too hot.

Using my topographical map, I directed Midge and Mac to what looked like a good spot to cross a stream we had come upon. This stream, which was just southeast of our destination, led into the <u>Song Quan River</u>.

After crossing the knee-deep waterway, our column continued another 500 meters before arriving at the back gate. The gate consisted of a narrow opening through the rolls of Concertina barbed wire that surrounded the base-camp. One at a time the men squeezed through the rows of barbed wire, stacked three coils high. All 105 soldiers, covered in sweat and grime, struggled through the multiple barriers and shuffled towards our company area under the watchful eyes of the base security soldiers. The humid, 115-degree weather was thick and oppressive. To me it felt like summertime in Yucatan, Mexico, or Miami, Florida. Walking into camp was tedious and hard, like treading on a dirt path inside a pressure cooker.

Delta Dogs Crossing a stream outside LZ Bronco.

I stopped for a minute, watching Midge as he continued on towards our company area. I observed the rest of my men staggering in, until I saw the last of them was inside the base-camp perimeter. It was 1650 hours. The infantrymen's pants were wet from wading across the shallow part of the stream; and their faces showed the harsh effect of the temperature, humidity, and the heavy backpacks. The two bandoleers of ammunition criss-crossing their chests, and the M-16 rifles they were carrying weighed them down and caused their shoulders to droop.

The battalion executive officer, Major Olgilvie, met us half-way towards our company location. He asked me to drop by the Battalion Operations Center after I had a meal. "Battalion has an operations order ready for you, so you can alert your men about tomorrow's operation," he said.

Our company barracks were nothing more than elevated wooden platforms covered with mosquito net lined tents. As we approached the barracks I noticed a couple USO ladies heading toward the helicopters for their return to <u>Chu</u> <u>Lai</u>. They had been at LZ Bronco giving out donuts and cookies to the men in the rear. Those out in the boonies seldom saw USO ladies, entertainers, the press, or any other visitors. Normally we infantrymen were too far forward for the visitors to venture. Even the men in the rear were lucky to see them today, because LZ Bronco was too far forward.

The USO ladies never stayed overnight at our base-camp -- it was too dangerous. But they were a sight for sore eyes, and the guys in the First Platoon perked up enough to whistle and hoot at them while trudging past the helicopter pad. The dirty grunts (the name of infantrymen who served in Vietnam), though tired and weighed down, stood tall with pride as if passing in review at a Fourth of July parade as they passed the ladies. To us, it was like watching the neighbors having a party. These men were happy for the lucky guys who had attended the party, but wished they could have joined the fun too.

The chopper was gone before even a third of the company had passed the helicopter pad. That was the way of war. Few of the goodies and perks reached the guys on the ground. Our men were lucky, because our company supply clerk and our orderly room clerk managed to grab a few of the large plastic bags the USO ladies had brought along for the troops. The large plastic bags that our company base-camp personnel got for us contained small packages which were filled with socks, stationery, pens, envelopes and pieces of candy.

Over an hour of sunlight remained, as sunset was at 1857 hours. I had a US Naval Observatory report to track of the daily sunrise, sunset, moonrise, moonset, and percent of moon visible. Those conditions played an important part in our day and night tactics.

After dropping our packs, everyone went to the mess hall for supper. Whenever I ate in the mess hall, I was always seated first and served first due to my rank. The army wasn't only rank conscious, it was also date-of-rank conscious. At both the jungle training in Panama and the in-country jungle training in Vietnam, I was assigned as the student company commander of all the troops being trained because I was the ranking Captain. I had six years seniority as a Captain, more time-in-grade than any other Captain with whom I served. This extensive prior experience that I brought to Vietnam provided an advantage for my company because I knew how to work the system to protect my men.

After supper, most of the men showered, changed into dry fatigues, and wrote letters home while I went to the Battalion Operations Center and picked up the operations order for the next day's mission. Afterwards I returned to my company orderly room and gave the waiting platoon leaders the warning order. The next day we were to conduct a combat assault by 'Hook' (the CH-47 Chinook medium lift helicopter) to Fire-Base Snoopy, located just north of LZ Bronco. The company was to sweep towards the hilly area east of Snoopy, called 'Big Red' because of its reddish terrain color. Lift-off time was scheduled for 0730 hours. Snoopy had received rocket and mortar fire from the Big Red area every day during the previous month. My company was ordered to conduct a search-and-destroy mission to relieve pressure for the artillery battery positioned on Snoopy.

The four platoon leaders departed to notify their men of the upcoming mission and the move-out time. While the leaders alerted their men, I scrutinized the topographical map of Snoopy and Big Red in my quarters, located just behind the orderly room. I wrote the five-paragraph operation order for the sweep of the land between Snoopy and Big Red and the assault on Big Red. At 2100 hours, I verbally gave the operation order to the four platoon leaders who had assembled again in the orderly room. After the platoon leaders understood the details for the next day's mission, we were all free for the night.

I showered and completed a few things I wanted to accomplish before the next day's mission. I wrote a short note to my eight-year-old son, letting him know I was all right and that I missed him. I inquired about his military school. Before I left for Vietnam, my son and I had come to an agreement, I would do my duty in Vietnam, and he would do his tour in a local military academy.

Just as I was finishing my letter, I was interrupted by a knock at the door that lead to the company orderly room.

"Enter," I barked.

First Lieutenant Larky D. Evans entered with a cold can of beer in each hand. "Would you like a cold one, Sir?" he asked. I put the finished letter aside and gladly accepted the beer. We chatted a bit about nothing important, just trying to get to know each other. Shortly after we started talking, two of the platoon leaders, First Lieutenant William Robert Wilson and First Lieutenant James Bradley Claybaugh joined us. I welcomed them. Lieutenant Evans, my company executive officer, got each of them a beer out of his ice chest.

Twenty-one year old Bill Wilson was a clean-cut, muscular, blonde. He looked as if he was a college cheerleader at the weekly football game. Bill had a fun personality with a friendly smile and was full of enthusiasm. His eyes sparkled as we talked about our lives. His smiling eyes pulled me in, as if I was now his best friend. Bill shared with us that he was the youngest child in his family. "At times," he said, "I feel embarrassed at all the attention I've gotten from my mom when I was in college. However, I confess I love every bit of the babying I've received."

"She's a great mom," he told me, and I could see in his face that he meant it. "I love her very much for the way she treated me."

Since I was brought up by my uncle and aunt, I envied him for his close family ties. I wished I was as young, handsome, and full of energy as Bill. I imagined he had no problem getting girlfriends. However, we did not discuss that aspect of each other's lives.

Twenty-five year old Jim Claybaugh talked about Idaho, skiing, and the fact that he had one leg shorter than the other. He wore a specially made boot, with the sole and heel thicker. I had been made aware of this before I came to the company, to prevent any unintentional embarrassing remarks. I didn't mention his condition, but he seemed to want to talk about it.

It turned out that Jim and I enjoyed a lot of the same things and I liked him right away. I offered to show him Los Angeles if he ever came to California and go skiing with him at some of the California ski areas. I, like Jim, loved to ski.

Bill had shared his family life with us, and Jim shared his extracurricular life style. We all drank another cold beer while we talked about nothing in particular before we turned in for the night. We all got along well together as if we were college buddies having a friendly evening conversation. It was as if we were in a different world from the one we had shared earlier in the day. It was nice to be back from the field in a safe place.

-   -   -   o   -   -   -

Just after 0600 hours, just 48 minutes before sunrise, on a damp, hot Monday morning, the 105 of us saddled up (putting on our backpacks, hooking on our cartridge belts and picking up our weapons) on the dirt street in front of our LZ Bronco company headquarters. Just before 0700 hours roll-calls were given, and the platoon leaders reported to me and the first sergeant, those present and would be moving out with us that day. Before going into combat, we both needed to know who was going with us so we could account for everyone before we left the battlefield.

The entire company, all 105 of us, marched off for the day's mission. We arrived at the heliport at 0715 hours and sat around waiting for the Chinook Medium Lift 'Hook' helicopter to arrive. Each man sat with legs outstretched, leaned back on his heavy backpack. The packs were fully loaded with enough ammo and food for three days. I spent the wait time updating my journal. Waiting for a helicopter was not unusual for us. Due to the dust and refuse hitting the helicopter blades when landing in parched rice paddies, the minimal maintenance time on an Army helicopter was five hours for each hour of flying time. Repairing damage from hostile fire caused additional down-time for the helicopter crews, running up to 20 to 30 hours. End result, the choppers rarely arrived on time. In the Army, especially during war times, 'hurry-up-and-wait' was a way of life.

The first sortie finally lifted off at 0810 hours. After about 10 minutes we landed at Snoopy, 25,000 meters (25 kilometers) north of Bronco (about 15 miles). The artillery fire base-camp was located 13,000 meters (less than 10 miles) southeast of the city of <u>Quang Ngai</u>, the capitol of Quang Ngai province.

I was on the first lift and met with the artillery officer when I arrived and I informed him of our mission. He pointed out the area from where the rockets and mortar rounds had been coming. The helicopter soon arrived with the Second Platoon and then returned to Bronco for the rest of the company. I don't know about other infantry company commanders, but I always made it a point to be on the first airlift into an assault

Hook - Chinook medium lift capability Helicopter

and on the last helicopter out from a scrimmage. I wanted to be at the point of contact when we arrived in order to get an accurate assessment of what was going on. When we departed

15

I wanted to be sure no one had been left behind. That was my manifesto. These were my men and I wanted to be sure everything possible had been done to protect them, even if they fell in battle. We left none of our men behind. These were things we didn't say out loud, but we each knew. It was unwritten but clearly understood.

When all the troops had been unloaded, I gave the final operations order to the platoon leaders. I pointed out two stands of trees, both on their maps and across the terrain, as we surveyed the area of operation from the hill named Snoopy. I pointed out the sources of the enemy fire the artillery officer had identified for me. I went over the routes each platoon would sweep.

Soon the First and Second Platoons moved into the first tree-line to the east of the Red Ball Highway. Then, the Third Platoon and the Weapons Platoon moved into the first tree-line to the west of the other two platoons. Lt. Bird's First Platoon moved out and Lt. Claybaugh's Second Platoon followed. After passing through the southern edge of <u>An Phong (2)</u>, they cut northeast, spread out with the two platoons side-by-side and swept through <u>Nho Lam (4)</u>.

Lt. Wilson's Third Platoon followed the first two platoons. Being short one lieutenant, Platoon Sergeant Glen H. Grimes commanded the Weapons Platoon. Lt. Wilson passed through <u>An Phong (2)</u>, and swept to the western edge of <u>Nho Lam (4)</u>, with his three rifle squads abreast, and then cut north of <u>Khien Khuong (2)</u>. Sgt. Grimes' platoon followed Lt. Wilson's platoon and spread out after passing <u>Nho Lam (4)</u> with Lt. Wilson's platoon on the left side and Lt. Bird's platoon to the right.

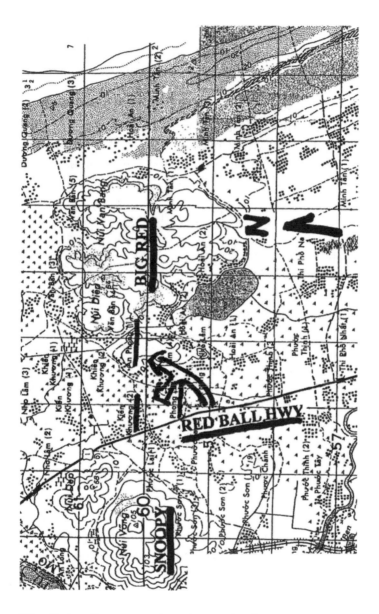

The Delta Dogs moving through villages on to Big Red.

As we moved forward, the battalion command helicopter swooped down and stopped a fleeing Vietnamese man who had appeared to be evading the advance of our men. After picking up the evader, the battalion command helicopter received small arms fire from the vicinity of <u>An Phong (1)</u>, just north of us. The two door-gunners in the Huey UH-1D helicopter returned fire as they pulled away. As they departed, the artillery forward observer in the battalion command helicopter directed artillery fire from Snoopy into the tree-line from where the snipers had been firing.

We observed the artillery rounds hitting near by, as the earth shook around us. My company command group blended into Lt. Wilson's platoon as we continued the sweep, two platoons abreast, while the First and Second Platoons swept two abreast to our right. This advance-on-line as scrimmagers was to assure that the enemy did not sneak by us as we advanced towards our objective.

Satisfied with the way the sweep by the Third Platoon and Weapons Platoon was going, I took the company command group with me to join the first two platoons. When I joined them, they had stopped for a break. The company command group and I dropped our packs and were just about to join the first two platoons for a drink and to take our salt tablets, when the battalion command and control chopper returned and asked us to pop smoke grenades to identify our locations.

Just as we popped a 'mellow-yellow' smoke grenade, I received a call from Lt. Wilson. "Delta Six, this is Delta Three. A large number of Vietnamese soldiers are operating here in my area. Are there supposed to be Romeo Victory November troops in the area? Over."

His report of Republic of South Vietnam troops (RVN) in the area caught me by surprise. I told Mac to report this to the battalion commander, and I radioed back to the Third Platoon,

18

"Delta Three, this is Delta Six. Hold your position and I'll verify with the operations center. Over."

After my company command group saddled up again, we chugged our water and took our salt tablets as we hurried to the Third Platoon's location while we listened for a reply from battalion.

"Delta Three, this is Delta Six. We are on our way to join you. Over," I informed Lt. Wilson as we moved towards him.

"Roger, Delta Six. We are going to take a break until you get here. Over," Lt. Wilson radioed back.

"Roger, out," I said as we continued northeast towards the Third Platoon. I had listened to Vietnamese language tapes for three months prior to my deployment, so I understood their language a little, but not much.

The battalion command helicopter headed for Lt. Wilson's position. Major Vaughn, who was on the chopper, spoke Vietnamese very well. Before the command chopper arrived at the Third Platoon's position, the helicopter crew spotted another man running away. They went after the fleeing black-pajama-clad man and the door gunner sprayed warning shots at the evading runner, but he didn't stop. When the door gunner circled the running Viet Cong suspect with fire, he stopped. The chopper landed and picked up the runner, then flew over to our location.

Vietnamese civilians wore black-pajama-type bottoms and white or black tops. This apparently was because the Vietnamese huts had dirt floors, with dusty roads and paths outside. Even Highway One, the main artery running north and south, was a dirt road. The black hid the dirt that soiled their clothing. NVA soldiers wore dark green army uniforms when in battle. The Viet Cong wore black tops and black bottoms, so it was hard to tell if a Vietnamese was VC or a civilian. Consequently, wearing black pajamas didn't define a person as a suspected Viet Cong. Being in the enemy's territory or not having RVN (Republic of South Vietnam) government identification papers did, however.

While the battalion command chopper was capturing the suspect, I arrived at the Third Platoon's location. As Lt. Wilson explained the situation, the command chopper flew back over our area. We had popped a 'goofy-grape' smoke grenade so they would know who and where we were. We verbally transmitted cryptic names for the color of our smoke so the enemy wouldn't pop a different colored smoke grenade to try to confuse our airmen.

The chopper landed and Lieutenant Colonel Walter Leo Pritchard, Junior, our Infantry Battalion Commander, climbed down from the chopper and informed me that they had a Viet Cong suspect. The man didn't have identification papers, so they were taking him back to our base-camp for interrogation. He asked if I could coordinate with the South Vietnamese soldiers. I thought I could, with the little Vietnamese I knew and my English-to-Vietnamese phrase book that I had with me. Being satisfied that I could handle the situation, he nodded his approval and headed back to LZ Bronco. I saluted him and headed for the Vietnamese troops. At least, I hoped they were South Vietnamese troops.

I led the Third Platoon and the Weapons Platoon along the dirt street through the Vietnamese soldiers who were taking a lunch break on each side of us. During the briefing the day before, we were told no RVN troops would be operating in this area. We all held our fingers on the triggers of our assault rifles, with the safeties in the off-position, at the ready just in case these soldiers were not South Vietnamese troops. As we passed the soldiers I asked, "Dye Wee?" which was Vietnamese for captain. In response, several of the men pointed in the direction we were going. As we continued forward in the direction they had pointed, I hoped they were RVN troops but I still wasn't sure. I wished that Lt. Hoa or Junior, our interpreters, were with us that day, but they weren't. Sunday was their day off and they hadn't returned yet.

I found the Vietnamese company commander and spoke to him in what little Vietnamese I knew, and he answered me in what little English he knew. As I talked in both Vietnamese and English, I still wasn't certain if we were among friendlies or the enemy disguised as RVN soldiers.

After many tries at communicating in both languages, I finally learned they were a South Vietnamese Army unit that had been patrolling the main highway which ran from north to south for the entire length of South Vietnam. They were ahead of schedule, which is why no one knew they were in this area of operation. While my battalion net radio operator was verifying this information with our battalion operations center at LZ Bronco, I asked the Vietnamese company commander if he had other troops operating in the area. He said he had one platoon to the east of us, in the direction we were going to sweep. It took a bit of time before I finally convinced him to order his platoon to come back and join him. I explained I wanted his entire company to move back to the Red Ball Highway so we would not engage them in battle by mistake.

Since he had witnessed the artillery shells falling and the helicopter machine-gunning, he appeared very willing to move back onto Highway One and remain clear of our operation. I ordered my company to take a break for an early lunch to give the Vietnamese troops time to clear out of our area. Before we had finished our lunch, the Vietnamese troops were back on the Red Ball, about 700 meters to our west. We were left alone with the villagers who lived in the hamlets we'd moved through and the Viet Cong to our northeast.

With the area of operation cleared of other friendly military forces, my four platoons moved again to the northeast. After leaving the occupied village, we swept to the east through the first line of trees.

We found a stack of hay next to a destroyed hut. I told the men to set fire to the haystack, since no haystack or rice caches were allowed outside hamlets or next to unoccupied hootches.

Leaving hay, rice, and food unattended, to be collected during the night by the enemy, was how villagers supplied the Viet Cong and North Vietnamese soldiers.

The area in which we operated was no-man's land, except for a handful of hamlets and small villages. After dark, no one was allowed outside the hamlets or villages, except for soldiers. It was said that the South Vietnamese and United States soldiers moved during the day while the Viet Cong and North Vietnamese soldiers moved at night. Our air superiority was the reason for this.

For about 500 meters in front of us (about four football fields long) we saw nothing but dried, parched, stubble-covered rice paddies. We crossed them single file, rather than in the shoulder-to-shoulder sweep formation. This column formation allowed us to move faster and make up for the time lost when we stopped to coordinate with the South Vietnamese forces. After arriving near the panhandle of the pork-chop-shaped wood-line at the far side of the rice paddies, we shifted back into a sweep formation. The four platoons advanced side-by-side, each soldier about four arms length from the other.

The battalion command chopper returned overhead. I got a call from the chopper, "Delta Six, this is Hotel Six. Over."

I grabbed the radio hand-mike from Mac and answered, "Hotel Six, this is Delta Six. Over."

"Your men aren't lined up," the Colonel answered. "Have your left element move to the right until all your troops are in

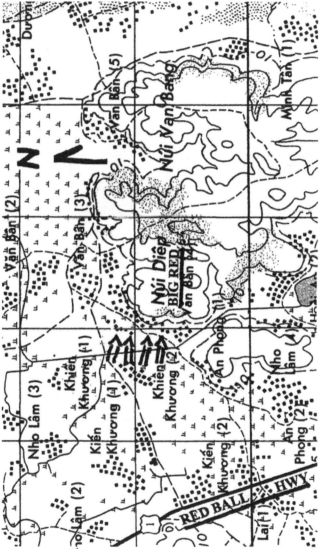

With the 1ˢᵗ Platoon right of the Weapons Platoon, the infantry company swept east towards Big Red.

contact with each other. Over"

"This is Delta Six. Wilco, out," I responded.

Controlling over a hundred men spread over a 1,000 feet front was the challenging task I faced daily. It helped to have an aero evaluation of our formation to identify that the right platoons were not abreast of, and in contact with, the Third and Weapons Platoon. I radioed Lt. Wilson and Sgt. Grimes to shift to the right and join up with the First and Second Platoons to assure we covered all the area we were sweeping.

After the realignment, I felt confident the enemy would be unable to slip through our platoons and escape the sweep. I radioed the First and Second Platoons and told them to pick up the pace so they could stay in line with the Third and Weapons Platoons. The battalion command chopper again informed me a Vietnamese dressed in black and wearing a straw hat, had been moving along the north edge of the woods. At the rate we had been moving, we would miss him. The chopper reported the Vietnamese man was carrying two baskets on a pole, much like a seesaw.

Getting 50 men to shift, without losing contact with the rest of the company, was a slow process, so I told Sgt. Grimes to send over a few men to catch the suspect. I ordered my company command group to break away from the rest of the men, and we also tried to head off the suspect.

The helicopter left the area following another Viet Cong suspect they had sighted south of us, outside the area we were sweeping. This suspect didn't stop when the chopper fired warning shots. The helicopter machine gunner killed him before he ran into a clump of trees.

Sgt. Grimes' men caught up with the Vietnamese man in black, walking with the two baskets. They found out he was a

70 year-old man. He explained that he was carrying his crops home to his hootch.

I joined them and asked, "VC?" pointing to the east.

The old man shook his head from side to side, as he uttered, "No VC." He claimed he didn't know about the Viet Cong. Considering all the mortar and rocket activity in the last month and his proclaimed lack of knowledge, I ordered him held for a helicopter evacuation. Since we had caught him in a fire-fight area, he was taken back to our base-camp for interrogation by our South Vietnamese Army interrogators.

Within a minute the chopper picked him up. After it departed, we resumed our sweep towards Big Red. We proceeded across the next set of dusty, empty rice paddies in the blistering noontime sun until we entered a second set of trees at the far end. When we were inside the wooded area, we stopped for another break. It was time to water down and take salt tablets again. It was 115-degrees that day, and we all sweated profusely. We needed plenty of water and salt tablets to replace the fluid we'd lost. We were taking five salt tablets a day, as the very hot and humid weather, plus our physical exertion, caused us to perspire excessively. I carried two canteens, one on my belt and one bota type plastic blivit slung over my shoulder, as did most of the other infantrymen. Because of the high humidity, even with all the sweating, we could not cool our bodies. The crotches of our pants and the arm pits of our fatigue jackets had large sedimentary salt rings on them where our body salts collected as we dripped with perspiration during the long hot days. At night it cooled down to a humid 85, or 90-degrees. Even with the 20 to 30-degrees cool down, it was still hot. The nearly 100 pounds of equipment we were each carrying only made it worse. By taking a break, we didn't burn as much energy and cooled our bodies down a little before we moved again and began burning more energy.

When we finished our break, we saddled up again. Before my company command group moved out, we heard a loud explosion that came from the vicinity of the Second Platoon.

"What was that?" I asked my company net radio telephone operator, Specialist Fourth Class Joe Dodson.

Joe was already on the radio calling the platoons. The Second Platoon reported, they needed a medical evacuation helicopter dust-off. Someone had tripped a booby-trap.

I asked for more information and Joe relayed the request to the platoon, while Mac called in a request to the battalion command post for a medical evacuation.

The Second Platoon operator radioed back, "Two men are wounded. One of the men stepped on a booby-trap."

Private First Class Roger Wilson and Pfc. Steven Hill were wounded. Wilson got the worst of it - - one of his legs was badly shattered. I told Mac to relay the information to the rear for the dust-off of the two men, not just one. The medical evacuation helicopter was already on its way to pick up the wounded when we gave them the casualty update.

We knew Wilson might lose a leg and Hill had received some shrapnel. Wilson was going home and in that regard, we were happy for him. Some of us would not be as lucky as he was. Some would leave in body-bags.

Hill would probably be back with us after they patched him up. Our war was not a battle between two persons, one winning, one losing. Much of the war was a matter of chance, luck, fate, God's will, or whatever one's belief is. If the two men on the right of Wilson and Hill had been hit by the booby-trap or the two soldiers on the left, one of them would have gone home instead of Wilson. As it was, at 1255 hours on Monday, 24 March 1969, Pfc. Roger Wilson and Pfc.

Steven Hill were wounded in the Quang Ngai Province of I-Corps, South Vietnam, while conducting an assault on the North Vietnamese forces. At 1318 hours, just 23 minutes after being wounded, both Wilson and Hill were airlifted back to base-camp Bronco and then to the Americal Division Army Hospital in <u>Chu</u> <u>Lai</u>.

I moved the First and Second Platoons back and ordered all the platoons to take cover after the dust-off by the medical evacuation helicopter was complete. I ordered Lt. Faust to call for an artillery barrage into the wooded area we were entering where Wilson had tripped the booby-trap.

These woods were not the kind of forests with which we were familiar in the United States. In the middle of the sea of rice paddies and the water dikes that separated them, small islands rose high above the rice paddies. Some of the islands were smaller, but the one we approached was about the size of half a football field. The high ground was about five to eight feet higher than the beds of the rice paddies and the water channels. The perimeter of the island was covered with mostly trees and hedgerows. Only about one-third of the island was covered with trees. The rest of the island consisted of several hedgerows separating the island into little yards with a hootch in each. Each hut's yard had a flat area used for drying rice, peanuts, and sliced potatoes.

The abandoned island was booby-trapped, like many others outside the government protected hamlets. The occupants had all moved into the protected villages next to the Red Ball Highway. In Quang Ngai Province, anyone not in the villages at night was considered an enemy and was shot. Also, during the night the artillery units, like the one on Snoopy, would fire artillery shells into randomly selected locations that were not occupied by the villagers, RVN soldiers or American troops.

While moving back to get out of the area the artillery barrage would hit, we heard another explosion. This one had come from the First Platoon's direction. I asked Joe to get on the radio again to find out what happened. The First Platoon radio operator reported one of their men had tripped a booby-trap. I told Mac to get back on the battalion radio net and request another dust-off.

The battalion command chopper was returning to our position after dropping off the old Vietnamese man they had taken back for interrogation. They radioed they would dust-off the booby-trap casualties. They were almost at our location when they offered to conduct the dust-off for the new casualties. However, the medical evacuation helicopter operator interrupted and squelched their offer of assistance. The medical chopper operator reported they were approaching our position, on the way to the Chu Lai field hospital with the other two casualities and said they would drop down and pick up the new casualties. They were better equipped to care for them in flight and at the Chu Lai field hospital. The medical evacuation chopper landed in our area five minutes after we had requested the second dust-off.

Specialist Fourth Class Marcos Rodriguez had tripped the land mine and the explosion had shattered his leg. Specialist Fourth Class Michael Jarmus and Robert Lombardo were hit with shrapnel from the blast. Rodriguez had a permanently injured leg and the prized ticket home, while Jarmus would be joining us again a month later after his wounds healed.

After the dust-off was complete and the artillery fire had saturated the area, I ordered Joe to radio the platoons and have them move out towards their objective. I hoped the artillery shells had ripped up any remaining booby-traps and destroyed any enemy who might have been there. With Lombardo still with us we moved out in a sweep formation as scrimmagers.

After we started moving forward, I heard a burst of fire from the east, about 100 meters away. We all hit the dirt and scurried forward until we were against the berm of the next hedgerow, then we lay in the dry, dusty rice paddy dirt waiting for the call for a medic. No call for help was heard, so I told Joe to get on the horn again to find out what was going on, and who'd made contact. We could tell by the sound of the gunfire that AK-47 assault rifles were fired, not our M-16 rifles or 30-caliber M-60 machine-guns.

The Third Platoon radioed they were in contact with the enemy and were returning fire. I told Mac to inform battalion, while Joe checked to verify that no one was hit. The report came back that none of our guys were hit during the exchange of fire.

Lt. Wilson's operator reported that after his platoon had swept through the wooded island, some of his men had jumped down into the dry field on the far side of the island and they came under AK-47 and enemy machine-gun fire as soon as they hit the floor of the empty rice paddy. While the rest of his platoon returned fire, the men scurried back on their bellies and up onto the dirt island where they took cover with the rest of the platoon behind the elevated hedgerow. The enemy fire had come from the next island, less than 100 meters east of them.

I ordered Lt. Faust, our Artillery Forward observer, to call in an artillery strike. We were lucky the artillery fire began moments after Lt. Faust requested it. The policy in I-Corps was that no artillery was to be applied to targets within 100 meters from friendly troops. We normally would not have received artillery fire support if we hadn't been working close with the artillery soldiers on Snoopy. Lt. Faust moved up to join the Third Platoon to better adjust the fire as it poured into the enemy's position. I moved the First and Second Platoon so they linked up with the Third Platoon.

After joining the Third Platoon, the other two infantry platoons were better deployed to fight the enemy. I told the company command group and the Weapons Platoon to move up to just behind the Third Platoon's position in case the Weapons Platoon's mortar was needed for indirect fire. Lt. Wilson's platoon was well dispersed and was exchanging fire with the enemy when I joined the Third Platoon. The First and Second Platoons started firing as they joined the Third Platoon.

Once the bombardment started, the artillery shells ripped through the air over our heads. We heard the 105-millimeter artillery rounds whistle past us before they hit their target. We were so close to the enemy, the shells' impact trembled through the hedgerow we were using for cover and shook the ground under us as the earth sprayed over us and turned day into night for a few minutes. As we hugged the ground, we couldn't help but worry that one of the shells would find us by mistake.

The artillery barrage continued while we engaged the enemy position with rifle and machine-gun fire. During the jittery assault by the artillery and my infantrymen, I received a call from the battalion command helicopter. They were on their way to our position. Their chopper would be in the path of the artillery fire if we didn't stop the barrage. Lt. Faust called off the fire from the artillery at Snoopy to assure that the battalion command helicopter would not be hit. The command chopper had us pop colored smoke grenades so they could identify our position.

I got a call from Lieutenant Colonel Pritchard. "Delta Six, This is Hotel Six. Over."

I rolled over on my back and while leaning against my backpack, I grabbed the mike and answered, "Hotel Six this is Delta Six. Over."

"This is Hotel Six. Move two of your elements to the Red Ball and secure a Lima Zulu for slicks that will pick up your unit. Over," the radio blurted out.

"This is Delta Six. Roger your message. Out," I answered.

He ordered me to have two platoons break contact with the enemy and move toward Highway One and secure a landing zone for slicks (what we called the Huey UH-1D helicopters

Huey - Light lift capability helicopter

which were configured to carry troops). They were coming to pick us up.

I gave the word to Lt. Bird and Lt. Claybaugh to move their platoons in columns towards the Red Ball and secure a landing zone (LZ). Each Huey could hold about a half dozen fully-equipped infantrymen. It would take six sorties of three helicopters to fly all of us back to our base-camp. With the First and Second Platoons at the LZ, one platoon could secure the LZ while the other platoon is lifted back to LZ Bronco. Then Lt. Wilson's platoon, Sgt. Grimes' platoon, and my company headquarters group would have time to complete the mission and get back to the Red Ball LZ before the first two platoons completed being ferried back to our base-camp.

I remained with Lt. Wilson and Sgt. Grimes to finish the engagement. I wanted the Weapons Platoon to stay with us to provide machine-gun and mortar fire. The two rifle platoons moved out while the Third and the Weapons Platoons continued firing on the enemy position. When Sgt. Grimes had his machine-guns and mortar set up, I ordered the Third Platoon to assault the enemy position about 100 meters east of our location.

As one of the Third Platoon's squads dropped down into the dry rice paddy, the other two squads of Lt. Wilson's platoon laid down a base of fire. As the squad leap-frogged across the open terrain, firing as they hit the ground to cover their buddies advance, Sgt. Grimes' machine-guns provided covering fire. When the first squad was across the open rice paddy and huddled against the next island's hedgerow, the next squad advanced. I followed the third squad across the open rice paddy and joined the Third Platoon as they entered the tree-line of the next island. Sgt. Grimes and his men maintained watch from our original position, ready to provide fire support as we searched the island. We moved cautiously through the island, checking for enemy hiding places, booby-traps, plus looking for equipment abandoned by the enemy.

While sweeping the island, I got a call from the command helicopter. Lieutenant Colonel (LTC) Pritchard observed that the two platoons moving toward the Red Ball were in columns. He wanted the platoons to sweep as scrimmagers, side-by-side, while they proceeded to the Red Ball.

Since I was trying to concentrate on the touchy situation around me, in the middle of the enemy's position with only one platoon, I quickly asked Joe to relay the message to the first two platoons. I continued to focus on the dangerous situation in which the Third Platoon and my company command group found ourselves in at that time. Then I got an order from the command chopper, telling us not to pursue the enemy up onto Big Red.

I was relieved to hear that order. I knew we weren't a strong enough force to effectively engage any concentrated enemy resistance. It was still a nervous time with only one infantry platoon in the middle of an enemy position and with only a Weapons Platoon as support. I relayed the order to Lt. Wilson and Sgt. Grimes.

While we were finishing the search of the island, Lt. Wilson let me know he had used all his Claymore mines and C-Four explosives destroying most of the enemy positions on the island. He'd found several more spider-holes and caves on the island he wanted to destroy. I directed the Weapons Platoon to join us and use their C-Four and Claymore mines to destroy the remaining spider-holes.

While the Weapons Platoon carried out my orders, Lt. Wilson's men destroyed all the hootches, hay stacks, and rice bins on the island. After mopping up the enemy location, the company command group, Weapons Platoon and the Third

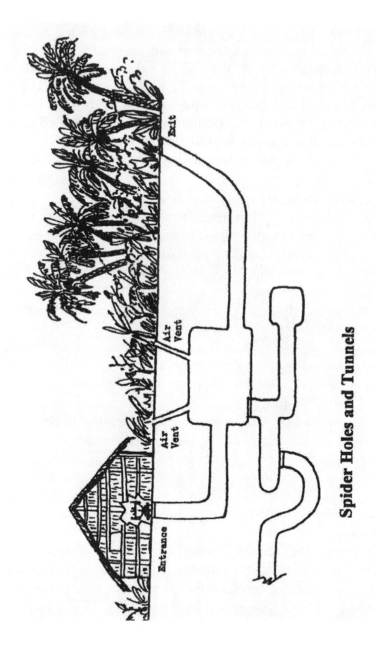

Spider Holes and Tunnels

Platoon headed back to the Red Ball. Since the command helicopter had already returned to our base-camp, we moved in column formation so we could reach the landing zone faster.

On the march back, rifle squad leader, Specialist Fourth Class (Spc.4) Ronald W. Isenhour (whom we called Ike), sprained his ankle when he fell into a spider-hole. Ike was lucky it was only a spider-hole and not a spike-pit. Doc Kelly, the Third Platoon medic, attended him.

All the medics were called Doc, because they were the closest thing we had to a doctor when we were in the field by ourselves. The Third Platoon medic, Private First Class Bernard Kelly, was a stocky, good-natured guy who enjoyed helping his buddies. Kelly and another soldier wrapped Ike's arms around their shoulders and let him use them as a brace so he could quickly hobble toward the Red Ball Highway with his platoon. While they did the five-legged race across the empty rice paddies, they encouraged Ike to keep going as fast as he could in order to get out of the enemy's territory and to make it to the pick-up point on time. As we hurried toward the LZ, one squad acted as the rear guard, firing to the rear as we moved. The rear guard made sure the enemy wasn't following us during our move towards the highway.

We started receiving enemy fire from what appeared to be a sniper just north of us as we maneuvered west. Lt. Faust called for artillery fire. As we rushed toward the highway, the artillery rounds crashed into the area where the enemy shots originated.

En route, we received word the Second Platoon had observed two Vietnamese running from the area of our last contact. Our men near the Red Ball fired a few rounds towards them, but they continued running. After our men laid down more fire, they stopped. The Second Platoon sent a squad to get the two, while the rest of the platoon formed a perimeter for the landing zone.

Once we had established a secure LZ, I received a message from battalion headquarters. They radioed that the slicks wouldn't be picking us up after all. They had been diverted for a priority mission. This meant we had to hump it up Snoopy and wait for the Hook (Chinook CH-47 Medium Lift Helicopter) to ferry us back.

The 2,000 meter hike back to the Red Ball seemed longer after a long, hard and hot day exchanging fire with the enemy, especially with the last 500 meters to Snoopy all uphill. We were already exhausted. To make matters worse, they wanted us to be there in half an hour for the first pick-up. I wasn't pleased, but that was the nature of combat operations. Things continually seemed to change.

I took the handset from the company net RTO and broadcasted, "Delta One and Delta Two, this is Delta Six, over."

Since the RTO's recognized my voice, they put their platoon leaders on the radios. "Delta One, Delta Two. There will be no slicks. Move to Snoopy ASAP for a Hook pick-up. Over," I ordered when they all had checked in.

"This is Delta One, roger. Out," Lt. Bird responded and started for Snoopy.

"This is Delta Two. Wilco, as soon as the squad I sent to pick up the two Vietnamese returns. Over," Lt. Claybaugh answered.

"This Delta Six. Roger, out," I answered them both.

The First Platoon moved toward Snoopy as fast as they could for the Hook pick-up. The Second Platoon was moving out as soon as their squad returned from picking up the two Vietnamese. The Third Platoon was moving too slowly, so I decided to call for a dust-off for Ike. Then we would high-tail it to Snoopy for the last set of lifts back to Bronco. I told Mac to call for a dust-off for Ike.

I ordered the Weapons Platoon to move out for Snoopy as fast as they could. I reasoned the Weapons Platoon would arrive while the First Platoon was being shuttled back to Bronco since they were the farthest of the two platoons away from Snoopy. I figured that would give my company headquarters group, the Second Platoon, and the Third Platoon a little more time before the fourth and fifth shuttles would be ready for us.

The good news was we were traveling a little lighter because we consumed most of our ammunition, water, and chow during the operation. This may not sound like a lot, but the 115-degree temperature, the humidity, and the afternoon sun made any lighting of the load a blessing. Every ounce we carried mattered; we even burned our mail after we read it because it became too heavy to carry. If the choice was one more bullet or mail we had already finished reading, the bullet won just about every time. The other bad news was we were carrying the backpacks and weapons of the four injured men.

Over the radio the Second Platoon reported that the two Vietnamese were an old man and a young girl. They had both been wounded when they didn't stop. I told them to let the platoon Doc check them out and let me know how bad the wounds were. We were heading towards the Second Platoon and we could get the two Vietnamese dusted-off with Ike if they could get there before the medevac helicopter arrived.

-   -   -   o   -   -   -

The policy for medical evacuation dust-offs priorities were:
HIGH   - EMERGENCY if a GI's life was dependent on immediate medical aid.

MEDIUM   -   PRIORITY if quick medical treatment was required for a GI.

LOW   -   ROUTINE for normal or delayed medical aid, such as x-rays, tooth aches, or other illnesses that would not hold up the mission if not treated right away. ROUTINE was also used for Vietnamese soldiers and civilians.

In addition, there was ROUTINE, WITH IMMEDIATE TACTICAL PRECEDENCE. This last one was the one we used for Ike's dust-off. We needed an immediate dust-off in order for us to complete our mission.

-    -   -   o   -   -   -

The First Platoon was the closest to Snoopy. The Weapons Platoon quickly moved past the Third Platoon and headed for Snoopy. The Second Platoon also started toward Snoopy, leaving one of their squads with the two wounded Vietnamese. I had let Lt. Claybaugh know the squad he left would move to Snoopy with the Third Platoon once we married-up with them.

Lt. Faust called the artillery men on Snoopy to let them know what was going on, so they wouldn't think we were the enemy advancing on their location. We were surprised and elated to see trucks driving down from Snoopy to meet my men and carry them up the hill. The guys from Snoopy said it was the first day in over a month they hadn't received incoming rocket or mortar fire. They hoped what we did, and the artillery rounds we directed towards the enemy, would prevent more incoming rockets and mortar rounds for several additional days. That's the way it was in combat. A day or two of rest seemed like a Godsend. The truck rides were a small way of showing how much they appreciated what we did for

The Delta Dogs moving towards Snoopy on the South Vietnamese Red Ball Highway Number 1.

them.

The dust-off arrived as the Third Platoon and my company command group joined the squad from the Second Platoon. We let the helicopter crew know we suspected the two wounded Vietnamese were either Viet Cong or Viet Cong sympathizers, as they had been wounded in the enemy territory. When a fire-fight took place, anyone found in the enemy's side of the battlefield were suspects. These two plus Ike were airlifted back to Bronco for medical attention, as well as for interrogation.

The squad from the Second Platoon, the Third Platoon, and my headquarters group scurried toward Snoopy in two columns. The Third Platoon on one side of the dirt highway and the headquarters group with the squad from the Second Platoon in the column on the other side. We didn't want to miss the last pick-up, or we would have to stay out there all night.

Before we arrived at the bottom of the hill, the artillerymen drove down the Red Ball highway and met us. They not only gave us a ride, they handed us ice cold cans of soda. After maneuvering and fighting in the sweltering rice paddies, the cold drinks tasted wonderful. Just after we arrived the last two Hook's arrived to pick us up.

We knew we had had a good day. We knew there was one enemy killed, several taken prisoner, and we were sure there were many killed or wounded by our gunfire, mortar rounds and artillery fire. We didn't stay around long enough to get a body count. Getting everyone safely back to base that day was more important than an enemy body count.

I arrived at Bronco at 1720 hours. Most of my men had already headed for the showers, then chow and finally to wherever they could get a tall, cool drink. I ate and then returned to my orderly room, got a cold soda, reflected on the last few days' activities and recorded the events in my journal. My first full day of combat in Vietnam. Only four wounded and nobody killed, and a mission successfully completed. I realized that I had five good officers, Lieutenants Bird, Claybaugh, Evans, Wilson, and Faust. I also had a good Weapons Platoon leader, Sergeant Grimes. After thinking about the day's activities, I realized I didn't know much about the men who were wounded. I ordered the company clerk to make a list of names of every man in the company and where they came from when the clerk had some free time.

- - - o - - -

First Lieutenant William Roger Wilson was drafted in 1966 after a short time in college. Upon completion of six months of basic and advanced infantry training, Bill Wilson from Alma, Arkansas, re-enlisted for four years in the Army. It was necessary for Bill to re-enlist in order to attend officers training school at Fort Benning, Georgia. Six months later he was commissioned as an Infantry Second Lieutenant in the US Army. He was promoted to First Lieutenant in January 1968. On 10 December 1968, Lt. Wilson shipped out to Vietnam. He was assigned as the infantry platoon leader of the Third Platoon, Company D, Third Battalion, First Infantry located at Duc Pho, Vietnam.

- - - o - - -

The following is the list of heroes who were identified in this chapter.

First Lieutenant Larky D. Evans, from Gainesville, Texas
First Lieutenant William Roger Wilson, from Alma, Arkansas
First Lieutenant James Bradley Claybaugh, from Caldwell, Idaho
First Lieutenant Roger R. Faust, from Chicago, Illinois
Platoon Sergeant Glen H. Grimes, from Wayneboro, Tennessee
Specialist Fourth Class Ronald W. Isenhour, (Ike), from Fort Myers, Florida
Private First Class Bernard Kelly, from Orange, New Jersey
Private First Class Millard (Midge) Ray Anderson, from Wooster, Ohio
Private First Class Roger Wilson ** Leg shattered by mortar round shrapnel
Private First Class Steven Hill ** Wounded by mortar round shrapnel
Specialist Fourth Class Marcos Rodriguez, from Bueonis, Puerto Rico ** booby-trap shattered his leg
Specialist Fourth Class Michael S. Jarmus, from Englishtown, New Jersey ** wounded by shrapnel from a booby-trap
Specialist Fourth Class Robert Lombardo, from New Haven, Connecticut ** Wounded for the third time by shrapnel.

Chapter Two
First Lieutenant William R. Wilson
Specialist First Class Richard Anastasio

Monday night I checked on the next day's assignments and found they hadn't firmed up the missions at that time. I volunteered to send out the ambush patrol from LZ Bronco. When they accepted my offer, it resulted in an opportunity for three of my four platoons to get time off. My men really needed time off. The men had been out humping (foot patrolling) ever since returning from a long assignment at LZ Cork, an isolated base-camp on top of a mountain to the west. For them, it had been several weeks since they had a day off. They needed to relax with a cool beer or soda, to smoke a cigarette, to play Ping-pong, or to watch a movie in the mess hall. The men also needed to take care of their equipment, do their laundry, get haircuts, write home, rest, and do whatever else they wanted to do within the vary large, and well defended base-camp, LZ Bronco. When fighting or patrolling in the boonies, clothing became torn. When soldiers hit the ground hard, their weapons were dinged. Equipment, like Claymore mines, bullets and bandages were consumed and had to be replaced. Infantrymen needed time to replace or clean their gear before the next engagement.

By accepting my offer of sending out the night ambush, three platoons had a chance to exchange equipment, get replacements for expended ammunition, and the opportunity to clean their weapons thoroughly. Since everyone fought during a battle, it was obvious none wanted to carry a dirty or damaged weapon. War wasn't just about fighting, but was also about being prepared to fight.

Down time was needed to accomplish these tasks. The DX day (direct exchange day) was a day set aside to take care of any equipment needing attention for three of the platoons. It was planned that the one platoon, which did not get the day off, would have time at a later date to take care of their equipment. I've listed the large amount of equipment we carried at the end of this chapter.

The platoon leaders assembled in the orderly room at 1900 hours to receive the tactical operation order. I gave them the good news, "Only one platoon is going out tomorrow. The rest will have a DX day."

Lieutenant Wilson spoke up, "The Third Platoon will go out tomorrow, if it's okay with you, Sir. We'll take our DX day later."

"Agreed," I answered. "The Third Platoon will patrol tomorrow and the remainder will have a DX day. Any questions?"

Since no one had a question, I said, "Lieutenant Wilson, I will give you the operation order after the rest leave. You are dismissed."

Everyone snapped to attention, saluted, and hurried back to give their men the good news. We seldom saluted in the field, except when a field grade officer (Major and above) landed in a secured landing zone. At the base-camp, everyone followed military protocol when addressing a superior officer.

Lt. Wilson and I looked at our maps as we discussed the deployment of his platoon for the next day. I recognized Bill Wilson was a natural leader. He was energetic, exuded a feeling of confidence, and was enthusiastic about performing his military assignments. He was ready to go out the next day, conduct patrols during the day, and provide both twiggies Tuesday night.

Twiggies were nighttime missions where teams of ten men set up a site. A platoon of 20 men, instead of the normal 25 to 35 platoon members, patrolled during the day and broke up into two different teams and waited for the enemy's night movement. Since our forces controlled the air, our ground elements could move freely during the day. The Viet Cong and North Vietnamese moved in darkness. Each twiggy sets up a killing-zone and waited to see if any 'night-crawlers' might enter their trap. If they did, covering fire would sweep the area. We wanted to kill as many of the enemy as possible. Sometimes the complete enemy force would enter the kill-zone before our men would open fire. Other times, only part of the enemy force was in the kill-zone when the fire-fight started. When that happened, while trying to kill as many as possible we had to also defend ourselves against the rest of the enemy soldiers.

After Lt. Wilson left, I showered, returned to my room, and entered additional information on the day's activities in my journal. Then I wrote a short letter home to my eight-year-old son, George, Junior, letting him know I was okay.

We eventually received word back from <u>Chu</u> <u>Lai</u> on the condition of my wounded men. Both Pfc. Wilson and Spc.4 Rodriguez lost legs. Pfc. Hill was going to be sent to Japan to have the shrapnel removed from his leg and body. Spc.4 Jarmus was treated and recuperating. He was to be back with us within a month. Except for the wounds Wilson and Rodriguez had received, I thought we had gotten out of our missions pretty cleanly.

The three platoon leaders and the executive officer showed up in my room and we shared a beer again. It soon became a tradition to get together in my orderly room on the nights we were in the base-camp. We drank and talked about not much of anything. We were getting to know each other better and just spending some quality time together.

-    -   -   o   -   -   -

Tet, the annual Vietnamese holiday season neared and the infantry companies from LZ Bronco conducted frequent sweeps to assure Charlie wouldn't get too close to our base-camp. The VC and NVA traditionally started their large-scale attacks during the Tet holidays, and we needed to be prepared.

At 0700 hours, Lt. Wilson and 19 members of his platoon left to sweep through an abandoned village just southeast of Bronco. An hour later the Third Platoon was in position and started their sweep near <u>An Lac (2)</u>, which was about 1,000 meters away from our location. A dozen of Lt. Wilson's men had to stay in the rear, since only twenty men were needed to conduct the patrol and the two ten-man ambushes. Lt. Wilson had let one of his squad leaders, Ike, who had the sprained ankle, stay in the rear with his platoon sergeant, Juan Espinoza, that day, because it was Juan's birthday.

I completed paperwork in the orderly room, while I monitored both the company radio net and the battalion net. At 1000 hours a call came in, "Delta Six, this is Delta Three. We have enemy contact. Over." We heard the popping sound of gun-fire in the background while listening to the message.

I quickly ordered the company administrative sergeant, Sgt. Brings, "Get on the land-line (field telephone line) and let battalion know."

I grabbed the company frequency radio microphone, "Delta Three, this is Delta Six. What is your situation? Over."

Private First Class Michael Chance, the platoon RTO, reported the Third Platoon had made contact with the enemy. In my orderly room, several of the company headquarters staff listened with me on the company radio net as the reports came in. Battalion headquarters switched one of their radios to our company net frequency so they could listen. Up to that point, the platoon had received and returned fire. I directed First Sergeant Arland L. Wheeler to contact members of the three

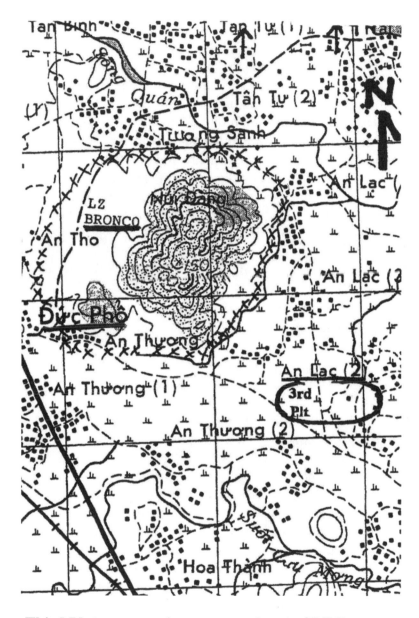

Third Platoon sweeping area southeast of LZ Bronco.

platoons to round up the rest of their men in case we needed to move out.

"One of the enemy ran out from the hedgerow," I heard Pfc. Chance report. "We fired at the Gook and are on our way to him now. I think we got him."

We later learned that when they arrived at the fallen enemy soldier, they saw that their gunfire had ripped his body open when the bullets from the platoon's M-60 machine-gun and their M-16 rifles tore into him. All firing stopped as Lt. Wilson moved one squad of his platoon forward, leap-frogging towards the enemy's location. Suddenly, the right side of the squad came under enemy fire again. All of them hit the ground. Lt. Wilson rushed to the point of contact and moved forward with his riflemen, accompanied by his RTO, Chance.

Wars involved nations and armies, but when the shooting started, the war narrowed down to the man on the ground at the point of contact, and that day it was 21-year-old First Lieutenant William Roger Wilson. He met the enemy face to face, along with Pfc. Chance, Spc.4 Richard Anastasio, Pfc.'s John Rozow and Jack Calamia. We, at the company area in the rear as well as the battalion operations center, witnessed the action that was happening on the battlefield over the radio.

The RTO reported Lt. Wilson and Spc.4 Anastasio fired at and hit the second enemy soldier. They proceeded, with the RTO tagging along, to the spider-hole where he had been hiding. Standing just outside, the two of them fired into the spider-hole. When they stopped, an enemy soldier jumped out of the hole and ran south between the RTO and Lt. Wilson, almost knocking them over. Spc.4 Anastasio and Lt. Wilson fired at the fleeing soldier, who returned fire with his AK-47 automatic rifle as he ran. Several rounds hit the North Vietnamese soldier and he fell, with his rifle still clutched in one of his hands. Lt. Wilson and Spc.4 Anastasio, keeping their weapons ready to fire, started towards the fallen man who lay motionless. As they approached the body, the rest of the squad kept their eyes open for additional enemy combatants.

When they got near him, the wounded enemy soldier turned and swung his AK-47 towards Lt. Bill Wilson with his right hand. Lt. Wilson was holding his M-16 with the barrel pointing up, so before the enemy could shoot his rifle at him, Lt. Wilson quickly bashed the head of the North Vietnamese soldier with the butt of his rifle, several times in quick succession. As he did, the fallen soldier slumped, dropped his automatic rifle and released a grenade he had been holding in his left hand. Someone shouted, "Grenade!"

Spc.4 Anastasio jumped for cover and Pfc. Chance, who was following Lt. Wilson, flattened himself on the ground. Lt. Wilson dived away from the fallen enemy soldier. Before Bill Wilson hit the ground, the grenade exploded. The shrapnel hit both Richard Anastasio and Lt. Wilson. The impact killed Bill Wilson instantly and wounded Spc.4 Anastasio in the foot.

The radio operator, 20-year-old Pfc. Chance was not hit, but he found himself in an open, dry rice paddy with a wounded buddy and a dead platoon leader. Apparently feeling he might be the next target, he called over the radio for help.

Pfc. Chance was with the rifle squad that was without a squad leader. Ike was the squad leader, but he was in the rear due to the sprained ankle he had sustained the previous day. The platoon sergeant, Espinoza, had been allowed to stay back in the base-camp for his birthday. Without a squad leader, a platoon sergeant, or a platoon leader, Pfc. Chance was alone and afraid. There was no one to protect him and no one to tell anyone else what to do. He continually squeezed the long black button on the radio's hand set, pleading for help as he blabbered out his fears over the company net. Alone in an empty rice paddy, out in the open with no place to hide, with a dead commander and a wounded companion, his radio calls revealed he was in a state of shock. Lying there in the open, the only contact he had with anyone was over the radio.

I had already grabbed my backpack and rifle and was out on the company street in the base-camp with Mac and Joe, my two radio operators. The first sergeant and company orderly room personnel were out helping the platoon leaders find their men. I instructed First Lieutenant Evans, my executive officer, to have the remaining three platoons ready to go on my order. I headed for the heliport pad to get a lift out to Pfc. Chance's location. I had already told the company orderly room RTO to call our battalion headquarters on the land-line and request an airlift for me and a dust-off for Anastasio and Wilson.

In the mean time, Lieutenant Colonel Pritchard was on the company radio net, trying to calm down Pfc. Chance. I listened on Joe's radio as we headed for the helicopter pad.

"Is the wounded soldier next to you still alive?" the battalion commander asked.

Chance checked with Anastasio and radioed back, "Yes, Sir. He's alive, but wounded."

"Okay," the battalion commander said, "the medevac chopper is on its way, and it will be there very soon. Look around and see if there are any other enemy soldiers around."

After a minute, Chance replied, "Negative."

"Are any of your platoon buddies near?" the Colonel asked.

Chance replied, "I don't know. I don't see anyone."

"Call out to your buddies to see if any of them are covering you," Colonel Pritchard told Chance.

Chance reported back, "There are several covering Anastasio and me."

The Colonel commented, "Good." Then he told Chance, "Crawl over and check your platoon leader. Find out, for sure, if he is dead or does he needs assistance."

Chance did as he was told and confirmed, "He's dead, Sir."

Then LTC Pritchard told Chance, "There is nothing anyone can do for him right now. All everyone is concerned with now is to get your wounded buddy medical help and to get you back under cover with the rest of your men. Do you feel everything is under control now, soldier?"

"Yes, Sir," Pfc. Chance replied.

Chance sounded better after the Colonel had calmed him down by reassuring him that it was all over and that his buddies were there covering him. By the time I arrived at the helicopter pad, I saw LTC Pritchard heading towards the pad, as he finished talking to Chance on his RTO's radio. We all climbed on the helicopter and headed for the Third Platoon's location. I informed the colonel my other three platoons were forming up and would move out to join the Third Platoon shortly. He concurred with that plan of action and directed me to sweep the contact area for more enemy spider-holes when the other platoons arrived at the contact location.

Sergeant Espinoza reached the helicopter pad the same time we did. He would take command of his platoon once we arrived at Chance's location. While in the air, LTC Pritchard told Sgt. Espinoza to set up a defensive position around the contact site and provide fire support for the helicopter. His main concern was to stabilize the Third Platoon. They had just lost their platoon leader and appeared to be disorganized. Sgt. Espinoza and I both assured the battalion commander we would take charge of the situation and continue the search and destroy mission, once the three other platoons joined us.

When we landed, Sgt. Espinoza took charge of his platoon. The three dead North Vietnamese soldiers were still lying on the ground. The medical evacuation helicopter had already extracted Anastasio and Wilson's body. That was a quick dust-off. Usually, the medical evacuation helicopter, as well as the resupply or the command helicopter would not land unless we gave them a secured landing zone.

No one wanted to die for their country. They wanted to live for it, so they could be around to fight another day. Dying was something that happened, not what we wanted to do. If the ground forces didn't secure a landing zone for the choppers, the pilots didn't risk trying to land in a hot LZ. They knew when we had secured a landing zone, there had still been a good chance they could receive enemy fire. Risks came with flying into a war zone. Without the secured landing zone, the chances of receiving excessive fire from the enemy were greater. That kind of risk was usually taken only in the movies, not on the battlefield. However, that day both the medevac helicopter and our command chopper landed in an unsecured landing zone, because LTC Pritchard had ordered them to do so.

Sgt. Espinoza deployed the remaining Third Platoon members into a defensive position. Pfc. Chance appeared to have gotten back to being his normal self. The platoon had used most of their grenades clearing spider-holes earlier in the day. The command and control chopper had a box of grenades and my men took several of them. The battalion commander flew out, leaving Joe, Mac (my two RTO's), the two squads from the Third Platoon and me on the ground.

Joe called our rear element for me, to see if the other three platoons were mustered. They were still in the base-camp, waiting for my order to move out. My men had run around the large brigade area to find as many of our men as they could. Some were still scattered all over LZ Bronco on what was supposed to be their day-off.

I gave the order for the other three platoons to move out and join us. While I waited for them to join with us, Specialist Fourth Class David I. Giles volunteered to go into the spider-hole that was located in the hedgerow. Usually, our 'tunnel rats' entered caves and spider-holes with pistols. Only officers and mortar crew members were issued pistols. The officers usually gave them to the company men who volunteered to be tunnel rats. I had given my forty-five-caliber pistol to one of the men in another platoon earlier and only carried an M-16 assault rifle. None in the Third Platoon at that time had a pistol, so Giles stripped off his rucksack, weapons belt, helmet, jacket, and his other extraneous items so he could squeeze into the tunnel. He removed the M-16 rifle carrying strap. Standing only in his boots, pants, olive drab T-shirt, a flashlight in one hand and his M-16 in the other, he was ready to crawl into the hole without his helmet.

He pulled the pin on one of the grenades they got from the Colonel's chopper and threw it into the hole. Nothing happened. The grenade had a pin to pull that held the handle onto the grenade. When thrown, the handle flew off. When the handle was off, the striker was released. The striker sprang forward and hit the igniter. After the striker hit the igniter, the delay fuse caused the grenade to explode several seconds later. That's the way it was supposed to work. However, when grenades were shipped, they also had a locking clamp that assured the handle would not come off if the grenade's pin had been accidentally knocked out during handling. Our armorer and supply sergeant removed the packing clamps before issuing the grenades to us. The ones we got from the command and control chopper didn't have the packing clamps removed. None of us realized this at first.

Giles checked his second grenade, removed the packing clamp, and then pulled the pin before he tossed the second grenade into the hole. That one went off, puffing out a cloud of dirt along with a big bang. As Giles started entering the hole, he bumped into an enemy soldier trying to come out. David Giles snapped his M-16 rifle on automatic and blasted all twenty rounds at the enemy soldier in the hole with him. Having expended his only magazine of ammunition, he quickly started backing out of the hole in the side of the hedgerow. While backing out as fast as he could, he caught his pants on some of the thorny overgrowth and tripped. He fell out of the hole on the side of the five-foot high dirt island, towards the dry rice paddy. We all aimed our rifles at the hole to protect the defenseless Giles. Giles was hanging up-side down from the brush, with his back against the mound and his legs elevated over his head, hollering, "Get me out! Get me out of here!"

We thought he was hit and rushed to assist him. When we got him down and heard that he was the only one in the hole who had fired and that he hollered for help to get him untangled from the brush, we laughed. After we got him upright, we waited to see if any more North Vietnamese Army (NVA) soldiers were going to come out of the hole.

While we were waiting, I received word the other three platoons were moving towards us as fast as they could. I knew it would take them almost an hour to reach us, considering they had to check for ambushes, spike-holes, spider-holes, and booby-traps as they maneuvered towards us.

Giles quickly recovered some of the ammo he had left outside with his gear and loaded a full magazine into his assault rifle. He had been afraid that some more NVA soldiers might come out fighting before he had reloaded and was able to fight back, if necessary. Giles' squad had used most of their grenades that day in the initial fire-fight and the day before outside Snoopy. They hadn't participated in the direct exchange (DX), so the other twiggy squad had to bring over some grenades before Giles could continue checking out the spider-hole. Sgt. Espinoza handed Giles a grenade he had received from the other squad, and Giles threw it into the hole. The burst of the grenade caused a perforation on the side of the dike where the spider-hole was located.

Sgt. Espinoza checked the rest of the platoon to see if anyone had any C-Four explosives and blasting caps. Each platoon usually carried both C-Four explosives and blasting caps with them when in the field. But, no DX meant no replenishing of the explosives that had been used the days before.

We talked over the plan for checking out the spider-hole again to be sure all the NVA soldiers in there were dead. We all knew the spider-holes sometimes led to tunnels and large underground rooms that could hold hundreds of enemy soldiers. We had no way of knowing how big this tunnel complex was.

I informed battalion about what we had found so far and was told the command chopper was on its way out to our location with C-Four explosives and blasting caps. Within ten minutes the chopper landed with Major Thomas B. Vaughn, the battalion operations officer.

Major Vaughn had graduated from the Infantry School's Officer Candidate Course at Fort Benning, Georgia in 1962, seven years after I graduated from the same OCS school.

While my men unloaded the explosives, I asked Major Vaughn if I could borrow his 45- Caliber pistol for tunnel-rat work. He gave me his pistol and two extra magazines of ammo. I gave them to Giles, while the others were distributing the explosives.

Giles took some of the explosives and enlarged the hole in the side of the hedgerow. Inside we could see a dead NVA soldier lying where Giles had left him. Not having any wire or

Concealed Tunnel Entrances

rope with which to pull the dead soldier out, we all took our slings off our M-16 rifles and gave them to Giles. He laced them together and made a lasso out of them. He was able to get the strap around one ankle of the dead NVA soldier. We all moved back to one side of the hole, just in case the dead soldier was lying on a grenade, with the pin pulled. This was one of the tricks the NVA used on both their fallen comrades' bodies and ours. We all grabbed the string of rifle straps and proceeded to pull out the dead body. The lassoed leg came out, but the other leg was caught in the hole. We all pulled harder until we heard the crack of his breaking bones, as the other leg folded back up towards the dead man's head. The dead NVA's face was completely disfigured as a result of Giles many shots to his face.

Sgt. Espinoza checked the dead man's wallet and found a picture of a NVA soldier in his dress uniform. We also found some papers, a notebook and a South Vietnamese government identification card showing he was allowed to work in Duc Pho (the hamlet just outside LZ Bronco, our base-camp), as well as Quang Ngai (the provincial capital) and Mao Duc, a hamlet just north of Duc Pho.

With the body out of the hole, Giles crawled back in and found three United States grenades, in addition to the one he threw in that didn't go off. He also retrieved two full M-14 rifle magazines, but no M-14 rifle. Giles also found what looked like a pearl-handled French 32 caliber pistol, with several pistol clips and about thirty rounds of ammunition. In addition, two M-79 grenade launcher rounds were found, as well as several NVA uniforms. We put a tag on the pistol with Giles' name on it. That way, he would claim it as a war trophy. Machine-guns and heavy weapons were not allowed to be taken home as war trophies, but pistols and non-firing enemy equipment were allowed to be claimed. We always asked for volunteers to be tunnel rats. There was seldom a problem finding a volunteer, because they would have first pick of any of the captured equipment that had been found.

The dead NVA soldier had two South Vietnam one-hundred Dong bills in his wallet. One of the men in the Third Platoon took them for the platoon soda and beer fund. In the field or in the rear, we had to pay for our sodas and beers. Putting the captured money in the platoon soda and beer fund prevented any argument that might arise over cash that was recovered. That way everyone in the platoon shared the booty.

We blew up the grenades and ammunition we found with our resupplied explosives. We never used captured ammunition or weapons, even if they were our own weapons that we had recovered, because they were sometimes tampered with and left as booby-traps for us to find. The most common booby-trap we found was the time-delay fuse taken out of grenade. This would cause the grenade to explode in the thrower's face instead of some distance away. Captured weapons were taken to the rear base-camp for inspection and refurbishment by our army ordinance specialists.

We didn't do anything with the dead NVA soldiers' bodies. The local Vietnamese farmers buried all the dead, enemy or friendly soldiers. It was their custom and most families were on both sides in this area of operation.

We left an Ace-of-Spades playing card with the bodies. The Vietnamese were superstitious and believed the Ace-of-Spades was a bad luck card. It was the US soldier's calling card, the infantryman's way of conducting psychological warfare. The playing cards companies had sent decks of cards with only the Ace-of-Spades in them when they heard what we were doing.

The other platoons from the base-camp linked up with us after we finished with the spider-hole. We returned Major

**David Giles in Chu Lai after being awarded the
Bronze Star and Army Commendation Medals.**

Vaughn's pistol and turned over the papers to him that we had found, for intelligence scrutiny to see if there was any useful information. I ordered the two fresh infantry platoons to search the two islands near the one we were on. The Weapons Platoon stayed with me so they would be available to support whichever platoon might need it. I ordered Sgt. Espinoza's Third Platoon to check out the island we were on to see if there were any other spider-holes in it. The Third Platoon didn't find anything else on this island and the other two platoons didn't find anyone on their islands. All four platoons headed back for base-camp with me after Major Vaughn and the captured documents were airlifted back to Bronco.

After chowing down at Bronco, the Second Platoon pulled the twiggies that night. The other platoons stood-down for the night. Lt. Bird and Lt. Claybaugh both took Lt. Wilson's death hard. I thought keeping them busy helped prevent them from dropping into a state of depression.

Of the officers I had met at LZ Bronco, I liked Lt. Wilson the most. He was straight talking and a nice guy that everyone and anyone would like. He must have been a charmer with the ladies, I reasoned. I knew we were going to miss him a lot.

That night I sat by myself, drinking a few beers while trying to write a letter to his family. But, I couldn't do justice to what a fine officer he was - - how he was right out there in the front, leading his men. He never asked his men to do anything he wasn't willing to do himself. There are military leaders and there are military administrators. Bill Wilson was a leader. I knew that someday I would be able to find the right words and write to his family, but I couldn't find the words that night.

The next day, the Second Platoon was the only one on patrol. I made arrangements with Captain Benson, the Brigade Chaplain, to give a memorial service for Lt. Wilson. Almost everyone in the company, except the platoon on patrol, attended. The company mess hall was packed for the memorial service.

The First Platoon leader asked if I wanted to say a few words. I declined and instead suggested he give the eulogy, as he had served with him the longest. He agreed and I stood in the back, with tears in my eyes. Both the lieutenant and Capt. Benson gave their prayers and shared their memories of Lt. Wilson with us.

I felt Lt. Wilson was the closest friend I had at LZ Bronco, and he was gone. The impact on me was much like when my high school buddy and fellow soldier, Kenneth Kaiser, was the first Southern California National Guardsman to be killed in the Korean War. At Ken's funeral, I felt like I was looking at a world shrouded in a gloomy haze. My gut was churning, and I felt like crying. But warriors aren't allowed to cry. I broke the rules. Tears trickled down my cheek back then and again the day of Bill's service. I shed a tear for my comrade who had fallen in battle, as I numbly went through the motions of a stoic professional soldier that day. It was as if I had been witnessing what was happening instead of being a part of it. After feeling that way again for Bill Wilson, I told myself, *Don't make friends again. It is too painful when one falls. George, don't do it again. Stay detached and act professional.*

- - - o - - -

The infantrymen normally carried the following equipment in the field:
Air mattress (to keep the soldier off the wet ground), Backpack (RuckSack), Bandoleer of Ammunition (2 each), Bayonet, Beer (3 cans), Can Opener, Candy, Canteen Case,

Infantryman with M-16 Assault Rifle

Canteen Cup, Cigarettes or Cigars, Cigarette Lighter, Combat Boots (with a steel plate on the bottom), Compass, Dog Tags, Envelopes, Fatigue Jacket, Fatigue Pants, First Aid Pouch and Field Bandage, Flashlight (L-shaped, with removable red filter for low visibility use), Garters (to keep the pants clinched against the boots), Percussion Grenades (2 each), Smoke Grenade (1 each), White Phosphorous Grenade (1 each), Cartage Belt, Handkerchief (olive-drab), Steel Helmet, Helmet Liner, Helmet Elastic Strap, Camouflage Helmet Cover, Entrenching Tool (Shovel), Halogen Water Purification Tablets, Malaria Tablets (Weekly & Daily), Mess Kit (2 Pans, Knife, Fork & Spoon), Mosquito Repellent, Poncho, Poncho Liner (Camouflaged Porous Blanket), Rations for 3 Days, Salt Tablets, Smoke Grenades, Soda-pop (3 cans), Socks (2 each), Stationary, Sterno Food Heating Tablets, Toilet Paper, Towel (olive-drab) (smaller than a shower towel, larger than a hand towel), Watch, Water Canteen (2 or 3 each), and Writing Pads for Messages.

Plus, every infantryman carried two or more of the following alternative equipment:
Binoculars, Blasting Caps, C-Four Plastic Explosives, Claymore Mines, Field First Aid Kit (for Medics), Daily Cryptic Code Tables, Daily Sun/Moon Rise/Set Tables, Maps, Map Grease Pencil, Pencil, Fuse (for explosives), Grappling line and hooks, Machete, M-14 Automatic Rifle, M-16 Assault Rifle, 45-Caliber Pistol, 66-Millimeter LAW (Light Antitank Weapon), Thin Trip Wire, Primer Cord (Exploding Cord for Explosives), Radio, Trip Flares, Vietnamese to English Dictionary, M-60 Machine-gun, M-79 Rifle Grenade Launcher, 60-millimeter Mortar, 60-Millimeter Mortar Base Plate and Ammunition for any of the above weapons.

- - - o - - -

Infantryman with M-79 Grenade Launcher

Specialist Fourth Class David I. Giles came from Saint Paul, Minnesota. He turned twenty-one just two months before he was drafted on 29 January 1968. He was single when he was sent to Fort Campbell, Kentucky for his basic training. He received his advanced infantry training at Fort Polk, Louisiana. Upon his arrival in Vietnam around the end of June 1968, he completed ten days of combat training at Chu Lai before being assigned to Company D. His first assignment was an infantryman in the Third Platoon. He became a 'tunnel rat' and the rifle squad's demolition man. After ten months of fighting as an infantryman, David was recognized as a proficient combatant and showed he had leadership ability. The result of his exemplary performance was Giles' promotion to Sergeant and being assigned as an infantry squad leader in the Third Platoon on 19 April 1969.

-    -   -   o   -   -   -

The following is a list of the Delta Dogs heroes who were identified in this chapter.

First Lieutenant William R. Wilson, from Alma, Arkansas ** Killed by enemy grenade

Specialist Fourth Class Richard Anastasio, from Belmont, Massachusetts ** wounded by grenade shrapnel

First Sergeant Arland L. Wheeler, from Leesville, Louisiana

Platoon Sergeant Juan Espinoza, from Texas

Private First Class Michael J. Chance, from Johnstown, Pennsylvania

Private First Class John (Jack) Rozow, from South Bend, Indiana

Private First Class Jack Calamia, from Glendale, New York.

Specialist Fourth Class David I. Giles, from Saint Paul, Minnesota

M18 CLAYMORE MINE

Chapter Three

Specialist Fourth Class William C. Gould

There have always been two kinds of military leaders, warriors and politicians. Generals Patton and Grant were warriors, while Generals Eisenhower and Bradley were politicians. Both types of leaders were needed, and each served well in their chosen roles. I believed I fit into the warrior category who wasn't 'just following orders.' I was an on-the-ground-commander who controlled my infantry company's tactical operation. Wars were won or lost by generals and their staff. Battles were won by the commander on-the-ground. For us, there were only 86 to 105 grunts against whatever number of enemy we came in contact with. For an infantry company, success was not winning the war. We were too small to win a war. Our objective was to cause as many deaths and wounded enemy as we could by any means available to us. Success was measured by killing or wounding more than the number of casualties we suffered. During the 1969 Tet battles we Company D infantrymen were very successful. We inflicted more deaths and casualties on the Viet Cong and North Vietnamese Regular Army soldiers than they inflicted on us. Sometimes the support we needed was not delivered. When that happened, the lack of support restricted our effectiveness and retarded our ability to perform optimally during an engagement, it also prevented us from conducting a post battle assessment to verify the extent of damages we had inflicted.

-    -   -   o   -   -   -

We were short two platoon leaders after losing Lt. Wilson, but our company's mission had not changed. The next day, Wednesday, 26 March 1969, the Second Platoon was in the field sweeping around the same area where Bill Wilson had been killed. I was back at the base-camp with the rest of the company. I received the following day's mission, and gave my orders to the First Platoon leader Lt. Bird, Third Platoon leader Sgt. Gourley and Weapons Platoon leader Sgt. Grimes. The Second Platoon was still out in the field, so I would issue the new mission to Lt. Claybaugh later.

Battalion directed our Weapons Platoon to stay behind and provide extra security for the defense of LZ Bronco. I was not happy about that. The loss of the Weapons Platoon took one dimension of my company's weapons firing ability away from us in the two-dimensional war. Our infantry platoons had M-16 rifles, M-60 machine-guns, M-79 rifle grenade launchers, and shoulder fired rocket launchers (LAW's). These armaments were all direct fire weapons. With these weapons we could only shoot at what we could see. The hand thrown grenades and mortar rounds were indirect fire weapons. Those armaments gave us the second dimension for laying down fire on the enemy from above them. Hand grenades could only be used against an enemy who was very close to us. Without the Weapons Platoon, we lost the indirect fire of their mortar, which could be propelled for a greater distance. We also lost the machine-gun fire they provided. We still had artillery fire available, but that had to be requested, and it was not always available, accurate, and could not be applied within 100 meters from our position. Battalion's decision assured the brigade base-camp better protection, but if our company came under attack, we were less capable of effectively fighting back. It was like robbing Peter to pay Paul, and we weren't Paul.

Tet, the lunar New Year, was the most important holiday in Vietnam. The four days were a time for celebration by the Vietnamese, and a time to remember their heritage. It was a business holiday and a time for ancestor worship. The Vietnamese worshippers gave obeisance to their ancestors, paid debts, and made fresh starts for the new year. During the war, Tet was frequently used to kickoff the new military offense by the Viet Cong and North Vietnamese communist forces. It was a prudent time for us to be cautious since it was highly likely they would launch new attacks. Where and when was the mystery. Would the enemy's major thrust be in the south, in the north, on the coast, or in the mountains? No one knew for sure, but everyone had been pretty certain in March, 1969 that a Tet offensive was coming.

-   -   -   o   -   -   -

I had replenished my supply of water and salt tablets the night before. In the hot climate we sweated a lot, so we had to drink plenty of liquids, and we took a lot of salt tablets. We had to be able to sweat. If we couldn't, the body's pH level would have gone out of kilter and caused all kinds of physical and mental problems. One could not maneuver well, fight well, and use logical thinking well when his pH was out of balance. While at the base-camp, cold beer or cold soda was a pleasant way of replenishing lost fluids. In the field, we had rice paddy water, warm sodas, and warm beers. The rice paddy water was the least desirable, since human waste was used as fertilizer. The water purification tablets killed the germs and bacteria in the water. However, the particles of human waste didn't disappear. We had to let the solids settle in the water before we drank from our canteens, being careful not to disturb the sediment. Water from the rear base-camp was brought out about once every three to four days. Since we couldn't carry more than a day's worth, we had to drink what was available, no matter how disgusting we found it.

The temperature would drop from 115-degrees during the day to 85-degrees at night, still with high humidity. The 30-degree difference was very noticeable, but drinking 85-degree sodas and beers was not the same as drinking it ice cold. We envied the guys in the rear, because they could get an ice cold drink just about any time they wanted, day or night. We couldn't get cold drinks in the field except on resupply days. When we were in the field for several days, the choppers would bring us water, Combat-rations (C-rations), ammo, plus the sodas and beers we paid for. I gave the supply clerk my monthly deposit and each time we were resupplied, I'd get my standard order of four sodas (one ice cold) and three beers. I drank the ice cold soda as soon as I got it. The next three sodas I saved for my morning breakfast. I found that after a can of soda had sat in my pack all night, it was a lot cooler. Each evening, I had a hot can of beer with my supper. Not my top choice, but it was the best I got as a foot soldier. That should make it pretty easy to understand why we grunts envied the guys in the rear.

-   -   -   o   -   -   -

The next day, Thursday, 27 March, the Second Platoon started out on a search-and-destroy mission in a different area than they searched the day before. The previous night, Lt. Claybaugh had deployed his troops by dividing them in two groups of ten each. Seven of his men stayed back at LZ Bronco with us, since they weren't needed for the twiggies. The men in the field took turns sleeping while they waited for any enemy to wonder into their ambush site. When daybreak arrived, the Second Platoon's mission was to sweep an area to the east located off Lt. Claybaugh's map.

If the Second Platoon encountered enemy forces, not having maps became a big problem. The location of friendly troops and the location of the enemy's position were given in degrees of longitude and latitude. These were determined by comparing the terrain with the topographical map. Locations were determined by comparing hill masses with elevation lines on the map. The locations were translated into longitudinal and latitude numbers by using the checkered lines on the map. This information was sent by radio, using a numbers-to-letters cryptic coding table that changed from day to day. Without a map, Lt. Claybaugh couldn't accurately call for artillery fire. His only indirect fire which was available had been reduced to hand grenades, since artillery fire was difficult to achieve without a map to identify target grid coordinates.

- - - o - - -

The night before, I called battalion and recommended that I take the rest of the company out before first light, around 0500 hours, to join the Second Platoon. Had we left then, as I suggested, we would have been with Lt. Claybaugh by 0730 hours, with his maps, but the battalion operations officer didn't like the idea fearing we might get caught in an enemy ambush. I explained I was familiar with the area, and had operated in that area with Company C before joining Company D. He still didn't buy my plan. Instead, Major Vaughn instructed me to have the Second Platoon move out of their twiggy locations at first-light and head east toward the new area of operation, off their map. The command and

71

control helicopter would drop Lt. Claybaugh his maps first thing in the morning.

Nothing is ever consistent in a combat zone and this was no exception. For some unknown reason, the command and control chopper was late. This was a frequent occurrence. Sometimes it was because of priority scheduling; and sometimes there were no helicopters available because of maintenance. For whatever reason, the chopper didn't show up to take the maps out as promised.

After waiting some time, battalion directed me to assure the Second Platoon was moving east on their assigned mission without maps. I radioed Lt. Claybaugh that morning and let him know he had to continue moving toward the assigned objective area and arrive there by 0800 hours. He complied with the orders, and at 1000 hours his 20 men were sweeping the new area when they came under enemy fire.

I was monitoring them by radio while I was in the company orderly room accomplishing some of the paperwork tasks that had been waiting for me. At 1000 hours, I got a call from the Second Platoon, "Delta Six, this is Delta Two. Over."

The company clerk answered the call, "Delta Two, this is Delta Six. Over."

"This is Delta Two. We have contact. We are receiving AK-47 and grenade fire from Charlie. Over," they radioed back.

I knew each weapon had its own distinct sound when fired, making it easy for the Second Platoon to identify the type of weapons the enemy was using when the fire-fight had started. Lt. Claybaugh maneuvered half the 20 men against the enemy, and Platoon Sergeant James H. Smith led the other half in a two pronged counterattack. They spread their men out and engaged the enemy with small arms fire. The enemy fire didn't diminish, so they had to call in artillery fire, as best they could.

Calling in artillery without a map was a tricky business. It required them to use the bracketing technique. Artillery rounds were fired, one at a time. The first round was called to strike a good distance away, then one up closer. By sighting were the rounds fell, it was then easy to adjust the fire either forward or back a little, or to move it to one side or another. Each succeeding round could be walked closer to the enemy by adjusting the fire from where the last artillery round fell. Once the correct location was hit by a single round, a 'fire-for-effect' was called. When the supporting artillerymen received an order for 'fire-for-effect,' they provided the normal amount of fire which was available for that engagement. It could be one cannon or the entire artillery battery of six cannons that would fire in and around the target location. If we were lucky and they were available, the entire artillery battalion might fire on the enemy's position. This could result in over 24 cannons firing into the enemy.

I sent men out to alert those in the base-camp that the Second Platoon was in contact with the enemy, and we would be moving out shortly. However, the artillery barrage was effective, the enemy broke off engagement with the Second Platoon, and reinforcements were not needed.

Before the rest of the company was assembled and ready to move out from LZ Bronco to join Lt. Claybaugh, battalion changed our company's mission. The remainder of the company at LZ Bronco was ordered to move out to a location west of LZ Bronco. We were to proceed west, passing Duc Pho. Then, we were to sweep south of Thanh Lam (1) to Thanh Lam (2). After sweeping the area, we were to set up a night logger position.

Loggering was an old western term for circling the wagons to provide all around protection. In the field, we loggered each night when we ate and when we bedded down for the night. The Second Platoon was to return to LZ Bronco, pick up more equipment and ammunition, then join us southwest of Duc Pho before we loggered for the night.

As we were on our way out, we passed the Second Platoon as they were on their way in. When I met Lt. Claybaugh, he asked, "Captain, can my men eat a hot meal before we move out?"

"Sure, as long as your platoon moves out before 1630 hours," I said.

Lt. Claybaugh confirmed the order and moved back into the base-camp for a warm meal, resupplies, maps and the replacement of his men's expended ammunition.

With the Second Platoon and the Weapons Platoon still in the base-camp, my command group and the two remaining platoons (First and Third Platoons) moved out, skirting Duc Pho village. As the 60 of us moved away from the village, children waved at us and started following us as we marched in a column-of-twos on the sides of the dirt road to our assigned area. We hadn't started our sweep yet, because we were too close to Duc Pho. We soon came to a railroad track berm. It appeared as if it had been a long time since trains had used the track, as the iron rails had been removed.

After awhile we stopped for a break and bought cold sodas and popsicles from the kids who were still following us. They had gotten ice from the ice house in Duc Pho and carried the buckets of iced soda with them. They sold the American brands of canned cool sodas to the South Vietnamese and American soldiers operating close to their village. They knew that soldiers were eager customers after marching in the hot weather with all their military gear weighing them down.

It may have also been their way of having fun. The villages didn't have television sets, radios, school yards, or parks. Every day of their lives were dangerous, living in a war torn countryside. Selling sodas to soldiers was no more dangerous

Vietnamese kids from Duc Pho following the Delta Dogs on the old railroad berm with popsicles and cold sodas.

for them than any other activity in their daily lives. Plus, we welcomed them and showered them with candy and gum. As far as I was concerned, we were in Vietnam to help the South

Vietnamese fight the communist invaders from the north, so I made sure we were friendly towards the villagers and their kids.

After the break we moved west, then we cut to the south. We spread out from our column formation and started looking for signs of the enemy's presence. We tried shaking the kids who had been following us, but they joyfully continued to follow, some distance away. We swept the area until we got to the southern end of the deserted village of <u>Thanh</u> <u>Lam</u> (2).

With the death of Lt. Wilson, I had Lt. Bird commanding the First Platoon, and I had assigned the First Platoon sergeant, Sergeant First Class Guy H. Gourley, to take charge of the Third Platoon. Gourley was a more senior non-commissioned officer (NCO rank of E-7) than Sgt. Espinoza (an E-5). Sgt. Gourley also was a regular army soldier with more years of active duty. Sgt. Espinoza was a fine sergeant. However, being a draftee who was promoted rapidly because of his leadership ability, he had only been in the army for a little over a year. Without an officer as a platoon leader, I felt a more experienced non-com was needed to be in charge of the Third Platoon. That was not taking anything away from Sgt. Espinoza. Even with the change, I still felt uncomfortable being in no-man's-land with only two of my four platoons, one commanded by an experienced officer and one by a new platoon leader, Sgt. Gourley. When Lt. Claybaugh's Second Platoon would join us, we were still left with only 86 men, instead of the 105 we would normally operate in the field.

- - - o - - -

LZ Bronco had about 10,000 soldiers in it, but only 10 to 15 percent were out in the bush like us. The rest were mechanics, staff personnel, artillerymen, medics, supply personnel, motor pool workers, cooks, engineers, helicopter crews, prison guards, infantrymen acting as base-camp security personnel, military police, intelligence interrogators, and dozens of other jobs that needed to be performed to support what we did in the field. Out of the 16 infantry companies operating out of LZ Bronco, one was taken out of the field to guard the Navy supply center south of us. That left about 1,500 infantrymen in the field.

The NVA army had two infantry divisions operating in Quang Ngai Providence, the Second and Third Divisions. Each division consisted of about 5,000 enemy soldiers. In addition, the local VC brought the number of enemy to well over 10,000 combatants in our area of operation. On our side, with the division support personnel and the US Navy, Army, Marine and Air Force air support, probably no more than five percent of the US forces in Vietnam were out in the field fighting the war in hand-to-hand combat, as we did.

I felt certain when all those rear echelon military personnel returned home, they would tell stories about the ordeal it had been for them during the war. Of course, I'm sure they left out the part about being able to have ice cold sodas, beers and being provided movies at night. It wasn't a big deal to them. I doubt they even talked about enjoying hot meals and showers. I'm sure they never knew what it was like to drink rice paddy water, not being able to change clothes for thirty days at a time, and not having refrigeration, fans, or mosquito nets to keep the pests away at night. The grunts who humped through the countryside carried home a very different picture of the war.

-   -   -   o   -   -   -

That day's mission was to make contact with the enemy and engage the enemy in battle, no matter how large the enemy force was. In Vietnam, we used the 'pile-on-tactics.' Once we engaged the enemy, additional troops who were not engaged in battle were to be rushed into the battle until we outnumbered the enemy. Superior numbers, plus having tactical air support and artillery fire available on demand, was supposed to assure our success. The economy-of-force mission, using pile-on-tactics, allowed our army units to use a force as small as our 86 men to find and fix a much larger enemy force. It was a risky proposition for our infantrymen because we could maneuver ourselves into a fight where we were out-numbered, out-positioned, and out-gunned. Then we would face the additional danger of not being reinforced in a timely manner. I knew if that happened, it would be disastrous for us.

We swept for a few more hours and then stopped to eat supper. As the day grew longer, the kids that had been following us finally went home. There was a curfew for the villagers, and no one was allowed outside the safe hamlets after dark except the enemy and us.

I wanted to give the Second Platoon time to catch up with us, so we ate earlier than usual. We sat in the hot, late afternoon sun, finding what little shade we could to eat our C-rations. I had canned ham and lima beans, a cracker that had twice a diameter as an Oreo cookie, but just about as thick. It was like eating a flat pretzel, rather than a soda cracker. Some men ate a cookie that was as big and hard as the cracker I ate. Others found a rock hard chocolate bar in their meal. It was as round and thick as the cracker and the cookie, but it was harder than either. It had to be hard so it wouldn't melt in the extreme temperatures we were continually operating in.

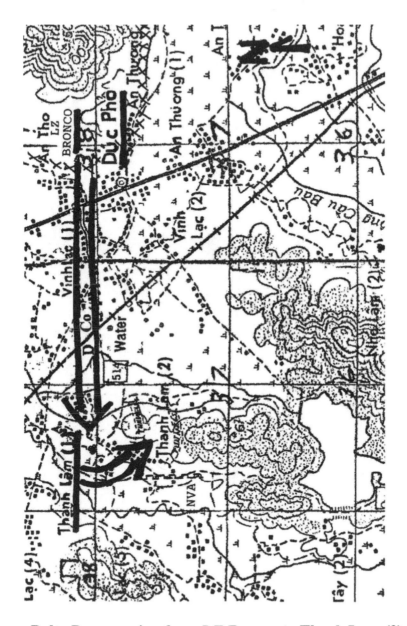

Delta Dogs moving from LZ Bronco to Thanh Lam (2).

This time of year was what we called their summer season. Due to the climatic conditions of this tropical land, the Vietnamese equivalent to summer was during the US winter. Their winter-like months were caused by the monsoon season. In July, the Monsoon rain caused the temperature to drop significantly when it rains day and night for 30 days at a time, without any let up. The coldest it got all year long was 74 degrees in July, at night.

-    -   -   o   -   -   -

We ate dinner in a dried, empty rice paddy. Some deserted islands surrounded us, with only house foundations left on them. After eating, we continued our slow sweep of the area, while we waited for the Second Platoon to join us. The First Platoon, which was on the right side of our sweep to the south, found an entrance to a large tunnel. Then the Third Platoon, sweeping to the left, reported finding another tunnel. Before we started investigating the two tunnels, the Second Platoon arrived.

The Second Platoon helped us in the search by covering the area between the other two platoons and discovered two more tunnels. I checked out the tunnel entrances, and they were major excavations about eight or nine feet tall with about the same width. Dirt ramps led down to some of the tunnel entrances. I had never seen tunnels that large or that long. They looked like mining shafts that I had seen when I visited the Calico Junction mine in California.

The sun was about to go down and the three platoons were spread out across 500 meters. I ordered the platoons to move back to where I was located, and we formed a logger defensive formation at a temporary location until after dark.

I was really nervous about the tunnels we found. A complex that large meant there could be an entire battalion, maybe even a regiment with several thousand NVA regulars hiding there. A force that large might easily overwhelm us, and every one of my men knew it. They also knew it was going to be our problem for awhile. The find was significant, and I knew battalion was going to want to know more about what we found. I called in the report and, as expected, we were ordered to remain there for the night and investigate further the next morning. Battalion let me know the next day they would send out engineers to destroy the tunnels. From then on I knew I had to proceed with extreme caution. The decisions I faced might well determine how many of my men would be able to leave the field alive. We continued to logger on the deserted island in the middle of the dry rice paddies until dark.

As the daylight was fading, I had the three platoon leaders join me. The entire company knew that we no longer took a logger position for the night at the same location where we ate supper. They also knew we no longer ate breakfast where we had formed a logger defensive position for the night. I showed the platoon leaders the location on the map where we would be loggering that night. Before we moved out, battalion called and wanted to know if we were in our night logger position yet. I reported we were still moving.

After dark I gave the order to move out. When I gave the order, I didn't talk on the company radio net. While at Chu Lai, I found that civilian radios with broad-band-width reception could pick up our military radio communications. After dark, we communicated by clicking the send button, not by talking into the handset. When we depressed the send button on the radio, it provided a clicking sound on all the receivers. The platoons heard the number of clicks that we had earlier agreed to. After Joe Dodson, my RTO sent the number of clicks for the move order, the First Platoon moved out, the Second Platoon followed them, the command group left next and the Third Platoon covered our rear.

The moon was already up by the time the sun went down, and it would be up until 0330 in the morning. We moved very cautiously and quietly into the night logger position. The First Platoon spread out and assumed the forward perimeter defensive position. The Second Platoon took fighting positions from the entrance point and to the right until they came in contact with the First Platoon. The Third Platoon found good fighting spots from the entrance to the left side until they came in contact with a First Platoon's soldier. The headquarters group formed in the center of the night position circle. The company night logger position was complete, and radio shifts were set so the radio operators would also sleep in shifts. We set up shifts, so one-fifth of our men would be awake at all times.

-     -   -   o   -   -   -

The 11th Light Infantry Brigade, to which we belonged, had wanted all troops operating out of LZ Bronco, to be in their night logger positions and have all their twiggies in position before dark, which was usually around 2000 hours at that time of year. As a cavalry officer who normally operated independently in the field, I learned long before Vietnam that if we slept where we ate or ate where we slept, there was a good chance the enemy would know our location. Several friendly outfits in our 11th Light Infantry Brigade operating area received incoming mortar rounds from the enemy while they slept because they had bedded down in the same location where they cooked their evening meal. I didn't want that happening to my company. To ensure that didn't happen, I had my men eat each evening before we moved into our final night logger position. I only moved into the final location in the dark, to keep the enemy from seeing where we bedded down.

Each morning, I had the men saddle-up and move to a new location before we had breakfast. In the morning, the move before breakfast assured all my men were packed and equipped for fighting when we stopped to eat. The battalion operations center personnel complained that their friendly forces locations report to the brigade operation center was always late. The US Army Artillery fired random barrages after dark into no-man's-land. Without knowing our location, they couldn't fire until an hour or so after dark. This was a few hours after they started randomly firing into other areas.

Our actions caused many rear echelon officers to have concerns about the ability of the commanders and our battalion operation centers officers' ability to control their lower echelon commanding officers. My concern, however, was not to disobey or belay an order, but to assure the safety of my men, even if we delayed our battalion, the brigade, and the artillery battalion's nightly operations. I was continually berated for my delay each night when I was the last one to report our night logger location and the company twiggy locations.

In case my maneuvering after dark didn't work, I took my boots off each night before falling asleep. I didn't care to die with my boots on. That's an old cavalry tradition. Even though I commanded an infantry company, I was still a cavalry officer. As a cavalry trooper, I felt a good way to die was in an old age home, in a hospital or at home in bed. Dying on the battlefield, with my boots on was not a good way to die. Each night I took off my boots, changed my socks from the ones I wore that day to the ones I had worn the day before. By changing socks each day I lessened the chance of getting foot-rot.

In the morning, I put my boots back on, packed the thin porous camouflaged blanket that I covered myself with to keep the mosquitoes away, rolled the poncho or air mattress that I used to keep off the moist ground, and packed everything in my backpack so we could move out. After moving to a morning logger position, everything I had was packed, and I was ready to maneuver if attacked, to either fight back or bug-out.

In all wars there are those who follow orders and those who do not. The military system is held together by the creed that orders must be obeyed. To not obey an order would bring charges of insubordination, dereliction of duty, cowardliness, performing conduct that is unbecoming an officer, disobeying a direct order, countermanding an order, rebellion, mutiny, usurping authority, being a traitor, and more. I had to come up with defensible reasons for delaying the execution of the order. To outright disobey an order on the battlefield during time of war would put me at great risk. The excuse I used almost every night was I hadn't completed maneuvering into a defensible position, or all my men hadn't arrived at the night logger position yet.

After I repeatedly reported in late, the operations center's responses let me know that it became obvious to the command that they had what we in the military called a loose-cannon commanding Company D, someone who would twist and bend their orders. In the military, as in industry, if one didn't support the objectives and desires of the boss and the boss' boss, they would soon become a thorn in their side. This was walking a thin line. The first time a loose-cannon stepped out of line, the hammer would drop on him hard. My not reporting our night logger or night ambush sites before dark embarrassed a lot of staff officers and commanders, whose ability to command was brought into question, to a point where they were making their feelings heard in our nightly communications. The fine line I had to walk was to only delay orders, not disobey them.

I thought at times, it would pay to have friends in high positions. When mistakes were made in the field, friends in the rear could gloss over the reports. Miscalculations and mistaken incidents could be viewed as either command errors or just the consequences of the many different obstacles that were ran into during combat. I knew any incident I might be involved in would not get much support from my battalion staff. I knew there was no champion for me, if I needed one, but I was wrong. My support came from the most unlikely person, when it was needed.

My extensive military experience let me avoid putting my men at risk without disobeying orders. On top of my lengthy military experience, I was probably the only officer in the battalion who had an article on military tactics published in an international military journal. My article, <u>From The Chessboard To The Battle Field</u>, was published years before in September 1965, in Armor Magazine.

As far as future recommendations for promotion from these senior officers were concerned, since I was an Army National Guard officer who was called to active duty for the Vietnam War, I was not worried about protecting my military career. Engineering was my vocation; military service was my avocation. I knew my future was in the civilian industry life, not the military life. Also, I was probably the only officer in the battalion who had served nine years as an enlisted man, from private to a sergeant first class platoon sergeant, before getting an officer's commission. I felt with my background as both an enlisted-man and as an officer, I could keep my men safe by delaying the reporting of our night logger position.

Sgt. Grimes was also a loose-cannon. Our infantry company was issued 81-millimeter mortars, which Sgt. Grimes never took into the field with us. The US Army Table Of Organization required an 81-millimeter mortar be issued to Infantry Company Weapons Platoons. The Weapons Platoon

U. S. Army 60-mm Mortar.

had been able to barter for a 60-millimeter mortar. It was unauthorized, but it had several advantages over the larger, more cumbersome 81-millimeter mortar.

The 81-mm mortar weighed 132 pounds. The 60-millimeter only 42 pounds. Units that tried to take the 81-millimeter mortar to the field with them could not maneuver as fast as we could. Not only did the large mortar weigh more, the seven pound mortar ammunition was heavier than the four pound 60-millimeter mortar round. In order to have the capability for fast maneuverability, some infantry companies would not take their 81-millimeter mortar out in the field with them, or they took fewer mortar rounds. With the 60-millimeter mortar, Sgt. Grimes could take his mortar into the boonies and carry twice as many mortar rounds to engage the enemy.

Keeping enough 60-millimeter mortar rounds was a challenge for Sgt. Grimes. The 60-mm mortar round was not a normal US Army supply channel item. In order to get the ammunition, Sgt. Grimes and our company personnel in the rear had to barter for mortar rounds. For some reason we didn't fully understand, Navy, Air Force, and the South Vietnamese soldiers liked our C-rations and LRRP rations (Long Range Reconnaissance Patrol rations). The LRRP rations were freeze dried meals where you just added hot water. We had rice and chili in a plastic bag and many other selections. The Combat-rations were canned food, like pork and beans, ham and lima beans, spaghetti and meatballs, beans and weenies, and other varieties of canned food. The C-rations came with canned candy, crackers and canned cookies. Plus, every month we received a 'goodies-box' called a Field Pack containing cigarettes, cigars, several kinds of candy, as well as other snacks and personables. These items are what we used to trade for 60-mm mortar rounds.

After a short night's sleep, we were up at first light the next morning. We moved back toward the tunnels and loggered in a good defensive position to eat breakfast. Friday morning, 28 March 1969, everyone was a little edgy, a little nervous, and a little moody. It was Tet. We had just lost a platoon leader and we were very close to a good hiding place for an NVA battalion, or worse yet, an entire enemy regiment. After breakfast, I was ready to move the company out when I got our orders from battalion. They ordered us to draw maps showing the locations of the tunnels. I asked each platoon to assign an artist and have him draw a map of the tunnels they had found the day before. When they completed their drawings, they were to join Lt. Faust, our artillery forward observer. Together they would make a map of the entire hill mass, showing the location of each tunnel's entrance.

The platoons guarded the tunnel entrances. Tunnel-rats went inside to see what was there and what direction the tunnels followed. They were armed with flashlights and 45-caliber pistols. The artists followed them into the tunnels and measured the widths, heights, distances and turns that the tunnels took. They also drew the locations and dimensions of the several underground rooms which were attached to the tunnels. There were about a dozen small, short tunnels. Plus, there were three long tunnels that spanned over 250 feet long. The three long tunnels were four to ten feet high, with 10 by 20 foot rooms attached and they were about 10 feet high. We added the tunnel routes and rooms to the tunnel entrance map.

The engineers had not arrived, so I called battalion and gave them the tunnel information and asked if we should continue sweeping to the south or wait at the tunnel location. Battalion instructed me to stay put while they assembled the engineer personnel who could fly out and join us. Then we were to check with battalion for our next assignment after the tunnels were sealed.

Not long after that, two men were flown out to join us. One was a demolition engineer and the other was a chemical unit soldier. They flew out 500 pounds of explosives with them and several bags of CN tear-gas powder. CN tear-gas was similar to what was used by the police to disperse crowds, only more potent and irritating. They used 100 pounds of the C-Four plastic explosives to see if it would seal one of the small tunnel entrances. First they placed some opened dry CN tear-gas powder bags inside the tunnel entrance. If anyone tried to dig into the tunnel, they would be gassed when they hit the powder. The explosives sealed the one small tunnel entrance. Next the engineer and chemical man attempted to destroy one of the larger tunnel entrances. The plan was to seal one entrance of a large tunnel, enter the tunnel from the other end, connect primer cord to the bags of CN tear-gas powder placed inside the sealed entrance, and then detonate the tear gas bags from the other end. After dispersing the gas in the larger tunnel, they would seal the other entrance with additional tear-gas bags inside the second entrance to the tunnel.

The engineer tried using 200 pounds of C-Four explosives to collapse the first side of a large tunnel and found that 200 pounds of explosive was not enough. The explosion only partially sealed the entrance. Only 200 pounds of explosives were left and were insufficient explosives to seal the large tunnel. The day's results were, we had one small tunnel entrance sealed, one large entrance partly closed and a bunch of tunnel entrances still open.

The demolition engineer reported back to me, "Sir, we don't have enough demo to seal the tunnels. We'll have to complete this job when we can get some more supplies."

"Roger that," I replied.

"Sir, I already opened two bags of CN. We'll have to bury them, then I'll have to get some more next time."

"Do you want to bury it yourself, or did you want my men to bury the CN?" I asked.

"It would be quicker if your men took care of it, Sir."

"How about if we buried it at the entrance to the tunnel we already sealed?" I asked.

"Yeah, that will increase the chances of someone hitting the tear gas if they tried to reopen the tunnel. Good idea, Sir."

"I'll have my RTO call for a chopper to pick you guys up," I said.

I reported the results to battalion, requested a chopper and had my men bury the opened bags of CN.

We had plenty of time to wait. Battalion wanted us to stay in the area another day. The chopper that came to pick up the two soldiers, brought us four insulated steel containers with two five-gallon packages of round drums of ice cream in each container. Each of the three platoons received one and the headquarters group the fourth one.

There were only eight of us in the headquarters group, so ten gallons of ice cream was to much for the eight of us. In the heat, there was no way we could save it for later so I asked Junior, the ex-NVA, and Lt. Hoa, the RVN officer, to offer our leftover ice cream to the kids who had come out to be with us again. After we had our fill of ice cream, the choppers came back out, bringing our mail and picked up the reusable empty ice cream containers. After the chopper left, I chased the kids away because I didn't want any Vietnamese nearby when we started forming our daytime logger position.

We idled away the rest of the day, watching for signs of the enemy, napping, writing home and in my case bringing my journal up to date. The day was one of our easiest and we took advantage of the slack time. After dark, we moved to a different island for our night defensive position. I rotated the platoons to offer each an opportunity to be the first, last or middle platoon in the order of march.

Again the moon rose in the middle of the afternoon. Even when the sun had set, the sky was not truly dark. Moving at night with 80 percent illumination from the moon, to the new location made it easy to see. However, I was uneasy about staying in one general area for several days and being visible during our night move. As our men walked stealthily across the rice paddies and onto the island, the only sound was the quiet trampling of the dry rice stalks. No one spoke. Each observed the silhouette of the man in front of him as they intermittently scanned the area around them for the enemy. Once each man was in their position at the night logger destination, no one moved or uttered a sound while they kept from being detected while taking turns sleeping.

At first light, 0535 hours on Saturday, 29 March 1969, we were up and packed. The company moved to another island about five hundred meters away, in a sea of dry empty rice paddies where we stopped for breakfast. After breakfast, we once again started to sweep the area where we had been the last two days, just to be sure no one placed land mines while we were sleeping. The night belonged to the Viet Cong and North Vietnamese Army soldiers, so we moved very cautiously.

Again, the First Platoon was to the right, with Lt. Bird in charge. The Second Platoon was in the middle, with Lt. Claybaugh. The Third Platoon was to the left, with Sgt. Gourley leading. I followed the Second Platoon, with my seven man headquarters group. We moved forward cautiously towards the tunnels. We all knew each step was bringing us closer to danger.

It was a hazy morning, so I knew the choppers would probably be late again. I felt we would have time to check each of the tunnels again to assure Charlie hadn't hidden a surprise in them during the night. We were very nervous and alert, having been in the area for three days. This was a long time to remain in one area for us. In a battle zone, consistency could get us killed. By being inconsistent, it was hard for the enemy to plan an attack. If enemy soldiers were nearby during the three days, I knew they probably had a pretty good idea we were going to be around the tunnels again. Charlie hadn't gone through all the trouble of building those tunnels for nothing. I suspected something was going to happen around the tunnel location, and we wanted to be ready for whatever Charlie had in mind.

As we neared the tunnel entrances, the sharp eye of the First Platoon's point man (the soldier who was in the forward most position of the advancing platoon), Specialist Fourth Class William (Bill) C. Gould, spotted a rifle barrel move in the hedgerow to the right of us. Half of Bill's First Platoon was out in the open in this empty rice paddy, with hedgerows on all four sides.

In a split second, Bill had to make a life or death decision. He could hit the dirt and hope the rest of his platoon would follow suit, or he could turn and shout, "Ambush!" He chose to sound the alarm. Bill Gould shouted, "Ambush!" so loud that everyone within a hundred meters from him could hear the warning. I was too far away from him to have seen what was going on, but I dropped to the dirt as I heard the enemy's AK-47 burst of fire just as Bill's shout reached me. The bullets were perfectly aimed, hitting Bill before he could reach the ground. His last word on Earth was, "Ambush!" He chose to save as many of his buddies that he could. Bill was the only one hit by the initial gun-fire. His unselfish, heroic action saved the lives of many of his buddies.

Bill's platoon leader maneuvered his platoon around and put down a base of fire in the direction of the enemy fire. I moved the headquarters group behind the First Platoon and directed the company RTO, Joe, to communicate with each of the other two platoons. I wanted to know how much enemy resistance we were up against. I received word back that we were receiving incoming rifle fire from three or four enemy soldiers and we were returning fire. One of our men was killed in hostile action, and we may have taken down two or three of the enemy.

The other two platoons circled around to assure we had a 360 degree perimeter, for all-around protection. I called battalion and let them know what was happening. Our company rear office personnel had been monitoring our company radio frequency, so they were also on the land-line to battalion headquarters to alert them we were in contact with the enemy.

Battalion called off the engineer tunnel operation and ordered us to maintain contact with the enemy. We were to keep battalion informed if we needed more troops. We were the first to report enemy contact for the day in the brigade's area of operation. As the day was one of the Tet holidays, all allied forces in Vietnam were expecting enemy contact and were eager to shift forces to overpower any resistance we encountered. Soon after our engagement started, the command and control helicopter was overhead.

I had the platoons spread out to provide security for a helicopter landing. Then we evacuated Bill's body and the documents from the one NVA we had killed during the scrimmage. Blood trails in the rice paddy indicated we wounded at least one other NVA soldier.

-    -   -   o   -   -   -

James Bradley Claybaugh was from Caldwell, Idaho. Jim graduated from Caldwell High School in 1962 where his mother was a high school teacher, then attended the University Of Idaho for one year, then Boise State University. He joined the Army in 1967 and after completing his basic training, he attended the Officer's Training Course at Fort Benning, Georgia. Upon completion of the Infantry Officers training he was commissioned a Second Lieutenant on 28 January 1968. After performing a tour as a member of the 101st Combat Brigade at Fort Benning, Georgia, he was shipped to Vietnam on 31 December 1968, when he was twenty-five years old. Jim Claybaugh was assigned as the infantry platoon leader of the Second Platoon in Company D in January 1969. On 22 January 1969 he was promoted to the officer rank of First Lieutenant.

-    -   -   o   -   -   -

This is a list of those Delta Dog's heroes who were identified in this chapter.

Specialist Fourth Class William C. (Bill) Gould, from Kingston, Massachusetts 22 Years old ** Killed by enemy gun-fire.
Specialist Fourth Class Joe W. Dodson, from Mayfield, Kentucky.

Chapter Four

First Lieutenant James B. Claybaugh, Specialist Fourth Class Michael L. Wilkins, Specialist Fourth Class David I. Styles, Platoon Sergeant Guy H. Gourley Platoon Sergeant James H. Smith

After Spc.4 Gould was killed and the enemy fire had ceased, the First Platoon moved forward into the enemy position. They found one dead NVA soldier and his AK-47. The rest of the company secured the landing zone for the incoming chopper. I joined the First Platoon and made sure the AK-47 and any papers found on the dead NVA soldier were placed on the helicopter for intelligence scrutinizing at the operations center. No one was allowed to claim the assault rifle as a war trophy.

The dead NVA soldier was left lying where we found him. We recovered three Chicom grenades. These were NVA type grenades, rather than the typical home-made appearing VC grenades. The grenades may have been tampered with and left as booby-traps, so we left them in-place until after the helicopter had left. The grenades found were Chicom Type 1 grenades, much like our own grenades.

-    -   -   o   -   -   -

The Viet Cong and North Vietnamese Army used six types of grenades. The Chicom (Chinese Communist) Type 1 grenade looked like a small, round pineapple, with a lever that flies off just like the US hand grenade.

95

Chinese Communist Type 1

Hand Grenade

Chinese Communist Type 42

Hand Grenade

Soviet RKG-3 HEAT Hand Grenade

Chinese Communist Type 59

Hand Grenade

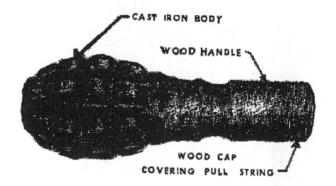

CAST IRON BODY

WOOD HANDLE

WOOD CAP
COVERING PULL STRING

STICK HAND GRENADE

Another Chicom grenade is the Type 42. The Viet Cong M32 grenade was a home-made looking version of the Type 42 grenade, made of metal soup cans, with a wood handle on one end. A string was coiled in the end of the wooden handle. When pulled, the string would ignite the fuse in the grenade.

The Soviet offensive hand grenade, Model RKG-3 looked like a large old-fashioned potato masher. When thrown, the small end popped off and a small parachute was deployed. The anti-tank and vehicle grenade parachuted down to the tank or truck. When it hit the top of the vehicle, the impact caused the grenade to explode. It contained a shaped charge which concentrated the explosion force into a narrow point and instantly melted the metal it contacted. A small hole was melted through the steel of the tank or truck and the molten metal blows through. Inside it solidifies and becomes shrapnel.

The fourth type grenade was the home-made pineapple looking stick grenade, which had a wooden handle with a string inside the capped end. When the string was pulled before throwing the grenade, the grenade fuse would ignite.

The fifth type grenade used by the NVA and Viet Cong was the Chicom Type 59 hand grenade. The Type 59 grenade was similar to the modern US percussion grenade.

The sixth type of grenade we encountered was the Soviet type shoulder launched anti-tank and personnel, Model RPG-40 self propelled rocket (not shown here). The RPG rounds had an anti-tank shaped charge, a percussion charge, or a fragment type configuration in the leading end of the rocket.

-    -   -   o   -   -   -

Before the chopper arrived to collect the captured documents and weapon, I received a report that Pfc. Billy R.

Franks, a rifle team leader in the Third Platoon, had sprained his ankle during the scrimmage. I made the decision to evacuate him along with the papers taken from the dead NVA soldier and Specialist Gould's body. We left the Chicom grenades to be blown up by a squad of the Third Platoon after we were finished in the area.

After completing the search of the enemy's location, I radioed battalion, updating them on what we knew, and asked for directions. Our battalion, the Third Battalion of the First Infantry, ordered me to pursue the fleeing NVA soldiers. At the time the Third Platoon was already engaged in securing the landing zone for the incoming helicopter, so I had the First Platoon move to the northwest and the Second Platoon move to the southwest. Soon the Second Platoon was advancing to the west just south of the First Platoon.

After we used smoke grenades to identify the landing zone and to show the airmen the wind direction, the battalion command and control helicopter picked up Pfc. Franks and Gould's body. The Second Platoon used some of their smoke grenades the day before to identify the landing zone for the engineers drop-off and for their pick-up. We didn't realize it then, but this usage by the platoons would affect us later.

While the extraction was going on, I was searching the area with one squad of the Third Platoon. We were inspecting the hiding places the NVA soldiers had used. A two and a half foot high wooden table was placed in position and then hay stacked on top to provide the camouflaged fighting position for the NVA soldiers. We found the old farmer who lived in the hootch on the island containing the NVA hiding place. There were two other Vietnamese old men with him. I told Lt. Hoa and Junior to interrogate them. The two interpreters told me the detainees weren't talking and suggested I send them back to the rear for further interrogation.

Any Vietnamese found in the enemy's area were considered part of the enemy operation. In this case, the farmers had allowed the NVA soldiers to use their property as an ambush site. I informed battalion of the three detainees. After delivering Gould's body and Pfc. Franks to the rear, the command and control helicopter returned to pick up the three Vietnamese men. We used more smoke grenades for determining wind direction for their pick-up. Lt. Hoa and Junior boarded the chopper with the three detainees and went back to LZ Bronco to interpret for the battalion staff before the detainees were turned over to the South Vietnamese troops in Duc Pho for further interrogation.

While watching the second extraction by the command and control helicopter, I saw the kids who had been following us and who had eaten ice cream with us the day before. They were kicking the dead NVA soldier. I told the Third Platoon to chase the children away. There were honorable soldiers on both sides of this war. Right or wrong, I felt the dead enemy was just like me and deserved some dignity in death. He was fighting for his people, just like I was fighting for all the Americans. He had a family and children just like I did. The only difference was he fought on the other side. I felt, except for the grace of God, that could have been me laying there.

I directed the squad from the Third Platoon that was searching the farmer's property with me, to burn the hay stack and the hootch. It was our policy to burn any structure used by the Viet Cong or NVA solders in an attack against US forces. If a house outside the government's redevelopment area was not used as a fire-base by the enemy, we let it stand. This house and the haystack, along with two other haystacks on the other side of the island, had been used by the NVA, so we burned them.

After the helicopter left the ground and the rest of the Third Platoon was returning from securing the LZ, an explosion blasted with a resounding boom. We all hit the ground. When we realized the explosion came from one of the burning haystacks, we scrambled to check the area again to be sure no enemy soldiers were at our location. We also wanted to be sure no more ammunition was left in the farmer's dirt island in the middle of the dried rice paddies.

Major Vaughn radioed from the command chopper and asked what the explosion was. I informed him we were burning the haystacks and the hootch the NVA had used in the attack on us. I reported it appeared the hay stack contained ammunition. Major Vaughn agreed that burning them was the right thing to do, but that we were not on a scorch-the-earth mission. I concurred and told him we only burned the locations from which we had received enemy fire.

"Good work," Major Vaughn replied and he continued back to LZ Bronco. During the scrimmages we were engaged in, battalion was always with us and it felt good to know that we weren't alone, plus we had the benefit of their aerial view.

All the men from the two squads of the Third Platoon who provided security for the helicopter landing were just about back with me. My command group and the one squad which stayed to burn the haystacks and farmer's hootch were waiting their return. With their arrival, we were ready to move to the west and join the First and Second Platoons.

-    -   -   o   -   -   -

The First Platoon was still patrolling to the northwest and crossed an open rice paddy before starting to enter a large line of trees. The Second Platoon had been having trouble finding a crossing point over the Song Quan River. The river was only about ten feet across and around four feet deep in this area. Searching for a crossing, they moved down into a deep dry irrigation ditch, which provided a good cover for them as they advanced towards the fleeing enemy. The trench skirted the river and took them farther south then originally planned.

The river was not deep enough to make it difficult to cross, but we tried to avoid crossing water more then two feet deep. Most bodies of fresh water in this part of Vietnam contained leeches that were up to two or three inches long. A leech on our private parts were something we wanted to avoid. Consequently, we only waded across deep water when it was absolutely necessary.

I radioed headquarters to verify the blue line on the map, representing the Song Quan River, was still our limiting boundary of operation. Battalion cleared us to operate another 5,000 meters to the west and south. We could now cross the Song Quan River west of Thanh Lam (2), just south of Vinh Lac (5). They informed me there were no friendly forces between Duc Pho to our east and 5,000 meters to the south and to the west of us. I passed this information on to the three platoons, and told the First and Second Platoons I wanted them to link up when they hit the river. They were about 300 meters or about two football field lengths apart.

Lt. Claybaugh requested permission to search further west for a crossing point over the river so they could link up with the First Platoon. I gave him the okay, but told him to be sure to link up with the First Platoon as soon as possible. I was already a little uneasy about the operation, plus being in the field without our Weapons Platoon put us at jeopardy.

A Second Platoon soldier, Specialist Fourth Class Ronnie L. Janes, crossed the waterway first. It was chest-deep. Lt. Claybaugh crossed behind Janes. He Called out, "Janes, help me up," when he reached the bank of the far side of the slow flowing river.

Ronnie Janes gave him a hand as he struggled to get out of the steep banked river. Spc.4 Michael L. Wilkins, the radio telephone operator, was the next to emerge. Janes assisted him. Next Janes helped Spc.4 David I. Styles, the medic, out of the water. Lt. Claybaugh and his RTO Wilkins advanced out of the hedgerow into the open rice farm. Soon the four infantrymen were advancing forward in the empty rice paddy.

The other squads continued their search for other crossing locations. Spc.4's Christopher O. Vavak, Wesley Rochelle, Donald J. Prochaska, and Pfc.'s Carl L. Paradis, and Franklin C. Horlback hadn't yet found a good crossing location.

Pfc. Freddie L. Frederick, and Spc.4 Resto J. Rivera found a crossing used by farmers. They crossed the waterway, as if they were tightrope walking, across a small log. When Spc.4 George M. Cato started to cross the river, all hell broke loose, sending him scrambling back to the original side of the river.

A loud explosion was heard and then 20 NVA soldiers opened fire with automatic assault rifles, light machine-guns, and grenades. Lt. Claybaugh was literally knocked off his feet and thrown back about three feet as the heavy enemy fire hit him. Spc.4 Janes dove to the ground in the dry field. Only his rucksack was visible above the top of the dike that separated the two dry rice paddies. He heard the bullets whistling over him and felt the enemy fire hitting his backpack.

"How are you guys?" Janes hollered to check on the others.

"I'm hit! It feels like my whole body is on fire," Lt. Claybaugh screamed, then he became silent, never to utter another sound again.

"I'm hit in the leg and arm," Spc.4 Wilkins shouted, but then he too became silent.

Ronnie James threw a grenade into the enemy's position in

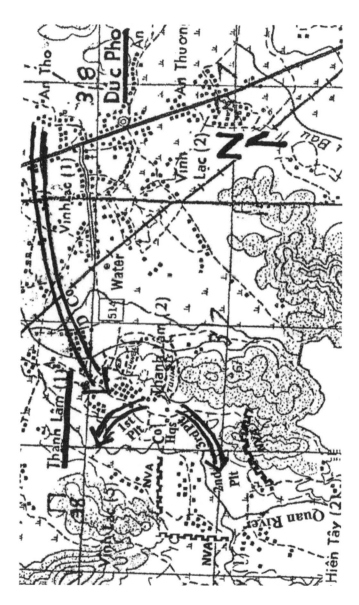

Delta Dogs battlefield of 29 March 1969.

the hedgerow some 15 meters in front of him. He could hear the screams after the debris stopped falling around him. But enemy fire continued from other locations in front of them.

The medic, Spc.4 Dave Styles was also hit next by enemy gunfire. He shouted that he was hit in the leg, arm and jaw. Then he started hollering for help.

"Shut up!" Janes hollered back. "Keep quiet! They are pinpointing your position when you holler."

Dave Styles kept hollering for help. Spc.4 Mike Wilkins had died depressing the send button on his radio and everyone on the company radio frequency could hear David's pleading for help, the sound of the gunfire, the incoming rounds smashing around them and the explosions. Ronnie yelled again for David to keep quiet but he didn't stop. After the next volley of enemy fire, David Styles never uttered another sound.

Ronnie Janes was still lying between Styles and Wilkins, about eight feet from each. Twenty-year old Ronnie knew he had received enemy fire each time he moved. He told me later he thought, "If I lay here motionless, maybe they will think I am dead."

Ronnie lay still for several hours, with the hot sun burning down on him. He prayed, "God of the universe who created all things, grant me mercy. If I get out of here alive, I will do only good things, Lord."

After a long period of time, with no bullets being fired in his direction, Ronnie slowly inched back to the hedgerow behind him. Once he was out of the rice paddy, he joined in the battle with the rest of his platoon.

Janes lived up to his promise. When he returned home he became a preacher and also owned a hardware store and an appliance store. His ministry would become his avocation, not his means of livelihood.

- - - o - - -

The enemy fire was so intense Frederick couldn't get over the dike to help his fallen comrades. His only option was to return fire and scoot back down his side of the dike until he reached the cover of the hedgerow next to the river they had crossed. Spc.4 Rivera slipped back into the water and returned to the original side, away from the enemy's location. Sgt. John L. Wheelan, the Second Platoon rifle squad leader, was behind Spc.4 Cato when the firing started. He dropped to the ground behind the hedgerow that ran along the stream, as did Spc.4 Michael D. Chappel. Just west of them, Spc.4 Ron Janes was a little farther away from the rest of the platoon. As he crawled back towards the river, enemy fire tore into the hedgerow where he tried to take cover and the rice paddy he had just crawled out of. Ronnie slipped back into the river and waded across the chest deep water to get back to the side farthest away from the enemy.

Before the fighting had begun, the Second Squad of Lt. Claybaugh's platoon was northeast of the platoon command group, a little west of my position. They were also searching for a way to cross the river. They stopped to take a break next to our side of the river dike. Suddenly a Chicom grenade landed in their midst. Spc.4 James R. Dourisseau saw the grenade and screamed, "Grenade!" in a startled, raspy voice. Only those near him heard the warning and dove for cover. The rest of us heard the explosion. Thanks to Dourisseau's warning, none of the men with him were hurt. After the fact, we concluded the grenade explosion set off the gunfire which hit the three casualties in the Second Platoon command group.

At that time we had no idea how large a force we were up against. My initial best estimate was there were about 50 Viet Cong or North Vietnamese Soldiers attacking us. What we had

107

received were the opening rounds of what would prove to be a much larger battle.

Second Platoon Sergeant James H. Smith moved the Second Squad back to the east to get out of grenade range. When the grenade exploded, Sgt. Smith had thought his squad was the only one in contact and all the enemy rifle and machine-gun fire he heard was being directed at them. Sgt. Wheelan also thought his Second Platoon squad was the only one in contact with the enemy.

Northeast of the Second Platoon, the First Platoon was moving out of an island, in an effort to link up with the Second Platoon at the time the fighting started. One squad of the First Platoon was in an open dry rice paddy when the shooting erupted. They immediately reported coming under enemy fire before the company radio net was jammed by Wilkins' radio. The First Platoon headed back to the wooded area from which they had maneuvered. Then, they deployed and took up positions for returning fire.

Platoon Sergeant Gourley and his Third Platoon joined my command group. We moved forward towards the west and started receiving enemy gun fire. Enemy fire rained down on both the Second and Third Platoons. Incoming fire from the high ground to the south of us and from the area north of our Second Platoon started hitting around our position. Then, shooting started coming from the west. It was obvious the enemy units had dug in positions on three sides of us. No matter which way the Second and Third Platoons maneuvered, they were meeting enemy resistance.

In order to assist the Second Platoon, Sgt. Gourley volunteered to move his Third Platoon men forward, to provide covering fire. I had him check on the deployment of his men first, to assure they were all intact and in good fighting positions.

I had reported the contact to battalion. Then, after Wilkins' grip on the transmitter button loosened, I called to get more information from the platoons. The First Platoon had no casualties. The Second Platoon knew their platoon leader was down and the RTO, Spc.4 Wilkins, was a casualty.

Meanwhile, when Sgt. Smith learned his platoon command group had been hit and needed help, he led his squad in a surge to the west to close the 150 meter gap between his squad and the platoon command group. Their route in the trench provided some cover. When they hit the eastwest trail, his RTO, Pfc. Bruce Holland, Spc.4's William Ferrell, William M. Donaldson, James Dourisseau, Marcelo Cruz, William N. Jasper, Gantt Thomas, and Daniel S. Payton were ready to fight.

Pfc. Horlback from the First Squad was trying to move east to link up with Sgt. Smith's squad but had to return to his squad's position when they started receiving fire from several directions.

As Sgt. Smith continued to lead his squad in a westerly direction to join the Second Squad, they came under heavy automatic weapons and small arms fire. Sgt. Smith was hit in the mouth. He fell to the ground, and couldn't crawl. His RTO, Pfc. Bruce Holland, dropped his radio and crawled to meet Sgt. Smith to give him first aid. Spc.4 Donaldson took the radio and communicated with us about what had happened.

Battalion was monitoring our company and battalion frequencies, since we were the first company to make contact that day.

Sgt. Gourley had verified all his men were back with him and again asked if he could take his men and assist them.

"Go," I told him. "I want you to extract as many of those men as you can, but don't get yourself trapped."

The company command group medic, "Doc" Jackson, usually stayed with me and the company command group. However, when he heard that the Second Platoon medic was hit and still lying in the rice paddy, he volunteered to go with Sgt. Gourley and join the Second Platoon as their medic for this engagement. They needed a medic.

The whole company was in jeopardy. The leader of the Second Platoon lay wounded in the open, and their platoon sergeant lay wounded on a trail. The First Platoon was the only platoon that was at full strength, with both a leader and platoon sergeant.

God, do we need our Weapons Platoon, I thought. *I wish they hadn't been taken from us.*

We appeared to be out-numbered and out-gunned, with no second dimension fire power available without our mortars. I figured, it was time to employ the battalion's pile-on theory. If there was ever a need to pile-on, it was now. I called battalion and asked for reinforcements. They acknowledged the request and said the battalion command chopper would be overhead shortly to assess our situation.

As Sgt. Gourley maneuvered his platoon forward, our company command group received heavy fire from a hill to the south of us. It rapidly started to look like there were a lot more NVA soldiers around us then I had originally estimated. We didn't know how many were there, but there were enough to block us, no matter which direction we tried to move. Even though there was no platoon leader for the Third Platoon, Sgt. Gourley was a fine soldier, and I had a lot of confidence in him. I was sure he would use sound tactics to assure the safety of his men. I was also confident he would be able to save many of the men in the Second Platoon. He took his three

North Vietnamese ambush site of 29 March 1969.

squads forward. Squad leader Sgt. Alfredo Zartuche and his rifle squad led the Third Platoon as they moved to the west.

I called battalion, requesting more men to join us in the battle. It was clear we made contact with a larger force than first thought. It was time for battalion to start building up our side until we out-numbered the enemy we had engaged, but that wasn't going to happen, at least not immediately. Battalion radioed to say they were supporting another company that had just made enemy contact and couldn't support us.

I feared I had lost my battalion's support. Then I was notified I was no longer under the command of the Third Battalion, First Infantry, but under the command of the First Battalion of the Twentieth Infantry. We had a tiger by the tail and so far, no one wanted to help us hold on to it.

The new battalion command and control helicopter flew overhead and asked us to pop smoke to identify our positions. I had each platoon pull a pin on a smoke grenade and throw it out in front of their position.

As the helicopter saw the smoke that we popped, we identified the color, so they knew the smoke was the one we popped and not one of the enemy's. The helicopter occupants verified our deployment and then flew off. Earlier we had used smoke grenades twice for our original battalion command and control helicopter to identify our positions. At the rate we were using smoke grenades, I was concerned about running low. One of the worst things that could happen in a battle was to run out of ammunition or smoke grenades.

Both commands were clamoring for more information, and I tried to keep them informed. Initially I reported each of the squads were under fire from what we believed were three or four enemy soldiers. The numbers were an estimate when the enemy first opened fire on us. The Second Platoon was now taking fire from several different locations and, the Third Platoon was still trying to lay surprising fires on the enemy locations in front of them. The First Platoon reported they were pinned down in a tree line north of the other two platoons. I again requested back-up forces. After receiving no response about the reinforcements from our new command group, I monitor the company frequency instead of the new battalion frequency and let Mac monitor the new battalion frequency net.

By then Sgt.'s Gourley and Zartuche had moved down the same trench-line used earlier by the Second Platoon. Sgt. Zartuche took the lead, as the riflemen cautiously moved forward to the contact point. Sgt. Gourley and Sgt. Zartuche split up and looked for the pinned-down Second Platoon. Sgt. Gourley took Pfc. John Davenport with him and they moved a little northwest. Sgt. Zartuche waded across the river and moved out onto the rice paddy with two men, RTO Spc.4 Robert O. (Rocky) Cole and Pfc. Coker B. Bonaparte. They were followed by several other squad members, who were still in the trench at that time. They were Sgt. Ronald Scribner, Spc.4 Charles Weaver, Spc.4 "Doc" Robert Lombardo, the Third Platoon aid-man, plus my medic Spc.4 "Doc" Gregory Jackson.

Sgt. Gourley and Pfc. Davenport crawled over a small dike on the enemy's side of the river, just west of where Sgt. Zartuche had taken his men. Another embankment ran perpendicular to the dike that the two sergeants had crawled over, and it separated the two groups. While crawling forward they could just see the tops of each other's packs in the opposite rice paddy.

A sudden burst of enemy fire erupted from somewhere and hit Sgt. Gourley. Sgt. Zartuche (his men called him by his nickname - Tuche) heard Sgt. Gourley groan in pain. He fell to the ground, and crawled a few meters back to the east to take cover. He had been hit in the leg by enemy fire and was still in the open. While crawling for cover, Sgt. Gourley was hit again, this time in the stomach and arm. He was wounded three times, the stomach wound being the most serious. Tuche jumped over the dike to Sgt. Gourley's side. He immediately saw how exposed he was when enemy fire sprayed into the almost empty rice paddy. Tuche jumped back to his original side of the dike and ordered Pfc. Bonaparte to set up his M-60 machine-gun to return fire on the hedgerow from where the enemy fire was coming. He shouted for Pfc. Davenport to cover him from the other side of the embankment. Sgt. Scribner and Spc.4 Weaver were still in the trench, so they took up positions to cover the men who were on the enemy's side of the river. Spc.4's Lombardo and Cole, the RTO, moved up a little further, to provide Tuche more covering fire. With covering fire to protect him, Sgt. Zartuche extracted the wounded Sgt. Gourley from the dry stubble filled rice paddy.

- - - o - - -

In the meantime, the First Platoon had consolidated all their men on the island north of where the action was taking place. I ordered them to move south and help the Second Platoon get out of the ambush. Lt. Bird, the First Platoon leader, reported they were pinned down by enemy fire. I asked if they had taken any casualties. He reported they had not, however he said they had one man who was suffering from heat-stroke. The man reported as the heat-stroke casualty was regarded by my two RTO's as a slacker who would come up with fabrications like this when it could get him out of a fight. Lt. Bird reported he couldn't move the rest of his platoon until this man was evacuated.

Since they had not been receiving heavy enemy fire like the rest of us, I requested a dust-off for the heat stroke casualty. I knew they wouldn't provide medical evacuation for the wounded in the Second and Third Platoons, because they were under enemy fire and could not provide a secured landing zone. Since the First Platoon was not under enemy fire, I reasoned they would be able to secure a safe landing area and get a chopper to land north of them.

The medical evacuation helicopter arrived within minutes after my request. They requested the First Platoon pop smoke where they had a secured landing zone. The First Platoon radioed back that they didn't have a secured landing zone. The dust-off helicopter left without picking up Lt. Bird's reported heat casualty. Lt. Bird and the First Platoon continued to stay in their safe position while the Third Platoon fought to extract as many of the Second Platoon from the ambush as they could.

Shortly after that, an Army Air-Forward-Observer checked in on our net and asked us to pop smoke to identify our position. He had a Gooney-bird en route to provide us with some cover. A Gooney-bird was a C-140 propeller transport plane with Gattling machine-guns mounted in the side window. They carried lots of ammunition and could fly slowly around the battleground laying down heavy machine-gun fire. Once again we identified our positions with smoke grenades and the Gooney-bird proceeded to spray the known enemy locations for about a half an hour. Their presence and the rain of bullets eased the pressure on us for a short time. After a while, they flew off, leaving us alone with the enemy.

If the air support we received caused any casualties, we didn't notice. The enemy still fired on us as if they hadn't been diminished at all. The situation had become less controllable for me and a lot more dangerous. Two rifle squad leaders had been left in the rear base-camp that day. Sgt. Larry Kepler was left behind because he had a high fever. Plus, rifle team leader Billy Franks was flown to the rear with a sprained ankle. We lost one platoon leader three days before, now Lt. Claybaugh, and two platoon sergeants were down. Two radio operators were hit by enemy fire, and the First Platoon leader wouldn't move to assist anyone because he had a soldier purportedly claiming to have a heat-stroke. To worsen the situation, we had two battalions who were NOT supporting us and our Weapons Platoon had been taken away from us to protect the rear during the Tet offensive. By now we were starting to run low on ammunition and smoke grenades. Midge said we were like the junkyard dogs who were doing what they were supposed to do, but no one seemed to be interested in giving us the support we needed. Maybe that's why we were known as the Delta Dogs.

My three platoons and my company command group were spread over 1,000 meters and in contact with an enemy force spread all around us. Experience told me the enemy needed a battalion size force or larger to cover so much area. A North Vietnamese battalion normally numbered 500 to 1,000 men. If that was what we were up against, 85 of us against so many enemy soldiers was tough odds. With the First Platoon not engaged in the combat, we were reduced to 60 against a much larger contingent of enemy soldiers.

We weren't the only ones taking note of the lack of support we were receiving. The enemy seemed to be getting bolder after they realized we had not received any reinforcements. AK-47 assault rifle fire, machine-gun rounds, shoulder fired RPG rockets, grenades, and sticks of dynamite rained on us. The enemy started yelling in English, "Stand up and fight, GI," and, "Are you cowards, GI?"

Each Communist unit had their propaganda officer in addition to a military commander. One communist officer did not overrule the other. Both had to agree on any action they took. A good number of the propaganda officers appeared to have been trained in the English language, just as I and several of our officers had trained in Vietnamese. They didn't speak perfect English, but they made themselves understood. They had us pinned down, and they knew it. Without reinforcements, we could only rely on ourselves to get us out of the mess. Even though we were out-numbered, out-maneuvered, and out-gunned, my first consideration was to provide enough resistance to discourage their over-running our position.

By then we were three hours into the fight. I was able to determine the locations of all my men well enough to be accurately plotted on my topographical map. That allowed me to get another dimension onto the battlefield. I told Lt. Faust to call in artillery fire on the enemy positions as close as 35 meters away. We couldn't give a false location because battalion already knew where we were. Unfortunately, the artillery refused the fire mission because we were too close to the enemy's position. I had Lt. Faust tell them we were going to move south and we would call back for artillery fire after we had re-established our position.

The Second and Third Platoons continued to fire at the enemy positions for about an hour, while the First Platoon stayed in their safe place. No battalion helicopters had been overhead for some time, so I directed Lt. Faust to call the supporting artillery unit again for artillery support, even though we were pinned down by the enemy and hadn't moved. Under my orders, he reported we had moved 100 meters south and that the North Vietnamese communists were crawling all over our former position. Since they thought we now met the division requirement of being 100 meters away from our former position, they granted our request.

Knowing artillery rounds were going to fall within 35 meters of our location, I told the platoons to take cover. Artillery rounds started slamming into the ground less then half a football field in front of us. The ground shook and dust flew all around us as 105 and 155-mm artillery rounds exploded right in front of us. Calling artillery fire in on our own position violated all the rules, and I knew it, but I didn't have a choice. Experience told me it was the only way we were going to get out of this trap. In my mind, I had to do it. Fortunately, it was the right thing to do because we had no casualties from the barrage. Unfortunately, I could not call artillery fire into the North Vietnamese Army positions on the high ground to the south of us. That was the location I told our artillery personnel we moved to in order to get an artillery bombardment into our position.

Lt. Faust had been a valuable assistant during the entire four-hour battle. He plotted each of our squad's locations. He also communicated with the two different battalions we were assigned to, while I was on the radio with the platoons. When I was busy, he communicated with the medical evacuation people, and with our company orderly room personnel. Lt. Faust was also communicating with the platoons at times to assure them we had control of the situation, and he requested they keep us informed of their situation and location. This was not the time to have someone panic or freeze-up, like the First Platoon had done.

Maintaining contact with each other served a real purpose. We knew we were engaged in a ferocious battle, but we knew we were not alone. We had each other. We could have withdrawn and left our wounded and dead comrades lying on the battlefield, but we didn't. We seemed to have the Antigone complex. We felt compelled to recover our fallen brothers. This was what we did because that is what we were - infantrymen. We fought together and we didn't leave our wounded and dead behind.

I radioed Lt. Evans, my executive officer, and told him to have the supply sergeant get some medical supplies, ammunition and smoke grenades ready. Then I wanted him to request a re-supply helicopter to make a run out to us. Once he got everything together, Larky radioed back that he had the supplies ready, but battalion wouldn't let a helicopter bring them to us because we couldn't secure a safe landing site.

I led the company command group into the trench where Sgt. Gourley had moved earlier. It provided good cover for us and allowed us to move closer to the Second and Third Platoons. As we moved into the contact point, we continued to receive fire from the high ground that was to the south of us. I checked on Sgt. Smith. It was a sight I will never forget. He was sitting in the trench, smoking a cigarette, with his lower jaw hanging loose. He could move his lips up and down to hold the cigarette in his mouth, but he couldn't move his jaw. Sgt. Gourley was lying a little further away, with a field bandage over his leg, arm and stomach wounds. I had the Second and Third Platoons consolidate and to tend to the wounded.

-　-　-　o　-　-　-

The end result of the platoons' maneuvers saved us. If we had moved forward in a column formation, we could have all been in the killing-zone before the enemy opened fire on us. So far, we had only three possibly killed in action and two wounded. If Lt. Bird had moved his men to assist the Second Platoon, we may have suffered many more casualties. When the battle is over, only then will we know how many we lost and how many the enemy lost during the battle.

Prior to coming to Vietnam I had studied NVA and VC tactics. I knew the enemy planned their engagement months ahead of time, and would not deviate from their plan. I was confident, even though the Second Platoon, Third Platoon, and my company command group were vastly outnumbered by the enemy force, they would not attack our position until after dark.

I believed it meant that staying in our defensive position was the best way to minimize casualties, as long as the sun was up. I checked my tables and sunset was around 1900 hours. The evening nautical twilight was 45 minutes later. That night we would have only around 40 percent illumination from the moon. It meant we would have to withdraw by 2000 hours, before darkness settled in. We didn't have any choice, we would have to leave the three fallen soldiers to be recovered the next day. It was a pretty sure bet they would booby-trap the bodies and leave snipers to take out as many of us as possible when we came back. As unpleasant and dangerous as the body recovery engagement would be, both the enemy and we knew it was a mission which had to be done. It was like both sides could see what the future would bring, but we could not refuse to do it. Our future was already written. We just had to go through the motions carefully before we saw what the price each of us would pay to bring our fallen comrades back home to their loved ones.

- - - o - - -

We continued to consolidate the scattered Second Platoon, tend to the wounded, and return fire for the next several hours. Around three in the afternoon, the Air Force Air-Traffic-

Controller flew over our location in a small single engine aircraft. He informed me that he had two marine jets coming in to give us air support. He wanted us to identify our locations with smoke grenades. We were almost out of smoke grenades. I contacted each platoon and had the men give me a count.

The First Platoon had enough smoke, one for each flank, as they hadn't lost any men carrying smoke grenades. In fact, they had no casualties whatsoever. The Second and Third Platoons, and the company command group didn't have enough smoke grenades. I had the men search their platoons for white phosphorous grenades, the infantryman's equivalent to napalm. They weren't perfect, but they would produce a large white smoke cloud. We distributed the smoke and white phosphorous grenades, and I let the Air Force pilot know that we were ready to identify our positions. I radioed our location and those of the enemy by using the daily cryptic code table. The pilot then wanted to visually verify the locations with our smoke bursts. When he was ready, we popped each grenade, and I identified the colors and the extremities they represented.

Soon, two jets swooped down low, close to the ground. They made a wide turn and came by for a second pass. On the second pass they dropped their napalm bombs, two from each jet. When the bombs hit the ground, a wall of flame erupted about three stories high and each covered an area the size of a football field. A giant wall of fire and smoke spread towards us in a rush, as the warm blast of air rolled over us.

If the heat didn't kill the NVA under those two blankets of flames, the lack of oxygen stripped from everything around them would. After the drop, the firing from the front stopped. We only received fire from the high ground south of us and west of us.

- - - o - - -

It turned out we were lucky our casualties were as light as they were. I learned later in the year that we had engaged two companies of the North Vietnamese regular army and one company of Viet Cong. In addition, they had a support company with the NVA infantry battalion.

From what we saw in the field and learned from their after-action report, they had set up a horseshoe ambush. Three NVA soldiers were sent out to make contact with us and withdraw. After wounding or killing some of our men, they knew we would pursue them, and expected us to be drawn into their killing-zone. Their 1,000 man battalion expected to have our 86 member infantry company out-numbered. The tactics I used resulted in a large gap between our platoons. This formation minimized our casualties. Only four of our men entered the killing-zone. One had escaped. Three were trapped. Our company had just touched the edge of the killing-zone, and most of my men were pretty well protected by the river's dikes and hedgerows on the south side and by the forest on the north side. We stayed out of the empty rice paddies they had set up as their target area, except for the three downed infantrymen.

The North Vietnamese soldiers and the Viet Cong carried out the battle tactics they had planned several months before this battle. Before the battle, they made a sand table model of the battlefield, went over the actions of each company, squad, and what each enemy soldier would do during the battle. They spent months digging the vast complex of tunnels, back-packing weapons and ammunitions and preparing their fighting positions around the ambush site. Their technique of fighting was to prepare and follow their rehearsed battle plan in every detail. If the ambush worked, then they would carry it to the finish. If their plan did not work, they would still follow it, as rehearsed, until the end. They did not deviate from their original plans.

-   -   -   o   -   -   -

My Artillery forward Observer, First Lieutenant Roger R. Faust, was drafted in 1966. After basic training, Roger decided he would rather serve as a Commissioned Officer rather than an enlisted-man. In 1966 young American men were drafted for two years. To become an officer, Roger enlisted for four more years in order to attend officer training. He attended the Artillery Officer's Candidate School at Fort Sill, Oklahoma. He served at Fort Irwin, California for some time. He married his sweetheart after being drafted. She moved out of Chicago to stay with her family in Manistique, Michigan when Roger shipped overseas. Lt. Faust was a big city man from Chicago, compared to a number of other Company D men from small towns throughout the United States. He was also older than most, being twenty-six when he arrived in Vietnam in October 1968. Being older and a sophisticated gentleman, Roger Faust was steadfast and efficient in performing his duties. He proved to be a strong right arm for me during the more difficult times.

-   -   -   o   -   -   -

This is a list of those Delta Dog's heroes who were identified in this chapter.

First Lieutenant James B. Claybaugh, from Caldwell, Idaho
25 Years old ** Killed in hostile action
Specialist Fourth Class Michael L. Wilkins, from Portland, Oregon 22 Years old ** Killed in hostile action
Specialist Fourth Class David I. Styles, from Blodgett, Oregon

20 Years old ** Killed in hostile action

Sergeant Alfredo R. Zartuche, from Pewaudkee Lake, Milwaukee, Wisconsin

Specialist Fourth Class Ronnie L. Janes, from Columbia, Kentucky

Specialist Fourth Class Christopher O. Vavak, from Robertsvillle, Missouri

Specialist Fourth Class Wesley Rochelle, from Bristal, Connecticut

Specialist Fourth Class Donald J. Prochaska, from David City, Nebraska

Private First Class Franklin C. Horlback, from Charleston, South Carolina

Specialist Fourth Class Resto J. Rivera, from Rio Piedras, Puerto Rico

Sergeant John L. Wheelan, from Hampton Hill, Illinois

Specialist Fourth Class James R. Dourisseau, from Palmettl, Louisiana

Platoon Sergeant Guy H. Gourley, from Greenback, Tennessee ** Wounded with gun shot in leg and stomach

Platoon Sergeant James H. Smith ** Wounded with a gunshot in the mouth

Private First Class Bruce E. Holland

Private First Class John D. Davenport, from Dallas, Texas

Specialist Fourth Class William N. Jasper, from Marthasville, Missouri

Private First Class Coker B. Bonaparte, from Darlington, South Carolina

Sergeant Ronald Scribner

Sergeant Larry E. Kepler, from Bassett, Nebraska

Private First Class Billy R. Franks

Chapter Five

Specialist Fourth Class Robert O. Cole
Specialist Fourth Class Freddie L. Frederick
Specialist Fourth Class William Ferrell
Specialist Fourth Class Michael D. Chappel
Specialist Fourth Class Gregory Jackson
Specialist Fourth Class Thomas E. Smith
Specialist Fourth Class Andrew Garcia
Specialist Fourth Class William M. Donaldson
Specialist Fourth Class Charles Weaver
Specialist Fourth Class Thomas W. Connelly
Specialist Fourth Class Robert Lombardo
Private First Class Carl L. Paradis

After the two napalm drops, I radioed Lt. Bird to leave a few men with the sick soldier and to move out and help the Second Platoon. We had been fighting for over seven hours, and I didn't want the company spread out like they were when darkness fell. Lt. Bird did not move and continued to wait for a helicopter dust-off.

The Second and Third Platoons were almost out of ammunition and smoke grenades, almost out of water, and almost out of hope for any reinforcements. The enemy had not charged our position, but I knew that would change as soon as darkness came. Night time was approaching. Within two hours the sun would be set, so I started planning the withdrawal of my men.

To my surprise an hour later, around 1700 hours, a United States Army Cavalry Troop, an armored unit the size of our company, pulled into our battlefield. They were riding in their armored personnel carriers, nicknamed 'tracks.' The cavalrymen came from the north, on the west side of the Song Quan River. They met the First Platoon before any of the rest of us. The first three armored personnel carriers picked up members of that platoon.

The First Battalion of the Twentieth Infantry, the second of the three infantry battalions we were passed on to for control during that battle, hadn't known how the battle had evolved. After some of the vehicles picked up the First Platoon, eight tracks, each of which could hold a rifle squad of ten men, proceeded south on the west side of the Song Quan River. The armored vehicles moved into the kill-zone to pick up the rest of us.

At first, the cavalry started picking up my men, wounded and unscathed alike. Two cavalry vehicles arrived to pick up the Second Platoon and two more the Third Platoon. Another track headed for my company command group.

Tuche saw the tracks heading towards him and guided the cavalry into his platoon's location. As they were preparing to recover our men, the enemy fired several RPG antitank rounds at the personnel carriers. The NVA had been hurt but were still fighting. The tracked vehicles stopped trying to pick up my men and maneuvered around to fire 30 and 50-caliber machine-guns at the NVA positions to the north of us.

Tuche and Davenport started dragging Ferrell, who had been wounded in the head, shoulder and buttocks, to Sgt. Smith's location at the edge of the rice paddy. Tuche yelled at Lombardo to join him. Spc.4 Lombardo, the Third Platoon medic, seemed dazed and unresponsive. Tuche stood there, with his fatigue jacket sleeve torn from a shell, which had just missed his arm. He yelled at Lombardo to get his attention above the sound of the NVA and cavalry machine-gun fire.

126

Cole and Lombardo finally joined Tuche, Davenport, and Ferrell. Enemy gunfire had started spraying them again and hit Cole. Cole, Tuche's RTO, fell forward, on top of Ferrell. Cole's body protected Ferrell from additional wounds, as the incoming rounds continued to hit Cole and his backpack.

Just to the right of Sgt. Smith lay Donaldson, Cruz, and others from the Second Platoon. Tuche crawled over to Sgt. Smith and grabbed him around the chest. He pulled him back out of the line of fire. While he was pulling Smith back, he called to Donaldson for help. Donaldson was not wounded, but wouldn't expose himself to help, so Tuche pulled Sgt. Smith to the hedgerow for cover.

Tuche dropped his backpack and weapon, and then headed for Cole, Ferrell, and Lombardo, who were still lying in the empty rice paddy with bullets flying around them. Tuche cut the straps holding Cole's pack to get his radio off his back. Cole was dead, so Tuche pulled Ferrell towards where he had left Sgt. Smith, as the burning hedgerow behind him poured black smoke into the air and bullets sprayed dust around them. Donaldson was screaming for Tuche to get down, but Sgt. Zartuche cared more about saving his buddies than he did his own safety.

When one of the track vehicles pulled up to where they were, Tuche pulled Ferrell and then Smith into the armored personnel carrier. Lombardo followed Tuche into the tracked vehicle.

Another armored vehicle pulled up and Vavak, Connelly, Rochelle, Paradis, and Prochaska carried Chappel, his backpack and rifle into the second armored cavalry assault vehicle. Chappel had been hit earlier in his leg, shattering his knee cap. He was in a lot of pain. Frederick helped them get Chappel and his gear over the dike, before they all entered the track vehicle.

Cato pulled Sgt. Gourley from the rice paddy and onto another tracked vehicle. Lombardo had shrapnel in his arm, his fourth purple heart. Doc Jackson had been hit in the leg while giving first aid to one of the men. The bullet passed through Doc Jackson's leg and shattered the bone.

This scrimmage was to be the last one for Doc Jackson. When he arrived back at the base hospital, he was diagnosed with a 'going-home' wound. It was little comfort for Doc Jackson, because he was scheduled to be transferred to a rear base aid station in a few days where he would be safe from the daily stress and violence of combat.

We were lucky that the napalm killed as many of the NVA as they did, otherwise this extraction could have been much worse.

No wonder the Communists and demonstrators back in the states are protesting and delaying shipments of napalm, I thought. *I'm sure the North Vietnamese soldiers appreciate each day a shipment is delayed as much as the artillerymen on Snoopy enjoyed each day that they were not mortared and rocketed. Thank goodness the shipment of the napalm used today got through. It sure saved a lot of American lives.*

While the wounded were being attended to in the track vehicle, Tuche went back out to drag Cole's body to the vehicle. Pfc. Weaver and Sgt. Scribner jumped into the tracked vehicle, but the cavalry troopers kicked them out, saying they only had room for the wounded. A wounded man took the seats of four to five men. The two men ran into the trench that they had previously occupied.

Tuche gasped for air in the smoke and dust filled battlefield, as he was single-handedly dragging Cole's lifeless body towards the armored vehicle. Then, Sgt. Zartuche heard the track vehicle rev its engines as it started to pull away. He screamed at them to wait, but they just continued pulling away. Tuche kept pulling Cole after the fleeing vehicle, while yelling at them to wait. Then he stopped and stood there for a moment, not believing they were going to leave him and his dead buddy in the middle of this dried rice paddy, with enemy bullets flying all around him.

I thought, *It is easy to do the fun things. It is hard to do the heroic things. That must be why there are so many fifth-columnists back in the States demonstrating for the enemy and so few men like Sergeant Zartuche.*

Note: Fifth-columnists are the anti-soldier persons described in Chapter 13.

- - - o - - -

Over thirty years later, I sometimes had difficulty sleeping nights as I relived this particular day of battle. I would be awakened from troubled dreams, by the picture of Sergeant Zartuche standing in the 115 degrees heat, covered with dirt and fire soot, dust flying everywhere from the armored vehicle's tracks, wet streams cutting through the grime that covered his face as he stood there in disbelief. It was hard to believe the armored personnel carriers were really leaving.

The Herculean effort this tired grunt had expended, first in battle with the hundred pounds of gear he carried during all the maneuvering, then dragging Smith, Ferrell, and finally Cole's body, was rewarded by the tracked vehicles leaving him behind in the kill-zone.

That late Saturday afternoon, a week before Palm Sunday, Tuche stood alone between our men and the enemy's line with his fatigue jacket smoldering where the tracer round had pierced his sleeve. I'm sure the same thing was going through all our minds, including Tuche's: why after ten hours of fighting had we been unable to get helicopter support for dust-offs or resupplies? Why had we received virtually no helicopter gun-ship support, and why had our battalion command helicopter not supported us any more? Where were the additional troops that were supposed to back us up when we fixed an enemy force ten times larger than us?

Tuche stood there too long, still holding Cole part way off the ground. He hardly seemed to notice he was alone with the body of his buddy Cole.

-　　-　　-　　o　　-　　-　　-

Suddenly realization hit him. He was in the middle of the dried rice paddy fully exposed to enemy fire, and dragging a dead body. He grabbed Rocky's weapon and ran to organize a defense. First he ordered, "Davenport, get up. Grab Ferrell's weapon, and get back into the trench."

Tuche scurried back to Bonaparte's position and told him, "Bonaparte, get back in the trench." He found Pfc. Weaver and Sgt. Scribner in the trench when he got there. Sgt. Zartuche got them all together and started them moving to the north-east. They soon ran into more track vehicles. The vehicles had circled up in a loggered formation after picking up our wounded.

With the cavalry providing a secure landing zone, an evacuation helicopter finally came to pick up some of our casualties. It landed in the center of the cavalry logger of circled armored personnel carriers. Even with the armored personnel carriers and their heavy machine-guns, the medical evacuation helicopter received enemy fire when it took off with our wounded. The first lift only evacuated about half of our wounded.

As the choppers flew away, the tracked vehicles started receiving enemy RPG anti-tank fire. Two of the armored personnel carriers were hit. Spc.4 Thomas E. Smith was hit in the thumb by the RPG shrapnel that had penetrated the vehicle's armor and ricocheted inside the personnel carrier. Spc.4 Andrew Garcia was also hit in the leg with shrapnel. A ricochet punctured Pfc. Carl Paradis' chest and lung. Spc.4 William M. Donaldson suffered a strike in the face by the shrapnel. In another vehicle, Spc.4 Charles Weaver was hit in the hand by RPG shrapnel. Spc.4 Thomas Connelly also was wounded by one of the RPG's.

The cavalry medics were taking care of our wounded and checking our men who were ill. No symptoms of heat stroke were found on the First Platoon's supposed victim. Spc.4 Gantt Thomas, of the Second Platoon, was spitting up green mucous. He had not complained of heat stroke, but was nevertheless evacuated by helicopter for heat exhaustion and a serious bronchial condition.

Before we left the battlefield, I confirmed with the platoons that everyone was accounted for. The Third Platoon confirmed that Cole was dead.

The Second Platoon confirmed that Lt. Claybaugh, Spc.4 Wilkins and Spc.4 Styles were dead. I reported the four American KIHA's (killed in hostile action) to our new battalion. The rest of the company was accounted for.

The new battalion, the First Battalion of the Twentieth Infantry, felt they were also too heavily engaged elsewhere, so we were transferred to a third command operation center, the Fourth Battalion of the Twenty-First Infantry.

The cavalry troop moved the company 300 meters to the north of the battlefield, for the second dust-off. All the remaining men boarded the tracks after the two helicopter dust-offs were complete. I hadn't been picked up yet, because I wanted to be sure all my men were extracted before I left the battlefield. My company command group was the last to board

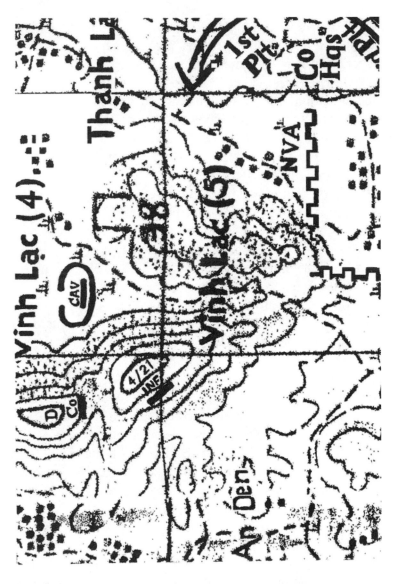

29 March battlefield with Cavalry position and location of Delta Dogs and other D Company.

the tracks, before we were driven 600 meters north.

The E Troop cavalry commander wanted to personally pick up the infantry company commander. He was directed by my men to our command post location, on the east side of the river. The cavalry troop commander came to the back and opened the swinging door of the armored personnel carrier and reached his hand out to help me aboard. The cavalry Captain stared at my lapels, and said, "Those aren't idiot sticks (slang for crossed rifles that infantry officers wear), they're sabers."

I responded, "Yes, I'm cav like you. Only you got the job I wanted, so I ended up an infantry company commander."

We both laughed at the irony of a cavalry commander saving an infantry company commander, who was also a cavalry officer. Considering all the RPG's the cavalry troop took during our extraction, it was hard to say which unit had the worst of it. Six of my company's casualties occurred after we were in the tracked vehicles, proving there was no safe place on the battlefield.

The cavalry troop dropped us off at the foot of the twin hills north of the battlefield. From there we waded across the stream and then hiked up the 100 meter high saddle-topped hill. It was approaching 1900 hours as we trudged up the hill, still hot, sweat-covered, grime-coated, exhausted, and dejected from our day-long beating by a superior force. When we arrived at the top, I had the remainder of our three platoons form a perimeter around the top of our peak. Even though we were all dog-tired, we had to dig in for the night.

Helicopters from the new battalion to which we were assigned landed one of their infantry companies on one of the two peaks of the hilltop. The two peaks were about equal height above the rice paddies on the rice-bowl floor. The other company was on the peak closest to the battlefield. We were on the peak farthest to the north. Company D of the Fourth

133

Battalion, Twenty-First Infantry acted as our security, so we could get a good night's sleep after our 14-hour long, painful day. I knew we needed a good night's rest, because the battle wasn't over for us yet. We still had to retrieve our dead comrades from the battlefield. But before we could turn in for the night, there were still tasks we had to complete.

Kepler and the Weapons Platoon joined us on the hilltop when a helicopter resupplied us. Ike's ankle was not completely healed, but he wanted to come to comfort and help his buddies. We needed every man we could get. We had lost 25 men during that past week, and our men in the rear knew how thin our ranks were. Those in the rear base-camp who could join us were flocking out to our hilltop to provide support to both our morale and our security. I told each platoon to take roll-call again and report to me the men present, those evacuated, and those killed in action. After I received the reports, I contacted the first sergeant at the base-camp and relayed the information to him. First Sergeant Wheeler and Lt. Evans would check on the wounded that we evacuated to follow their progress.

Those who could, ate. Those who were too exhausted or emotionally drained couldn't eat, so we kept busy preparing our fox-holes for the night. A special kind of nervousness took over. We kept digging before nightfall. Despite the extreme fatigue and being joined by skilled fighters, a kind of animal instinct took over and made us prepare to fight for survival that night by digging deeper. After we dug in and secured the perimeter, some of us were finally able to think about eating and resting.

Spc.4 Freddie L. Frederick had to relieve himself, and went down the side of the hill. He passed a spot where several other men had gone and settled for a spot a little further down the hill. While looking for a good spot, he stumbled across a tripwire and a booby-trap exploded. It completely peppered his whole body on one side with shrapnel. As our medic attended Freddie, I ordered the men to check the entire top of the hill for more booby-traps, before it was too dark to see anything.

The remaining Delta Dogs infantrymen scoured the hill top, looking for spike-pits and booby-traps. We found a bouncing-betty, which is an anti-personnel mine that shoots up about head height before it exploded. One of the men blew it up with his C-Four explosives.

- - - o - - -

As a basis for ordering more equipment and requesting more infantrymen and aidmen, I made a list of our equipment lost and of the men killed or wounded during the battle. With a lack of medics and equipment, we were not well prepared for further enemy action. I sent the results to the rear on one of the resupply helicopters.

The casualty list was as follows: Five killed in hostile action and twelve wounded in hostile action. Six of the wounded occurred during the extraction by the cavalry.

A check of our equipment revealed that we had lost the following equipment during the battle and extraction: 2 each AN/PRC 25 radios, 2 each 45-caliber pistols, 8 M-16 rifles, 23 Rucksacks, 3 Damaged Rucksacks (due to enemy fire), 3 Compasses, 1 M-72 LAW (Light Antitank Weapon), 1 M-79 grenade launcher, 5 Claymore mines, 10 pounds of C-Four plastic explosives, 25 feet of DET Detonation Cord (explosive cord for detonating C-Four), 25 feet of Time Fuse, 1 M-60 machine gun, 23 sets of equipment in the rucksacks (ponchos, air mattresses, canteens, entrenching tools, food, shaving gear and personal belongings).

-    -   -   o   -   -   -

A couple months later, I saw an intelligence report on the losses suffered by one NVA company opposing us on the north. I didn't see a report on the enemy companies on the west and on the high ground to the south of us. The main NVA company we were in contact with lost one man due to rifle fire, he must have been the one in the hay stack. They lost 16 from the napalm strike. They had 21 wounded by our gunfire or the Gooney-bird's gunfire.

Their 17 killed exceeded our five killed. Their 21 wounded exceeded our twelve wounded. Not counting the enemy's casualties in the companies to the south and west of us, we were successful in inflicting more KIA's and more wounded enemy soldiers than they inflicted on us. That was our objective, kill and wound more of them than they would kill or wound of us. It was impossible for me to think of my men as numbers or statistics. No matter how we did the math, I still lost five good men, and too many wounded. It hadn't been a good day for us.

-    -   -   o   -   -   -

We settled in for the night, after ensuring there were no more booby-traps in our area. Each of us dealt with the ramifications of the day's action in our own way. The First Platoon leader, the only platoon leader officer left, lamented over the radio to the battalion intelligence officer, his remorse, his feeling of loss, his hopelessness and his agony of losing the two fellow lieutenants.

Each officer in the army spent about half of their one-year tour in Vietnam as a field officer and one-half as a rear assignment officer. Our battalion S-2 (Intelligence Officer)

136

was the Delta Company Commander prior to the commander before me. He had known Lt. Wilson, Lt. Claybaugh and Lt. Bird. He sympathized with the First Platoon leader, Lt. Bird, and the loss of his comrades. For over an hour the First Platoon leader poured his heart out over the radio for all those on the company frequency and those close enough to him to hear about his fears, his emptiness due to the losses, and his remorse for not being able to help his fallen buddies. Maybe the fact that the S-2 was providing him a friendly ear for the release of his pent-up feeling was the best thing for him, but I didn't think his whining was good for the morale of all those listening to this radio broadcast. I had already experienced that the enemy could pick up our radio transmissions on their commercial radios If the enemy were listening, I surmised, this would surely inflate their morale. I felt like putting a stop to the transmissions, but I decided that I needed some sleep and that this would have to be dealt with at a later time.

I thought, *Adversity does not make a man; it exposes who that man really is. Tuche showed he was a brave, heroic, fearless fighting infantryman that day on the battlefield. The adversity of facing a superior enemy force demonstrated his courage when he led his men into the fight, when he fought bravely when outnumbered, when he exposed himself to danger as he pulled his buddies off the battlefield while under fire from the enemy, and when he tried to take care of his dead buddy's body. He was not one to stay in a safe place by coming up with an excuse for not engaging the enemy. Instead, he used every bit of his energy to save his fellow soldiers and to take care of the brave men who had fallen. The man of the day, the soldier with whom I was proud to serve, was Sergeant Alfredo R. Zartuche from Milwaukee.*

The day was done, and my lungs ached to be able to sing out a cry of joy that I lived through it. I had endured the lousy food, the warm beer and sodas, the repetitive hot nights and blistering days, the endless toiling while carrying this heavy load of equipment, the mosquitoes, and the leech-infested waters. The exhilaration of having survived a ferocious battle was almost overwhelming. I don't know if every man in the field that day felt the same, but in my heart I believed I had come to Vietnam to die. It had long been said those who reap fame quickly die young. At 36 I had achieved more in my life than I ever dreamed possible as a boy. I believed I truly had exceeded all my childhood expectations. I was sure my life had been so successful I was destined to die here defending the good life I and so many others had enjoyed back home. However, this day was not the day. I was alive.

-     -   -   o   -   -   -

The next morning the commander of the new battalion flew in by chopper to our position at one of the peaks of the saddle hill. He told me the cavalry was going to assist in the search for our fallen comrades and retrieving our equipment. He asked me who knew where the dead Delta Company men had fallen.

Spc.4 Daniel S. Payton said he knew where the Second Platoon's bodies lay. Lt. Bird also volunteered, offering that he knew where his platoon had left their rucksacks. I knew where the Second and Third Platoons had fought and could look for rifles and equipment in their former locations. My two RTO's and Lt. Faust, plus his RTO, were ready to assist in the recovery.

After we all gathered at the command and control chopper, the Lieutenant Colonel said he could only take three soldiers to the cavalry for the recovery of our equipment.

I asked the men if any of them knew all the locations. None did. I stayed with the company on the hill and let Lt. Bird, Spc.4 Payton and one other soldier go with the chopper. The command and control chopper made an aerial reconnaissance of the area, then returned and directed me to send 20 men with the cavalry unit at the foot of the hill to recover our equipment. The cavalry and my men would ride into the battlefield, and if they were hit by any enemy fire, they would pull back. Then the Fourth Battalion, Twenty First Infantry company on the other peak would descend from their location and engage the enemy. I was told this new infantry battalion also had two infantry companies north of us that could be air-lifted into the battle, if necessary.

The First and Third Platoons could each send 10 men. Lt. Bird volunteered to be one of the 10 from his platoon. He would be the officer in charge of our men during this recovery mission. I let the men going know the rest of us on the hill would be ready to come down to help them if they ran into any enemy resistance.

Lt. Bird plus the 19 men from the Third and First Platoons inched their way down the hill, trying not to trip any booby-traps. They crossed the stream we had crossed the night before and joined five of the armored personnel carriers from the cavalry troop. The tracked vehicles, with our men mounted on four of them, moved around the high ground near the battlefield. Then they moved towards the charred, still smoldering battle location where the napalm bombs had fell the day before.

Some of the enemy were still there, and fired a RPG round at the armored personal carriers, but missed the vehicles. The cavalrymen unloaded our infantrymen and retreated, leaving my men alone to assault the enemy position.

While watching through my binoculars, I monitored both

Capt. Durgin observing the recovery of their fallen comrades. Joe Dodson is sitting on this side of the Captain while is in contact with his men on the radio.

our company and the new battalion radio frequencies to keep track of how the recovery was going. When I heard the RPG explosion, Lt. Bird called me, "Delta Six, this is Delta One. What's going on? Over."

"Delta one, this is Delta Six. What do you mean? Over," I said.

"The track vehicle personnel had us dismount. They want us to assault the enemy on foot without them."

I ordered him to retreat to the location of the tracked vehicles.

Sgt. Zartuche called back on his platoon radio and said he didn't think it was a good idea for him and his nine men to assault a dug-in enemy. I agreed, and instructed him to also join the armored personnel carriers.

Before Tuche withdrew, he had his men shoot a number of LAW rounds at the enemy's dug-in position, destroying the bunker from where the RPG was shot.

Sgt. Zartuche and his men returned to get on the tracked vehicle they had been riding in. The cavalrymen informed them the infantry would have to assault on foot while advancing alongside the armored personal carriers. That was a reasonable request. From my vantage point on the hill top, it looked like a textbook assault formation used to attack an enemy position.

Three tracked vehicles were advancing on the enemy, with 10 men walking as scrimmagers between each set of armored personnel carriers. As they advanced, the 50-caliber machine guns, plus the 30-caliber machine guns mounted on the tracked vehicles were fired at the enemy position. The infantrymen between the tracks were firing their rifles as they advanced next to the armored personnel carriers. Two other tracks remained in a position to the rear to give them fire-support if needed.

Battlefield of 29 March 1969.

When the tracks came to a dike the commander told the infantrymen to continue the assault without them. The tracks continued providing supporting machine-gun fire. The infantrymen continued advancing another 50 meters without the armored personnel carriers.

Lt. Bird radioed me again. "Why do we have to attack an enemy position with 20 men, when a whole company couldn't accomplish the mission yesterday?"

I radioed the new battalion operation center and asked the same question. While I was on the radio, I had my men on the hilltop put on their gear, and get ready to join our men in the rice bowl.

The battalion commander called the cavalry commander on the ground from his chopper and instructed the track commander to mount my men on his tracks and get on with his mission to recover the bodies and gear from the battlefield.

Several tracks drove over to the location where the troops waited and picked them up. The armored vehicles didn't seem to be bothered by the previously reported impediment. Then the tracked vehicles traversed the low berm and headed towards our fallen comrades. No more enemy fire came from their prior location.

Two of the armored personnel carriers stopped near the three bodies on the battlefield while the others were searching elsewhere. Our men jumped off the tracks and checked the bodies of Lt. Claybaugh, Spc.4 Wilkins and Spc.4 Styles. They tied a long tether line to the first body's foot and everyone took cover behind the tracks or hugged the ground. Then the cord was tugged. They did the same to each of the other two bodies. None of the bodies were booby-trapped. When our men searched the bodies, they found their wallets, watches, weapons, and all their personal belongings were gone. Even though our artillery had fired endless barrages of artillery fire into the battle zone all night long, the NVA and VC still combed the battlefield for our equipment and any valuables our dead buddies had on them.

My men wrapped the bodies of the dead in ponchos and carried them back to the tracked vehicles. Then they checked the locations where the Second and Third Platoons' rucksacks and equipment were left. None were found. Lt. Bird and his First Platoon men searched until they found Cole's body. Spc.4 Donald Prochaska attached a tether line to his leg and pulled it, after taking cover. This time a tremendous explosion reverberated from the booby-trapped body. The loud explosion could be heard all over the battlefield and even up on our hill, which was over 1,000 meters away.

No enemy fire was received after the first RPG round exploded; however, the cavalrymen on the tracks got jittery again after the explosion and radioed our men. They wanted to get out of there and informed the infantrymen if they didn't get back on the tracks right away, they were going to leave without them. Some very foul language crossed the air waves, as our First Platoon men strongly requested that the cavalry men get off the tracked vehicle and help collect Cole's body if they wanted to get out of this area fast. The cavalrymen would have nothing to do with leaving the protection of their armored personnel carriers.

Even though his body was blown up, my men were not going to leave Cole on the battlefield. They gathered the body parts to be sent home to his family, just as they would want if it were one of them.

Lt. Bird led the tracks to the location where his First Platoon men had left their rucksacks. The equipment was still there. They checked for booby-traps and found nothing was touched by the enemy. It was obvious the NVA and VC didn't even know the First Platoon was there. If they had known, their gear would have been gone too. The VC did not leave any gear they found on the battlefield.

The armored personnel carriers brought the 20 men back to the foot of the hill where we had spent the night. A helicopter dust-off came to the logger of tracked vehicles for the bodies of the four men killed in action the previous day. The rest of the First Platoon came down from the hill to claim their rucksacks.

Half a dozen of my men from the Second and Third Platoons were without backpack and needed field equipment to sustain them. Some resupplies were sent out for those who had lost their rucksacks. We had enough individual weapons. Soldiers held onto their rifle above anything. During combat, a soldier did not want to be caught without a weapon to defend himself.

There was a difference in opinion between our new and original battalion operation centers about what our next assignment would be. Our company's strength and fire power was reduced by the heavy casualties we suffered, 25 men in all. We were short three medics and four RTO's, plus their radios and medical packs. The third battalion we were attached to now wasn't sure how to deploy us. The original battalion operation control center let us know we would stay put on the hilltop until we were air-lifted out in the afternoon. We were to return to LZ Bronco for equipment exchange and refurbishment.

The battalion to which we were currently attached said we would stay on the hill another night and that two more companies would join us on two nearby hill tops to provide a number of blocking-positions for the NVA and VC forces, which were still in the area. The mission didn't make any sense to me. We had too few men and lacked the field-gear to provide an effective force for a blocking-position mission.

The enemy assessment didn't make sense to me either. With us in the north, the US and South Vietnamese army locations to the east, plus the air and artillery bombardments falling in the west valley, the NVA and VC forces would probably move to the mountain range to the south of us. It was the only area not occupied by our forces or being peppered with artillery and air strikes. I didn't express my concerns with the new battalion staff, but the plan for one more night on this hill was doable even though undesirable. In order for us to achieve their objective, however, we needed replacements and a lot of supplies before we could effectively commit to meet further hostile action.

My thoughts were validated six months later when numerous intelligence reports from US ground troops, aerial sightings and South Vietnamese Army initiated intelligence reports pin-pointed the North Vietnamese Division headquarters in the mountain range just to the south of us.

We waited on the hilltop most of the afternoon, not knowing if we were to spend the night there, move down from the hilltop to a blocking position, or we would be air-lifted back to Bronco. I was concerned that several of my men were still without rucksacks, ponchos, air mattresses, mosquito nets, eating utensils and other necessities. With the two battalions sending contradicting orders, I had no choice but to wait and see what our mission would be.

I got the order from the Fourth Battalion, Twenty-First Infantry to move down from the hill and join their Company D, which was also moving down from the other peak of our hill. Together, we would both sweep the battlefield. Our participation was needed because we knew the battlefield and the enemy's positions. I let them know that we needed to be re-equipped first.

I ordered additional supplies from our company supply sergeant and requested they be air-lifted to us immediately. Some of our men had only their rifles and the ammo we had received on the morning supply run. Specifically, I ordered Claymore mines, C-Four plastic explosives, primer cord, blasting caps, detonating cord, smoke grenades, field bandages, LAW's (Light Anti-tank Weapons), radios, and percussion grenades. I also let our rear support people know we needed three aid-men, entrenching tools, M-79 rifle grenade launchers, radio batteries, flashlights, canteens, insect repellent, the small packets of toilet paper each of us carried, water purification tablets, rucksacks, malaria and salt tablets to replace what had been lost when Charlie captured our equipment, as well as three days worth of C-rations.

I finally received word from the new battalion command post in the rear that we would be air-extracted and returned to LZ Bronco after all their infantry companies were air-lifted into their positions. I guess when our men in the rear ordered so much equipment to be brought out to us, someone finally figured out we were not equipped well enough to sweep or block an enemy force of any kind.

Our company let out a loud roar of approval when I had the platoon leaders let them know we were going to be airlifted back to Bronco for a direct exchange day. They quickly got their gear together and stacked all the resupplies that were not distributed yet in a pile for quick loading onto the helicopters when they arrived. Spirits were soaring and the men were keyed up. They recovered their fallen comrades, evacuated all the wounded, managed to get a full night's sleep, and were going back to a rear fire-base.

LZ Bronco, although far forward, was a lot safer and more comfortable than what we experienced in the field. I was looking forward to being able to shower away the grit and dirt of the battle, change into some clean fatigues, and have a hot meal complete with cold ice cream (the infantryman's gift from the Gods).

I can look back on it now and remember how the little things made us so happy. There was no joy greater than getting cookies from home, a letter from a loved one, or ice cream. Any sign of appreciation was cherished. Adversity changes everything. Back in the States some of us would find it disgusting to use an out-house, especially when three or four other men used it at the same time. The four-holer out-house was standard accommodations in our rear fire-base-camp. A four-holer was nothing more than a large wooden box with its bottom removed and four circular holes cut in the top. We sat there in the open, side-by-side, with nothing between, above or around us. That made it easier to escape if a rocket or enemy attack started while we were otherwise occupied. For all their shortcomings, the base-camp out-houses were much better than what we had when operating in the field.

I was able to enjoy a cold soda and an ice cold beer for a change. On top of that, in the base-camp we would be able to get a mosquito-free night's sleep. In the field I slept troubled, waking every hour or so to be sure each platoon and twiggy reported when expected and made sure our company command group soldier was awake. Then there was always the possibility we were being infiltrated by the enemy. There was no routine night in the field.

I hiked over to the other peak of our hill and thanked the Company D commander for his support the night before by offering us a safe night's sleep by sharing the hilltop with us.

After the last incoming infantry company was dropped off, the choppers started picking us up. The night was darkening around us. At 1830 hours, while the sun was setting, I got on the last chopper with my company command group. A lot of men met us when we got off the choppers at Bronco. Our company rear support personnel, the battalion chaplain, the regiment medical personnel, and some of the battalion staff wanted to share their sorrow for our losses and the joy of our safe return from a hard-fought battle. I didn't know how to respond. I really didn't want to say anything, because I was afraid the tears would start flowing - - tears of sorrow for those who died, tears of sorrow for those who were wounded, and tears of joy for those of us who were coming back safe. As a survivor, I felt a jumble of emotions. I just wanted to keep quiet, take a shower, have a good hot meal, some cold beer, and get a good night's sleep.

It was after sunset when we arrived at Bronco. Most of us had already eaten something on the hilltop but the idea of a good hot meal was too tempting to turn down. Almost all of us went to the mess hall and enjoyed not only the steak, mashed potatoes, vegetables, and salad, but the other things we never got in the field - - salsa, Tabasco, steak sauce, catsup, mustard, mayonnaise, butter, fresh bread or rolls, and iced tea or cold milk. No matter how full we were, we could not turn down such a pleasant spread. To me, it felt like Thanksgiving, Christmas, and a birthday party all rolled into one. I looked at the faces of my men. They didn't have the Christmas festive meal look on their faces. Most had the 100-meter stare. They were not focusing on the soldier sitting opposite them, nor at the objects around them. It appeared as if these tired, emotionally drained young men were concentrating on something 100 meters away. We all ate in silence.

After eating, our men stationed in the rear brought ice cold sodas and beers for us. They had listened, both day and night on our company radio net, as well as on the battalion radio net when each report had been broadcasted back from the battlefield. Now, they wanted us to know how much they felt our pain. These fellow soldiers wanted to make our return as enjoyable as they could.

We ate, we drank, we showered, we changed clothes, we wrote home, but we didn't talk about the battle much. We did a lot of thinking but it was hard to find the right things to say about the engagement with a larger force. I resented the lack of fire support and the lack of more men coming to fight with us. I grieved for the loss of life, the loss due to wounds, and the feeling of abandonment as we were being shifted from one battalion to another. None of the commands provided the supplies and medical evacuations we needed. I thought about the 'what-ifs.' Could we have saved those four men if additional troops had arrived to join in the fight with us? No one will ever know, but none of us would ever stop asking that question.

-    -   -   o   -   -   -

Specialist Fourth Class Robert O. Cole from Sacramento, California, and Private First Class Bernard Kelly were much alike, yet they were distinctly different in some ways. Robert Cole went by his three initials, ROC. His buddies back home in the states as well as in Company D just called him Rocky. He was against the war but when his country called, he answered the call. He loved his country more than he hated the war.

Kelly, on the other hand, was a regular-army soldier. Yet he also was an anti-war guy. He had enlisted instead of being drafted so he would have a choice of assignments. He wanted to be a medic, not a rifleman. He continually wore the inverted cross which the war protesters were using as the 'peace symbol.'

The two were anti-war soldiers, one drafted and one enlisted. Rocky Cole was drafted in 1968 from Sacramento, California and sent to Vietnam in September 1968. Bernard Kelly joined the army in May 1968 from South Orange, New Jersey. Kelly arrived in Vietnam around the first part of November 1968.

They were both good soldiers. Their anti-war feelings didn't interfere with what they had to do in the field.

-   -   -   o   -   -   -

This is a list of those Delta Dog's heroes who were identified in this chapter.

Sergeant Alfredo R. Zartuche, from Pewaudkee Lake, Milwaukee, Wisconsin

Specialist Fourth Class Ronnie L. Janes, from Columbia, Kentucky

Private First Class Carl L. Paradis ** Wounded with shrapnel in the chest and lung

Specialist Fourth Class Thomas W. Connelly ** Wounded by shrapnel

Private First Class Freddie L. Frederick, from Coffeeville, Kansas ** Wounded by shrapnel in one side of body

Specialist Fourth Class Thomas B. Smith ** Wounded in the thumb by shrapnel

Specialist Fourth Class George M. Cato

Specialist Fourth Class Michael D. Chappel ** Wounded by a gun shot in knee cap

Specialist Fourth Class Andrew Garcia ** Wounded in leg by shrapnel

Specialist Fourth Class William Ferrell , from Wylliesburg, Va ** Wounded in head, shoulder and rear end

Specialist Fourth Class William M. Donaldson, from Los Angeles, California ** Wounded in the face with shrapnel
Specialist Fourth Class Marcelo Cruz, from Tucson, Arizona,
Specialist Fourth Class Daniel S. Payton, from Louisville, Kentucky.
Specialist Fourth Class Gantt Thomas, from Opelousas, Louisiana ** Heat stroke, but continued to fight in battle
Specialist Fourth Class Robert O. Cole, from Sacramento, California ** Killed by enemy fire in hostile action, 20 Years old
Private First Class Charles Weaver, from West Springfield, Massachusetts ** Wounded with RPG shrapnel in hand
Specialist Fourth Class "Doc" Robert Lombardo, from New Haven, Connecticut ** Fourth wound, shrapnel in the arm
Specialist Fourth Class "Doc" Gregory Jackson, from Houston, Texas ** Wounded, shot in leg, broken bone
Private First Class Bernard Kelly, from South Orange, New Jersey

Chapter Six

The Water Crossing

One of the men waiting for us when we returned from the twin peaks was a replacement for Lieutenant Wilson, First Lieutenant James Gregory (Greg) Miller. I had other things I wanted to do first. I asked my executive officer, Larky, to have Lt. Miller report to the orderly room at 2000 hours (8 PM). I spent the early part of Palm Sunday evening replenishing my field supplies and getting my gear ready for the next mission. I showered and since it wasn't time for our meeting yet, I relaxed a little with a nice cold beer. I reviewed Miller's file. His date of rank (the date he was promoted to First Lieutenant) was 2 March 1969, not even a month earlier.

At 2000 hours I met with Lt. Miller in the company orderly room. I assigned him to the Third Platoon and gave him four pieces of advice: "Lieutenant, use the basic tactics that you were taught during your officer's training. Keep in mind the success of your platoon depends on your leadership, not your sacrifices, so be a platoon leader, not a point man. Third, use the chain of command and delegate. And most of all, don't try to do everything yourself."

"Yes, Sir," he replied.

I shared that I believed we had come out ahead during our battles because we used sound tactics, and we had the support of our artillery, gun-ships, Gooney-birds, Air Force, plus Navy and Marine air support when we needed it. Lt. Miller assured me he knew military tactics. He was very self-confident and eager to lead men. My initial evaluation was that he would be an effective platoon leader.

Lt. Evans took Lt. Miller to meet his platoon sergeant and then stayed with him until he was properly equipped and ready for any mission we would be assigned.

The next day, Monday, 31 March, 1969, the company spent the day reorganizing, resupplying, and enjoying the security of the base-camp that allowed the men to shower, write, change clothes and have a smoke without fear of being detected by the enemy. Lt. Evans, First Sgt. Weaver, Sgt. Shea, and I spent most of the day writing reports. We had to complete reports for each man wounded or killed. Transfer orders had to be prepared, signed, distributed, and filed in each man's personnel file. All participants in the battle had to have their personnel files reviewed to see if they were previously awarded the Combat Infantryman's Badge. This included the files of those killed, wounded and not wounded. Requests for orders had to be prepared for those who had not previously been awarded the Combat Infantryman's Badge. Requests also had to be initiated for the Purple Heart awards for each man wounded or killed in the battle. The orders were issued from the higher headquarters, but we had to initiate the requests.

An inventory of the equipment that each survivor still possessed was made and the serial numbers of all weapons were verified. The weapons that were inadvertently swapped, while evacuating the wounded, were returned to the original assignee or the paperwork was generated and signed to transfer the weapon to the new person. Paperwork had to be generated to get the additional equipment needed to replace what was lost and the equipment had to be secured, transported to the company area, and then issued. On top of all the paperwork, each man had to prepare for any up-coming tactical assignment. We didn't know whether the battle we had just experienced was the worst battle we would see, or if there would be greater battles ahead of us. Each of us had to get ready as quickly as we could for whatever awaited us.

When most of the paperwork was completed, Lt. Evans took the half hour flight to <u>Chu</u> <u>Lai</u>, where he visited our men in the military hospital. He visited each wounded man to assure he was receiving everything that he needed. Larky made a list of the personal belongings each man still had at LZ Bronco so he could send each item to them or to their home.

Purple Hearts and Combat Infantryman's Badges were awarded to these brave young men who fought so valiantly for their fellow countrymen. Battalion still believed what the battalion intelligence officer had concluded. In his report, Delta Company had been ambushed by six to twelve enemy fighters. Clearly, our battalion staff had a different opinion than I did. However, time would reveal Delta Company had been up against a reinforced North Vietnamese Infantry Battalion.

The battalion chaplain held a memorial service for those we lost. All the men of our company and a few others from the battalion attended. After the services, I tried to write to Lieutenant Claybaugh's family, but I couldn't do justice to how bravely this young man had served. I knew that someday I would write the letter, but I was depressed and incapable of doing it correctly at that time.

-    -   -   o   -   -   -

On Tuesday, 1 April 1969, we were scheduled to have an additional day to get completely resupplied, finish our paperwork, and put the new company chain of command in place. Sgt. Zartuche became the First Platoon leader, Sgt. John L. Wheelan the Second Platoon leader, Lt. Miller the Third Platoon leader, and Sgt. Grimes was still the Weapons Platoon leader. The two new medics, Pfc.'s William Wordell and Vaughn McClendon, were assigned to their platoons.

Battalion thought it would be best if Lt. Bird was transferred to the battalion staff. I agreed. His performance on the battlefield and his long whining session over the airwaves after the battle may have left doubt in his platoon members' minds about his capabilities as a platoon leader. It certainly did create doubts in mine.

At 1400 hours I received an order to move out immediately to the rice bowl to the north of LZ Bronco. We had operated in the mountains, in the jungle, and in the coastal rice bowls like the one where LZ Bronco was located. I preferred operating in the mountains and on the seashore, more than in the rice bowls. A cool breeze blew on the beach and in the mountains. The rice bowl, which was the flat land between the mountains and the sand berms near the shoreline, was full of stale, hot, humid, and stagnant air.

At 1430 hours the company fell out on the dirt street in front of the orderly room, ready to move out. We were not up to full strength because of our losses and those conducting DX activities whom we hadn't found yet. However, those of us who were notified were ready. The Delta Dogs were to head north and join Company B on the north side of LZ Bronco. Company D was to replace Company B in a joint sweep with Company A to the north of LZ Bronco.

My First Sergeant, Company Clerk, and Supply Sergeant scurried around the base-camp looking for the rest of our men. Lt. Miller, the new platoon leader was one of the men we hadn't been able to notify. We had not received the operation order the day before, as was the usual practice, and the last minute order was somewhat of a surprise. Consequently, we were not completely ready to move out and join Company A when the order came.

Delta Dogs moving north on Tuesday, 1 April 1969.

Before we arrived at the rear gate, we found some of our men on their way back to our company area. While talking to them, our company jeep pulled up to us with Lt. Miller, Sgt. Espinoza, and some more of our men who were picked up while returning from the barbershop. I told all those not geared up for the field to meet us by the fuel storage tank by the back gate. The jeep took off to let them grab their weapons and gear. They would be driven to the back gate when they were geared up. We continued our trek in that direction. We were short-handed and needed everyone that we could muster to go on this mission with us.

I gathered the men into a small half circle. While waiting for the others to join us, I told them how proud I was of their performance on the battlefield. I concluded we could learn two things from that engagement. First, we had to stay spread out, but had to stay linked up with the other platoons. Second, we had to carry more smoke grenades and more ammunition with us. My men agreed about those two points. But no one accepted the S-2 report.

Before ending the impromptu meeting, I told them the battalion commander said the whole battalion was proud of the way we fought. I reminded them our battle plan remained the same. When we find a superior force of enemy, we make contact and hold them. We will be reinforced until we out-number the enemy. The reason it didn't work earlier was because our S-2 thought we had out-numbered the enemy, and most of the other units were in contact somewhere else after the Tet offensive began.

When the other men joined us, I ended the small gathering. We trudged out the back gate and headed towards the river north of LZ Bronco. At 1500 hours we were leaving the base-camp. I was not comfortable with the force I was leading into the field. Our casualties had not been replaced, and I had men who were not able to exchange damaged and expended equipment. There were only 73 of us, instead of the 106 we had a few days ago.

Soon after just exiting the base-camp, battalion started sending us messages to move faster. I thought it was like a bad April Fool's day joke. Battalion wanted Company B to move back before dark. At 1530 hours we had barely moved 500 meters from LZ Bronco and had 4,000 meters more to go before we would reach Company B.

We waded across a shallow point where the <u>Song Quan River</u> was only ankle deep, instead of the waist-deep river we crossed the previous week, or the chest-deep river south of the battlefield. We snaked our way through the sea of rice paddies and islands. We passed a few Vietnamese boys who were tending a half dozen grazing water buffaloes. Our pace was steady, but not back-breaking. We were operating with less enthusiasm than we had on previous days. I had to keep the Delta Dogs moving quickly, but it was more important to be cautious.

When we came to the large <u>Song Cau River</u> that led into the <u>Song Tra Cau Lake</u> north of Bronco, we found what I expected. The bridge marked on the map, did not exist. This was the story of this war. Towns and bridges shown on the maps no longer existed. Most prominent structures, such as schools, town halls, and other large buildings had disappeared. In this no-man's land, these structures were either destroyed during the Indo-China War, or during the current conflict.

We saw people fishing and kids swimming in the large lake formed by the river before it flowed into the sea to our east. It looked like it would be quite awhile before we could get the entire company across the river. I started to move the company back to the south, to form a perimeter so we could have our

Delta Dogs Crossing the Song Cau River.

supper before crossing the water. Just as we started to move to form our logger position, the fishermen and kids began heading for their homes. They crossed the river at a shallow spot. I immediately moved the company down to that location and started moving them across.

While the company was crossing, the battalion command and control chopper arrived. The helicopter landed on the south side of the river, where I was located. They gave me the daily SOI's (Signal Operating Instructions) which changed every month. We had left so quickly, we hadn't received April's codes for sending information over the radio. The SOI gave us the new daily cryptic codes.

I also received a change in mission. Instead of moving north to replace Company B, we were to move east towards the sea. We were to logger for the night and then be prepared to move north in the morning to cordon off a village.

Most of the company had waded across the river. My command group personnel were the only ones yet to cross the river when the chopper left. The river was only about knee-deep at this location. Some of the shorter men walked on their tip-toes to prevent the water from wetting their crotches.

When I reached the other side, I gathered the platoon leaders together and informed them of the change in mission. Then we moved towards the South China Sea with each platoon following the one in front of them. The lead platoon observed a Dink evading our approach. My RTO called in the report to our operations center. The command chopper that was still in our vicinity, flew over our area and couldn't find any sign of the Dink.

Dinks were Vietnamese, not known to be enemy or friendly. We called them Dinks because of their diminutive stature. Gooks or Charlie were what we called known enemy

Viet Cong or North Vietnamese Army (NVA) soldiers. RVN troops were Republic of South Vietnam soldiers.

We continued east, then up a 30-foot high sand berm that separated the farmland in the rice bowl from the sandy beach. We struggled up the steep embankment on the hot, sunny late afternoon, sliding back a little with each step we took. After we climbed over the top of the berm, the sand dropped more gradually to the ocean. There was about a 100 meters of brush and trees covering the flat stretch of land between the bottom of the berm and the water. The South China Sea spread out before us.

With the hot temperature and the surf pounding the shore, it seemed like we were in Florida during summer. The cool surf was a tempting sight. *A paradise in the midst of hell*, I thought. *This would be a nice vacation spot, if there wasn't a war going on.* It felt good to feel the soft, cool ocean breeze brush across my face as I took a moment to enjoy the pleasant seashore view.

For dinner we loggercd in a clump of pine trees, part way up the berm on the water side. After we ate and the darkness was about to cover us, one of the men at the southern end of our logger saw a Vietnamese man strolling along the beach. The Vietnamese suddenly noticed us and started hightailing it south, away from us. Our men shouted at him to stop in Vietnamese and for him to come back. The Vietnamese man continued trying to evade us. The men fired a warning shot, but he still wouldn't stop. He was just about to run out of our sight when my men opened fire on him with an M-60 machine-gun. He fell and our men hurried to his location to see who he was and the extent of his injuries. He was of military age, not in uniform, and had no identification papers. A bullet had hit him in the spine and he was in a lot of pain. I told Spc.4 Jimmy Cumbee, my new battalion net RTO who had previously served as one of the Second Platoon RTO's, to call the battalion operation center for a dust-off. The operator at the battalion command post who had received our earlier reports wanted to know why we wanted a dust-off for a wounded Vietnamese man, especially since he didn't have proper identification papers and was evading us after dark.

All the local Vietnamese knew there was a curfew in our area of operation. No one was to be outside a safe hamlet after dark unless they had a torch and proper identification papers. There was no doubt in the command post operator's mind we had wounded a VC.

I headed over to join the men with the Vietnamese man to check on his status. I could see the man was in a lot of pain, so I got on the radio myself to talk to the operations center operator to get the wounded man medical attention. I told the command post operator that the suspect had to be dusted-off, since he could probably provide intelligence information. Both the American and RVN troops that were operating in this area would benefit from his capture. The operations center radio operator finally agreed and called for a medevac dust-off, but as the medical evacuation helicopter was lifting off the ground the VC suspect died from the wound. I canceled the request. I felt sorry for him. We left the dead body on the beach. The local Vietnamese buried all dead, theirs or ours if we didn't recover our fatalities. Burying him would have taken time and might have exposed us to enemy detection.

I ordered the company to mount up and move out from our dinner position logger. Battalion called to receive our night logger coordinates, and I told my RTO Cumbee to report that we were just leaving and that we would report in as soon as we could establish our night logger position after our twiggies were in place. The operator informed Cumbee they wanted us to arrive at our night logger position as soon as possible. They were already late in reporting to brigade where all the troops in the field were located.

We moved to another grove of pine trees to the north and loggered for the night. I had each platoon, except the Weapons Platoon, send a twiggy out in front of them. The four platoons set up a night perimeter. Cumbee used our SOI to send in the coordinates I had given him.

I dug a foxhole in the sand and bunched a pile of pine needles next to it to sleep on. I didn't like sleeping in a hole, but I wanted it nearby if I needed it. A barrage of random artillery fire falling some distance away started lulling us to sleep.

-    -   -   o   -   -   -

As I lay on the pine needles by the sea, under the pine tree canopy, I listened to the surf pounding and the artillery shells bursting. My thoughts drifted back to North Carolina. When I was a young paratrooper stationed at Fort Bragg, a number of us rode motorcycles to the Asheville-Waynesville racetrack and spent the night before the race sleeping on the ground with just pine needles as mattresses and the pine tree canopy as our roof. Only back then, there weren't artillery shells bursting in the distance.

I fell asleep around 1900 hours only to be awakened two hours later by Cumbee reporting that battalion called with instructions on the next day's mission. I couldn't help but wonder if the late awakening was part of their payback for my not reporting our night position until late. I got on the radio and was ordered to move out at 0200 hours and be in position at 0500 hours to cordon-off <u>Phan</u> <u>That</u> (1). At sunrise we were to search the village. I left word with Cumbee to wake me at 0100 hours. I didn't want to wake the platoon leaders up to tell them what I could let them know when it was near time to get ready to move out.

My three radio operators and the company command group medic took turns on radio watch. Each hour they checked by clicking the radio send button to be sure someone in each platoon was awake. I went back to sleep and was awakened at 0100 hours.

I told Joe and Cumbee to call each of the platoon leaders so I could talk to them on the radio. I ordered them to wake up their men, call in their twiggies, and while their men were getting ready to move out, they were to join me at my location.

As everyone was getting up and preparing to move out, the four platoon leaders and I hunched under our ponchos and used our red filter-lens flashlights to look at our maps. I told them about our mission, and I showed them our location and the village location over 4,000 meters away (two and a half miles) to our north. I gave the order-of-march. Lt. Miller's Third Platoon would lead the march. The command group followed the Third Platoon. The Weapons Platoon, then the First Platoon, and the Second Platoon followed us, in that order. We moved out cautiously at 0200 hours, everyone keeping their eyes open for enemy activity and booby-traps. We all knew we could very easily bump into the enemy in the dark. The full moon was a mixed blessing. We had better visibility, but so did Charlie. We cautiously crossed the open farmland, one platoon closely following the other so we could move fast and follow the path cleared by the lead platoon.

We had to search a 500 by 700 meter area. The Third and First Platoons deployed along the 700-meter side of the village. The Second and Weapons Platoons spread out along the 500 meters side, forming an 'L' shape.

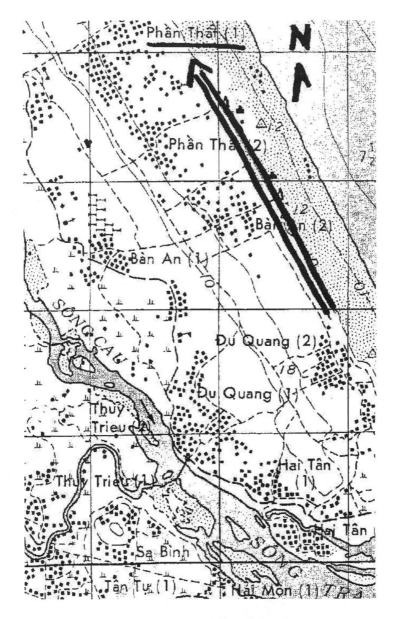

Delta Company moving north to Phan That (1) village.

We had the cordon in place by 0500 hours. The men took turns sleeping and watching until 0630 hours. When it was light enough, we started the search. All the platoons held their positions while Lt. Miller and his Third Platoon searched the village. I gave Lt. Miller's platoon the more crucial tasks because his platoon was the only platoon commanded by an officer at that time.

The village was typical of most Vietnamese villages outside the protected hamlets. The old men and woman in the village chewed red berries that killed the pain of rotting teeth and kept them high enough so they didn't worry about the way of life they were forced to live. In addition to the old men and women, the village contained several girls about 16 years old who were pregnant and had one or two children each and no husband.

That was the way Charlie operated. The men had to leave their families in North Vietnam and they frequently created a second family in the south. When the village boys in Quang Ngai Province were only 13 or 14-years old, they had to choose if they were going to be South Vietnamese soldiers or North Vietnamese soldiers. Those who chose to be South Vietnamese soldiers moved their family to a South Vietnamese safe hamlet. Those who chose to be North Vietnamese soldiers would leave their families in these unprotected villages.

I felt sorry for the kids. My eight-year old son was enjoying a carefree childhood. These kids were not as fortunate. They were in a war zone every day, and had to choose a side when they became teenagers. They had to grow up too fast and under harsh circumstances.

At the end of the village we found a 70-year old lady with a three-year old boy. In her yard was an old, unexploded 105-millimeter howitzer shell. The fuse was still attached and the

167

explosives were still in it. I put a demolition team on it and took the old lady and kid with us. They didn't want to go, but for their own good we forced them to leave. I didn't want them to get hurt by the explosion. We cleared everyone else out of the area.

While I was waiting for the demo team to explode the artillery round, I reached into my C-rations and took out a paper packet of cocoa. I tore open the end, poured a little powder in my hand, and then looked at the young boy before licking the brown powder. Then I took the small boy's hand, poured a little pile of powder into his hand and waited for him to lick it. He did and then looked at me with a big smile on his face. He liked it and held out his hand for more. I poured a little more in his hand and then handed the paper pouch to his grandmother. I took out a candy bar from my C-ration package and did the same thing with the chocolate candy bar. I knew life wasn't always going to be good for this kid. That day, I was doing what I could to make his life a little better by sharing my cocoa powder and chocolate bar with him. I hoped he would remember this small kindness if he ever grew up to be forced into military service.

While the grandmother and boy were enjoying the cocoa and candy bar, I opened a can of applesauce and ate my breakfast of applesauce and crackers. After the artillery round was exploded, we let the villagers back into their village.

As I was reporting the results of the cordon and sweep of the village, the command helicopter arrived overhead and landed. I boarded and they took me on an aerial visual reconnaissance of the area. LTC Pritchard pointed out all the likely VC positions as we flew south 10,000 meters and then east 3,000 meters. The chopper headed back toward my company's location, and I was given our new mission. We would sweep south and set up a night logger position just north of the mouth of the lake where it emptied into the South China Sea. The next day we were to cross the river again and check out the area just south of the lake. We were to look for caves and spider holes. Then we were to move south to An Lac villages 1, 2, and 3, and search that area for spider-holes and caves.

An Lac was in the vicinity where Lt. Claybaugh had received enemy fire when he didn't have maps with which to direct artillery fire the week before. I was instructed that after sweeping the An Lac villages, we were to move towards the mountain near LZ Bronco and east of the Song Cau Bau River.

After the 25-minute visual reconnaissance flight, they dropped me off with my company. LTC Pritchard stepped out of the helicopter with me, and we both walked a good number of feet away so we could talk without shouting. The battalion commander asked me a personal question, "Captain, is it important to you to keep your mustache?"

"No, Sir," I said

"Then I would like you to shave it, if you don't mind."

I had a mustache when at Fort Lewis, Washington. It wasn't important for me to keep it, but I wondered why it was important to the battalion commander. "Why is that, Sir?"

The Colonel pointed towards my men. "Look how many are starting to grow mustaches."

I looked at the men and to my surprise most had stubble's under their nose on their otherwise clean-shaven faces. "No problem, Sir. I'll shave it right away."

I saluted him and he headed back to his chopper.

Everyone had finished his morning rations and was ready to move out by the time I returned. I gave the four platoon leaders the day's mission to sweep south and then logger north of the Song Tra Cau Lake.

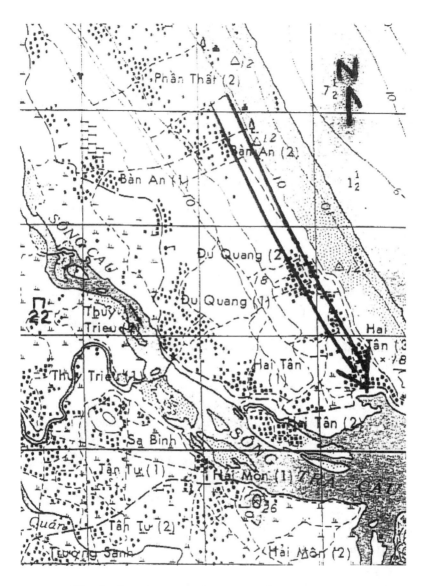

**The infantry company sweeping
toward the Song Tra Cau Lake.**

Lt. Faust, the Artillery Forward Observer, attended all the company command meetings when I gave the operation orders. He also acted as my advisor and understudy, so he could take over if I was incapacitated. Battalion would appoint a new company commander if anything happened to me. However, when all the platoons were in contact, Lt. Faust could temporarily coordinate the platoons' efforts and communicate with battalion while the battle was still in progress. The change in command would occur only after the battle was over and control of all our men had stabilized.

When the platoon leaders departed to brief their men on the day's mission, the six of us in the company command group huddled together so I could brief them on our move south. Lt. Hoa and Junior, my interpreters, were not available when we got the quick order to move out from LZ Bronco, because they were observing the Tet holidays with family and friends. The six men included in the company command group were Lt. Faust, Midge (his RTO) and Spc.4 Cumbee (who had replaced my RTO battalion net operator Spc.4 McBurnett), Joe (my other RTO), Spc.4 Vandermeer, and myself. Being a short timer, Mac had been reassigned to a rear RTO position. Spc.4 Vaughn S. Vandermeer was our new command group medic, replacing Spc.4 Jackson who had been wounded four days earlier.

I always kept the command group briefed. It was important because the three RTO's did most of the communicating with the platoons and the rear base for me. I gave my orders and requests to the two company radio operators who relayed them to the platoons or to battalion. For that reason, they always stayed close to me 24 hours a day. I only got on the horn when things were not getting done, when I wanted to communicate to a platoon leader personally, or when someone at battalion wanted to talk directly with me. When things got hot, I was very busy encrypting messages, encrypting map location coordinates of both the enemy and us, plotting locations on the tactical map, writing operation orders before I gave them, and maneuvering myself and the command group to a location where I could better observe and assess the tactical situation. Combat was not a one-man show or a static operation. Success required close teamwork at every level. Each soldier performed his tasks professionally, and each had to be ready to perform their buddies' tasks in case something happened to them.

We moved south, with Sgt. Zartuche leading us with his First Platoon. They swept as scrimmagers on the right flank. Sgt. Wheelan, who was the leader of the Second Platoon, swept just east of the First Platoon. The Third, commanded by Lt. Miller and with Sgt. Espinoza as his platoon sergeant, swept on the left flank. The Weapons Platoon, led by Sgt. Grimes, and the company command group followed behind the other three as we moved south.

When we moved out, Midge still didn't have a radio, so the artillery forward observer's radio telephone operator volunteered to act as our company command group point man, as we followed the three rifle platoons. His commander, Lt. Faust, shared one of my radios when artillery fire was needed. Usually my medic acted as the company command group rear guard, since I wanted my two radio operators and Lt. Faust close to me.

We swept south for 2,000 meters and stopped at a dirt island in the sea of rice paddies, with trees along the hedge-row that bordered it. We got out of the noonday sun to eat our lunch and rest a little. I ordered the platoons to logger to provide all-around security while we ate. We spent an entire hour for lunch, instead of the brief 15 to 20 minutes we normally took for lunch.

Each C-ration package came with a single use roll of toilet paper. I tucked my roll between my helmet cover and the thick elastic band that also held the insect repellent. The white toilet paper sheets were neatly packaged in a light brown wrapper so they would blend in with the olive-drab helmet cover.

If we became too nauseous from humping all day in the very hot climate with no shade, we might not feel like eating the canned foods. So we opened the cans, dumped the contents out, crushed the can and buried everything. Sometimes we just ate the crackers and jelly so we could get some energy. That happened quite frequently when we were forced to maneuver, even though our bodies were telling us we were too tired to continue moving.

We carried sterno to heat our C-rations with. When it was a very hot day, we just ate them out of the can without further heating. When we ran out of sterno, we set fire to a chunk of the Velveeta Cheese size block of C-Four plastic explosive to heat our meals. C-Four exploded when shocked with a blasting cap, not by the impact of a bullet or by setting it on fire. When set on fire, it just burned, a little brighter than sterno. We crushed the cans and burned the trash after we ate. Then, we buried everything. We didn't want to leave anything around for Charlie to use to make booby-traps. Any coffee, sugar, or salt that wasn't used was given to another soldier or destroyed to prevent Charlie from finding and using our discards.

I stopped smoking cigarettes during my jungle training in Panama. I stopped for three reasons: (1) the enemy could detect the smell of cigarette smoke easily; (2) lighting the cigarette during the day or night gave a bright signal to the enemy indicating our location; and (3) I didn't think smoking was very healthy. I didn't want to completely stop, so I switched to cigars. I felt it was a good way to cut back, because they were hard to get in the field. I didn't think smoking cigars was as harmful as smoking the bleached-paper wrapped cigarettes.

After we finished lunch, we continued south. We called this area the Gaza Strip. The South China Sea was to the east, the <u>Song</u> <u>Cau</u> <u>River</u> to the west and the <u>Song</u> <u>Tra</u> <u>Cau</u> <u>Lake</u> was to the south. This was fertile farmland with a large sand bar to the east and a sloping wooded beach on the other side of the sand bar. The farmland was used to grow a variety of crops, including rice, potatoes, bananas, peanuts, berries, pineapple, and coconuts. The low land closer to the three rivers that flowed into the <u>Song</u> <u>Tra</u> <u>Cau</u> <u>Lake</u> consisted of a vast sea of rice paddies, separated with the islands and dikes. Most of the rice paddies were dry, but many were full of water and rice plants. This area was farmed by both those who lived in the government hamlets, such as <u>Duc</u> <u>Pho</u>, and those who lived in non-government villages, such as the one we had cordoned that morning.

After lunch we burned our discarded flammable material, like the C-ration boxes and unused paper packets. We didn't stick around until everything burned out. We were concerned about the smoke pin-pointing our position to any enemy forces in the area. As we continued south, the wind whipped up the small fire from the pile Spc.4 David Giles had left burning. An ocean breeze spread the small fire into the dry fields and the fire spread north through the almost empty fields. The smoke from the burning dry farm fields rose into the sky as the fire moved away from us. This may have been a concern for some, but for us it gave a secure feeling. We knew that no VC would be following us from that direction, because of the burning fire spreading about 1,000 meters across and about 2,000 meters to the north.

We reached a small cove of the <u>Song</u> <u>Tra</u> <u>Cau</u> <u>Lake</u> a few hours before sunset. The men asked if they could take a dip. I

Trees in the background hidden by the fire's smoke.

ordered two platoons to set up a half circle around our location at the water's edge and let the other two platoons take an hour-long dip. Then they switched places.

I was bringing my logbook up to date, when the battalion command chopper flew overhead. They wanted to know what all the burning was about. I got on the radio and reported we were burning our trash, and the wind spread the fire. Since the fields were empty and we had a mission to accomplish, I just let it burn it's self out. Major Vaughn, who had questioned the hootch burning a week earlier, was evidently concerned that we may be conducting a scorched earth action. I assured him we were not burning the fields; the fire was an accident. Major Vaughn said he was glad to hear that and flew off to check on the battalion's other companies.

Rumor had it the commander before LTC Pritchard enjoyed killing Dinks. The prior battalion commander considered any Dink found outside the sanctioned hamlets to be VC. Rumor was that he would go out 'Dink hunting' each day, to see how many he could kill. That commander, it was said, liked to accompany the sweeps, like the one we had been conducting. When the grunts (infantrymen) flushed out anyone, he would have his command chopper swoop down so he could shoot them. When he flew over areas being swept, he expected to see hootches, fields and haystacks in no-man's land being burned. If he saw burning, he was happy.

LTC Pritchard was not like that. He was a people person. He understood that some Vietnamese would like to live on their own land, instead of in the safe South Vietnamese Government hamlets. His policy was, if we receive fire from a hootch or if we found ammo or supplies being stored in a hootch for the NVA or VC, we should burn down the hootch. In other words, live and let live.

176

Sergeants Gerald D. Gerlach, Robert C. Reed, Wheelan, and Zartuche, plus dozens of their men went swimming in the nude. Jungle warriors did not wear underwear, since they

Delta Dogs swimming in the Song Tra Cau Lake.

caused chafing. While the men were enjoying them selves, a chopper flew over us, circled and landed about 50 meters from me. I grabbed my rifle and headed for the chopper. As I approached the helicopter, I was surprised to see Colonel Jack L. Treadwell, the commanding officer of the 11th Light Infantry Brigade disembark with his aide and a couple brigade staff officers. I was shaken, and yet in a state of euphoria. I figured I did something very good or very wrong. Colonel Treadwell was one of the very few Congressional Medal of Honor winners in the world. The Medal of Honor was the highest US award for bravery anyone could receive. Colonel Treadwell's visit was like having an audience with the Pope.

I immediately sent one of my radio operators to ensure we had our security on the alert. I didn't want any enemy surprises while such a distinguished visitor was with our company. My other RTO was concerned, "What if he doesn't like our men swimming?"

"It's too late now. Maybe that is why he's landed," I said.

When I reached the chopper, I saluted the colonel and reported, "Captain George Durgin, Delta Company Command, Sir. How may I be of service, Sir."

Colonel Treadwell returned the salute and asked what we were doing. I told him we had completed our mission and were taking turns swimming in the lake, before moving to our night logger position. I pointed to the smoldering area north of us and explained how we had just completed cordoning off a village and sweeping 3,000 meters south after searching the village. As I spoke, we could still see the smoldering land, with less smoke now rising into the air. I thought this might be why he landed. I was sure that he was going to chastise me for the fire we started. I quickly pointed to where the two platoons were securing the beach area, hoping to distract him from the fire.

He asked what mission we had coming up. I reported we would logger on this side of the lake tonight, then proceed to sweep to the south side of the lake tomorrow, looking for caves and spider-holes.

"Very good, Captain. Carry on," he commented, then the colonel headed for the chopper.

One of the Majors with him stayed a moment to ask a question. "Captain, were you the unit that was in the fire fight southwest of Duc Pho on the 29th of March?"

"Yes, Sir," I said.

"You were in quite a tight spot then, weren't you?"

"Yes, Sir. We were lucky we only lost as few as we did."

"We were all listening to your communications then and thought your men did a good job. I think that's why the Colonel wanted to come out and meet you."

He saluted me, "Good luck, Captain."

After I returned his salute, he turned and returned to the chopper. It seemed strange to me that the Major would salute me. We salute the most senior officer first as a way of showing respect. It is very seldom that a senior officer saluted an officer junior to him unless he wants to show respect for the junior officer. This situation was puzzling to me at the time. Then the chopper took off.

I didn't know if the colonel and his staff were pleased or displeased with my men taking a swim in the lake. I also didn't know I had just completed a mini-interview and would be on the Brigade Commander's staff in a few months.

-    -   -   o   -   -   -

The men were finished with their swimming, and we were getting ready to saddle up. I didn't swim because I was afraid of water. My older brother and I almost drowned when I was seven years old. If the lifeguard at the Detroit swimming pool hadn't discovered that I was still in the water after pulling my

179

brother out, I would have drowned. After that experience, I didn't like going into the water.

Not being able to swim proved to be quite a challenge during my jungle training in Panama. We had to cross five rivers on the last part of our two weeks of jungle fighter's training. Army Special Forces personnel were tracking us down, and we had to move fast to evade them. Using the roads and bridges would mean we would be captured. Taking the hard route through dense jungle and across the five rivers would give our three-man team a good chance of not being captured. At the first river we found a tree that had fallen or someone had chopped so it would fall across the river. The next river was not too deep, so I cut a small tree and used it as a staff to probe for where the boulders were in the river. I was able to step on them to cross. I was lucky on the next river. We scaled the face of a cliff and crossed the river at its origin where it was shallower.

My teammates were very supportive of me then. At the next river, we cut a lot of brush and grass. Then we used our ponchos to make a floating ball filled with grass that I held onto while the other two swam and pulled me across. I helped by kicking my legs while holding on for dear life to the makeshift raft. The last river we crossed by cutting a thin, tall tree so it fell across the river. Then we tightrope walked across the last river.

All the excess effort to help me cross the five rivers without having to swim, didn't delay us too much. We were in the top ten percent for arriving at the other end of the island at the Gatun Locks in Panama. Some didn't make it across until 20 hours after we completed the evasion maneuver, and we had already enjoyed a full night's sleep back at the army facility.

Because of my hydrophobia, swimming in the <u>Song</u> <u>Tra</u> <u>Cau</u> <u>Lake</u> with my infantry company men was the last thing I had wanted to do, even in the over 115-degrees weather.

- - - o - - -

At 1600 hours, before we moved out, Lt. Evans radioed us and informed us he had arranged a helicopter resupply run so he could transport some of the men who had missed our last minute departure. He was on the chopper when it landed. We all got a nice cold soda and whatever standing beer and soda orders we had. To make up for the last two days' worth we had consumed, we also received C-rations and fresh water. A new man joined us, Pfc. Richard McConnel.

Lt. Evans came out because someone else in the brigade had lost the SOI (Signal Operating Instructions), and the one I had wasn't good any more. As the SOI was a top-secret document, he brought our copies out himself. The Supply Clerk also brought us our mail.

We loaded our resupplies in our rucksacks, drank the cool soda while we read our mail, and then we were ready to move out. I gave the platoon leaders my operation order to move north a few hundred meters, then to the east where the sand dune berm was located.

We were to find a secure location for our evening meal, then locate a secure night logger position after dark. We had been in the area for some time and if there were any enemy forces around, they would have been following our movements. It would make us a good target if we moved predictably.

Shortly after eating our evening chow, and before moving out at 1915 hours Sgt. Grimes reported observing several Vietnamese men. The sun had set at 1858 hours and evening nautical twilight was at 1944 hours, about a half an hour from then. I asked Sgt. Grimes why his men didn't shoot at the men.

"They didn't think it was after dark yet," he said.

That was the way war was, everyone had a different opinion on when darkness occurred, so I had to agree with his men. I had the light tables and they didn't.

I figured they were probably VC, but they could have been farmers who were late getting back from their fields. In any case it presented a problem. Their presence meant we couldn't move north to a night logger position without revealing our nighttime location. I had the company move east over the large sand berm to the ocean side. We were close to where we had killed the VC suspect the night before.

Prior to forming our night logger position, one of the men saw movement to the north of us on the beach. The South China Sea was to our east. We had unknown men to the north and unknown men to the west. It appeared we had only one way to go - south. I wasn't fearful of the four or five men we had seen but was concerned they were VC or NVA soldiers and could lob mortar or rocket rounds into our night logger position.

This presented a problem, particularly for me. We were on a peninsula with the <u>Song</u> <u>Tra</u> <u>Cau</u> <u>Lake</u> inlet to the south of us. Being afraid of water, moving south was a very difficult decision for me to make. I didn't share my apprehension with anyone, because I didn't want them overly concerned with my problem. Going south meant we had to cross the inlet. Crossing the waterway appeared to be the only course that could take us away from the unknown Vietnamese we had seen.

I ordered the four platoon leaders to join me. Under our ponchos, we looked at the map. I informed them of the situation and told them to take their tallest men and start

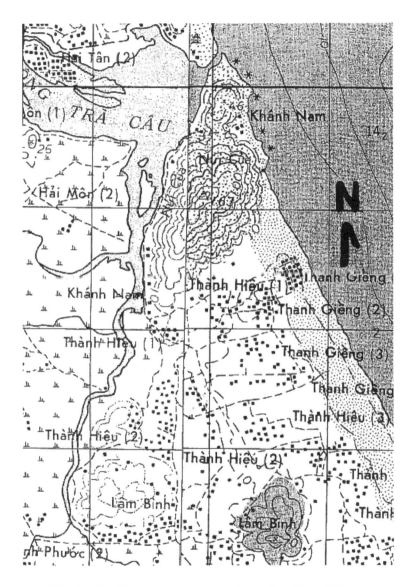

The Delta Dogs were located on the tip of the
peninsula located on the north side of the inlet
of the South China Sea into Song Tra Cau Lake.

across the waterway connecting the lake and the sea. As a number of our men were short, we would have to station the taller men in the water to heft the shorter grunts up so they could catch their breath if the water was too deep for them.

The platoons started toward the inlet. Some of the men took their letters, wallets, toilet paper, stationary and whatever they didn't want to get wet and stuck them under the olive-drab elastic band that we all had on our helmet covers. We held our weapons and ammunition in our hands so we could raise them up out of the salt water, as well.

The almost full moon had risen an hour earlier. It was 2015 hours when we started to cross the 60-meter wide watery divide in the dark. My command group was behind the first platoon to cross, so I could see if there was a suitable night logger position on the peninsula south of us. Some men pulled their pant legs up past their knees in a futile attempt to try to keep them dry. Several were sweating and breathing as heavily as I was. In the moonlit night, we stepped into the water not knowing how deep it was or how forceful the tide was going to be.

As I stepped into the ocean, my fear, anxiety, and apprehension caused sweat to flow from my entire body. The surging cool seawater washed away the dust-saturated sweat, but it didn't cleanse the state of panic from me. Each step, each wave, each minute brought a new influx of panic for me. Only my sense of duty and the knowledge of what we were fleeing from superseded my fear of the water as I forced myself forward, the pulsating waves washing over me.

While crossing the inlet, I struggled with the war within me. One fear was of drowning, the other fear was being mortared or ambushed by the enemy. Memories were still fresh in my mind from our 29 March battle. Both fears engulfed me cyclically as the swells rose and subsided. While

Looking towards the inlet from the South China Sea on the east side of the Song Tra Cau Lake.

immerged, the fear of drowning prevailed. When the water level dropped, our exposure to possible enemy detection brought the second fear upon me.

I couldn't let my emotions get the better of me. I had to maintain the confidence of my men. I felt that I could not shatter their conviction that I was a leader to be followed by letting my fears become known. I felt if there was a hell on Earth, I was experiencing it. I felt I might have been walking to a watery grave in order to evade a sandy grave on the peninsula north of us.

That night, the enemy and the seawater were the fire of fear that hardened the fiber of my being. After the crossing, I knew I could suffer any ordeal that would result in the protection of my men. However, I was glad my men didn't know the hidden battle I was facing as I led them away from danger.

In the moonlight I could see the soldiers moving in a single file ahead of me. Each had his weapon and ammo raised as high as they could in an effort to keep them out of the corrosive salt water. The three to four foot high swells covered the heads of the men in front of me as we reached what I hoped was the deepest part of the inlet. I held my breath as the waves washed over my head. After the wave passed, I took a few steps forward, stopped, waited for the next swell to submerge me before moving a couple more steps.

The soldiers not tall enough had to be steadied by the taller men stationed at the deep part of the inlet. After they took a deep breath, they took their next couple of steps. Then the next tall guy would grab them and steady them so they could gasp another deep breath before continuing across the deep part of the waterway. Sgt. Grimes was one of the taller men in the company who had stationed him self in the middle of the inlet to help the shorter ones get across.

The shifting sand caused by the tide surging in and out caused the movement forward to be a slow, painstaking task for each of us. I took my fatigue jacket off and put the SOI, maps, my three writing pads, toilet paper, my wallet, stationary, and anything else I wanted to keep dry in the four buttoned-down pockets of my jacket. I held my two ammo belts and my M-16 automatic assault rifle in one hand and the loaded fatigue jacket in the other. I had both arms raised as high as I could while the tide surged over my head. With difficulty and extreme anxiety, I moved forward between waves. I am five foot eleven and the waves rushed over my head. One could imagine what it would be like for those under five foot nine. They were under water a good deal of the time.

All 87 of us crossed the inlet that night. Some crossed with all their clothing on, some took their jackets off, and some took everything off except their boots, steel pots, and rucksacks for the crossing. While we were crossing, the rear platoon kept watch for the enemy until it was their turn to cross. The first ones across took up security positions to watch for the enemy. Some watched to the north from where we were coming, the rest to the south and west side of the peninsula we moved onto. We loggered until everyone had crossed. Once everyone was accounted for, we dressed and prepared to move again. We kept watch to the north to be sure that Charlie didn't cross the inlet too. We kept a sharp eye out for any mortar fire that may be launched from the north of us.

The battalion operations center had been calling us for over two hours asking for our night logger coordinates. Fortunately our radios were waterproof. We continually let them know we were being followed and continuing to move. The Battalion Operations Officer, Major Vaughn, radioed and requested to talk to me.

When I finally felt our position was secure, I answered his call.

"Well, since you like to move after dark, here is your new mission," he said. Then he gave us the coordinates of the village <u>Thanh</u> <u>Hieu</u> (1), almost 2,000 meters south of us. Traveling 2,000 meters should normally take us a couple hours, I thought, so it would not be a problem. Major Vaughn told me that we could get some sleep after we had cordoned the village.

There was no question, this was payback time for not loggering before sunset. The battalion operations personnel didn't like reporting our location late yet one more night. For me, this was a small price to pay for not letting Charlie know where we were sleeping.

- - - o - - -

First Lieutenant Larky D. Evans was drafted into the army in 1968 from Gainesville, Texas. Like Lt. Faust, he wanted to serve his country as a Commissioned Officer instead of an enlisted-man. To become an officer, he completed his basic training and then enlisted for four years so he could attend officer training at the Infantry Officer's Candidate School at Fort Benning, Georgia. He arrived in Vietnam in October 1968. Lt. Evans was assigned to Company D as the Second Platoon leader. Combat officers only served half their tour in Vietnam in the field. Captain Walters was the D Company commander for five months, then reassigned as the battalion Intelligence Officer (S-2). Larky was assigned as the Company D Executive Officer after half his tour was completed as an infantry platoon leader. He appeared to me to be a true southern gentleman, not just by an act of congress, but also in his actions. He was very cooperative and pleasant to work with. He performed his tasks efficiently and always acted as professionally as any career officer.

-    -   -   o   -   -   -

This is a list of those Delta Dogs heroes who were identified in this chapter.

First Lieutenant Larky D. Evans, from Gainesville, Texas
First Lieutenant James G. (Greg) Miller, from Newark, Ohio
Specialist Fourth Class Vaughn S. Vander Meer, from Grand Rapids, Michigan
Sergeant Gerald D. Gerlach, from Mount Vernon, South Dakota
Sergeant Robert C. Reed, from Lathrup Village, Michigan
Sergeant David E. Curry, from Liberty Lake, Washington
Specialist Fourth Class Jimmy D. Cumbee, from Twin City, Georgia
Sergeant John L. Wheelan, from Hampton Hills, Illinois
Private First Class Vaughn C. McClendon, from Saint Luis, Missouri
Private First Class William A. Wordell, from Lakesville, Massachusetts

**Sgt. Juan Espinoza moving on the
Red Ball Highway with Company D.**

Chapter Seven

Specialist Fourth Class Daniel M. Butler
Private First Class John M. Gilmore

After suppressing my fear of water and crossing the inlet, I calmed myself down while I deployed my men into a defensive position on the south side of the waterway. Having ensured all my men were accounted for, I gave the order for our change in mission to the four platoon leaders. We moved east until we were at the land's end. While we moved to the east, I had a thought. I asked Joe Dodson, my radio operator, "Why didn't we blow up our air mattresses and float our weapons and the belongings we wanted to keep dry when we crossed the inlet?"

"Good idea, Sir. I guess we just wanted to get away from Charlie so fast that we didn't think of it." We both laughed at the idea, which we hadn't thought of earlier.

"Why didn't you ask me that question before we crossed the water, Sir?" Joe asked.

We laughed again. "I didn't think of it then."

There wasn't any complaining from the men. They just appeared to be pleased we had evaded the enemy, even if the water crossing was more challenging and fearful for some of us. We were safe and had gotten out of a tight situation quickly. It's always easy to do Monday-morning quarterbacking where you can always come up with some better alternatives. But, when the heat was on, I had to do something and quick. Crossing the inlet was a successful answer. We probably could have done it better. What was done was done.

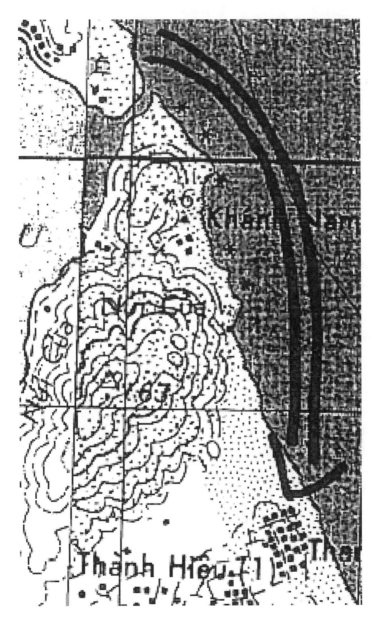

The all night move south to Thanh Hieu.

Second-guessing was a good mind game to play, and it was a lesson learned.

As we proceeded south along the shoreline, we heard the mortar rounds exploding in the night logger position we would have been in north of the inlet. I was glad we had crossed the waterway before the enemy's rain of mortar rounds started. Our water crossing had saved us from having men injured or worse. Not letting the enemy know where we were going to spend the night paid off, whether Major Vaughn liked it or not.

When we were a little south of the northeasterly edge of the peninsula, we discovered the beach was covered with large boulders, four to twenty feet in diameter. The eroded cliffs had fallen onto the beach. We couldn't see how far the thick piles of granite blocks extended to the south, so we climbed onto the rubble and continued south.

While climbing over the rocks, we slipped and banged ourselves against the large wet boulders. Because of the uneven piling of the huge fallen pieces of dark granite, we zigzagged over what looked like the easiest path to climb. At times, we had to stop, go back a little and take a different path. It was difficult climbing the huge boulders, either in the up or down direction.

We were tired, and had been up since 0100 hours the day before. We had gone 26 hours without sleep as we continued our march towards the assigned village south of us. We couldn't stop anyplace for a break, because there was no suitable location to rest or from which to fight if we met the enemy. Even though we continually watched our rear to be sure we weren't being followed, an attack from the rear was always a possibility. We had to keep going in order to arrive at our assigned objective by 0600 hours.

Most of us were in good physical shape, some not quite as fit as others. However, the men who carried the mortar, the mortar base plate, or the mortar ammunition had the heaviest loads to haul and they tired more quickly. The backtracking efforts gave them time to catch up with the rest of us. The 87 men following each other made quite a long line of tired, over loaded grunts negotiating nature's very difficult obstacle course.

Our mission was to be positioned east of <u>Thanh</u> <u>Hieu</u> (1) village, with one platoon on the high ground north of the village before morning nautical twilight, which was 0553 hours. We were to wait for the South Vietnamese PRU's to join us. The PRU's (South Vietnamese Provincial Recon Unit men) were a unique lot of mercenaries. They were ex-VC and ex-NVA soldiers who were paid proportionally to the number of VC and NVA soldiers they killed or captured. The PRU's would conduct the search of the village and the surrounding area for caves, spider-holes and enemy food or ammo caches.

Originally, I thought the 2,000-meters walk down the beach to the village would take two to three hours. But after climbing rocks for over four hours, we were not even halfway to our objective. I knew we would have to pick up the pace if we were to get to the village before sunrise.

During our water crossing of the inlet, one man had sprained his ankle and I left Sgt. Espinoza and his squad of men with him. Sgt. Grimes and his mortar-men were also left behind to pick up stragglers. I disconnected the two groups from the rest of us. The main group needed to move south much faster then I thought the others could. I didn't worry about the rear groups. We had radio communications with them. Both Sgt.'s Espinoza, and Grimes were good soldiers. I knew they would ensure their men were protected during the march south. Joe Dodson was not as confident. He worried about the stragglers. I knew the two sergeants were the best soldiers that could be found anywhere, and they would join with the rest of us as quickly as possible.

At last we came to a sandy beach and started moving faster over the dunes and scattered brush. We ached from the bruises and cuts from the sharp rocks. Even though we were sore and exhausted, we moved quickly south a few hundred meters on the sand until I saw a tall lanky American solider come ambling out of the brush on the side of the hill to our west.

As the lanky Tennessee Sergeant First Class Grimes approached us, with a moonlit smile on his face, he asked, "What took you guys so long?"

"I guess we're just a little tired and took our time." I answered. "Where's your platoon?"

He told me they were on the hillside, sleeping. He said he had been waiting for us for two hours. I thought he was joking, but he may not have been. I told him his platoon would be the last one in our order of march, so he could let his men sleep until the last of our guys passed. The company started moving south again, as the sergeant went back into the brush to rejoin his men. Sgt. Grimes' arrival ahead of us validated my earlier feelings that we had been moving too slowly.

As we proceeded south, we found VC or NVA-type boot prints in the wet sand. The tide would have washed them out if they were old tracks. When we came to an open space, I ordered the company to logger and, after a short break, I told Lt. Miller to take the lead with his platoon. I believed we had to move more cautiously after the discovery of the fresh footprints. We were out in the open and I knew the enemy was close by.

Sgt. Espinoza was in the back with one squad and the soldier with the sprained ankle. I let the platoon leaders know that Espinoza's squad would be the one to take the high

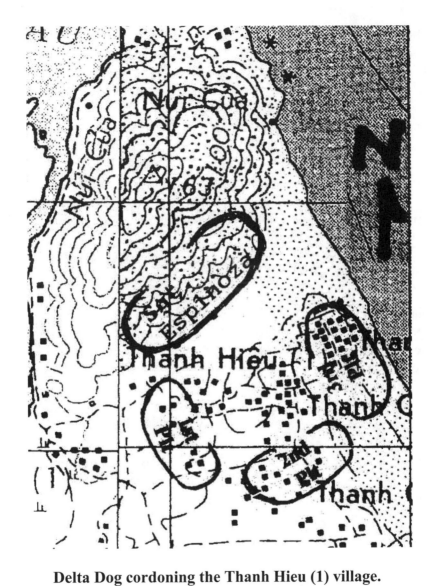

Delta Dog cordoning the Thanh Hieu (1) village.

ground just north of the village when he caught up with us.

Sgt. Reed, one of Lt. Miller's squad leaders, sent half his squad to one side of a high ground of sand, small rocks, and brush and the other half of his squad to another clump of rocks, sand, and brush on the far side of the clearing. The two groups of men were deployed as a covering force for the rest of us when we crossed the clearing. After they gave us the all clear, we crossed the clearing and started to move inland to cordon the village on both the south and east side. Sgt. Espinoza's squad was now on the side of the mountain, north of the village. This gave us the three-sided cordon battalion had wanted.

We needed a safe place to rest before the South Vietnamese PRU's arrived. I saw a wooded area west of the village and headed for it with the company command group. It gave us good cover and would allow us a safe location to catch a few winks. When we stopped, instead of assuming fighting positions, everyone just fell down to rest. It was almost 0400 hours, 27 hours since we had any sleep. We also had carried nearly 100 pounds of gear over steep, slippery rocks, and dry shifting sand. The men had started to complain.

"What in the hell do they think we are? Are we dumb animals, robots, or what? Don't they know that a God-damn guy has to have some sleep?"

Griping was a common thing in any organization, but this time it was justified. The men had been pushed too far by battalion and we all knew it. They were exhausted. They had earned the right to let everyone else know how they felt and I was too tired to defend battalion. I wasn't inclined to do so anyway, so I let it slide.

I knew the men wouldn't be very effective if Charlie were to hit us now. I told the platoon leaders to keep at least two men awake at all times while the rest got some sleep. The men were all too tired to expect the watch-guy to stay awake without some help from one of his buddies. They ate candy, chewed gum, or wrote letters home while on watch, to keep their minds busy so they wouldn't fall asleep. I hoped that the choppers would be late again for their pick up of the PRU's so we would have a little more time to catch up on our sleep.

At 0500 hours I had the RTO radio the platoons and have them wake up their men. Then I ordered the men to move into their cordon positions around the two sides of the village. We were in good fighting positions by 0530 hours, and took turns sleeping while waiting for the PRU's to arrive.

At 0600 hours, I got the call from battalion. They ordered me to start the search of the village without the PRU's. The South Vietnamese soldiers would join us later.

I relayed the orders to the three rifle platoon leaders. Almost immediately, we found an old woman trying to hide some papers when my men entered her hootch. The documents turned out to be four South Vietnamese Government Identification Cards.

All the villagers were required to carry their own ID papers. No one was allowed to carry another person's identification papers. All the ID's she was trying to hide were for women 20 to 25 years old. If the women exited, then they would have the ID cards with them. Suspecting that these were fraudulent ID cards for NVA women, I called in our find to battalion and requested they send a chopper out to pick the old woman up for interrogation.

When the chopper landed for the pickup, LTC Pritchard disembarked and began to reprimand me because some of my men were congregating under the shade of the trees, instead of being spread out to provide a good cordon of the village. I assured him I would see that the men were in fact spread out; covering the three sides while the fourth platoon conducted the search of the village. As the chopper took off with the old woman, I radioed the platoons and had them check to be sure their men were spread out and not clustered in the shaded areas during the search.

I speculated that my men were trying to catch a few winks in the shade while the one platoon was conducting the search. I knew the command chopper would probably be returning shortly to check on our progress, and I wanted to make sure we were properly deployed when they returned. Being an infantry company commander was not an easy task. There always seemed to be some anomaly occurrence.

The First and Second Platoons were spread out to provide full coverage of the hamlet while the Third Platoon continued searching. Sgt. Espinoza's men stayed on the hill mass to the north of the village providing the third side of the cordon. During the search, I received a call to inform me the PRU's were on their way and would be joining us shortly. Since the PRU's were South Vietnamese troops who were formally VC soldiers, they were familiar with the techniques the NVA and VC used to hide. I was cautioned to treat them well, since they could be very uncooperative if not treated with respect. I let battalion know I worked well with the Vietnamese forces, and that I would make them feel welcomed.

Not long after our conversation, two brigade choppers arrived with the South Vietnamese Provincial Recon Unit (PRU) men. The 10 men were clad in black Vietnamese pajama-type tops and bottoms. My men were happy they were finally here with us and we knew these men could make our work a lot easier and less dangerous. Gathered on a shaded path, which ran down the middle of a hedgerow, we offered them sodas and beers and I conversed with them in the little Vietnamese I knew and the small amount of English they knew.

Danh, the team leader, didn't want my men to continue their sweep of the village. He wanted us to pull back and form a big square around the outside of the village while his men conducted the search.

This was a break for us, because I knew my men needed sleep, and so did I. We had only two hours sleep in the past thirty-one hours. With Danh's men conducting the search, we could take turns sleeping and providing security for the area. I told Joe, my RTO, to call the platoon leaders and ask them to join us. I continued talking to Danh while I was waiting for them to arrive. I passed my phrase book back and forth to Danh. Between his English, my Vietnamese and the English-to-Vietnamese phrase book, we continued to communicate.

When Lt. Miller, Sgt.'s Grimes, Wheelan and Zartuche arrived, I discussed how we were going to assist the PRU's while they searched the village. While the platoon leaders were returning to their platoons, I joined the PRU's and the rest of my company command group.

To my surprise, some of the PRU's were smoking marijuana. The PRU's were feared and hated by both the South Vietnamese and North Vietnamese soldiers, and when the war was over, they had to live with whichever former enemy won the war. I knew they used marijuana to tune out their everyday life, but I hadn't expected them to use it so openly, particularly in a combat situation.

We had very few infantrymen who used dope in the field. It was a sure way of getting themselves and their buddies killed. During a battle everyone needed to be sharp. Smoking grass was something some rear echelon troops might do. But in the field, nobody touched the stuff.

Once the platoon leaders radioed they were in position, I informed the PRU's we were ready for them to start their search. I walked around the perimeter to ensure my men were positioned so none of the villagers could get out during the operation. Some of the men at a Third Platoon observation post were watching the PRU's performing their search, instead of watching for possible evaders or any in-coming enemy troops. Lt. Miller corrected the deficiency. Then Lt. Miller and I watched the shortest and sneakiest-looking of the PRU's, poking a long stick into one of the hedgerows. His name was Phou. To me, he was an oriental version of the old time movie actor, Peter Lorie. Phou seemed to be the best of the group. He took out one of his grenades, pulled the pin and threw it into the hedgerow where he had just poked. We all observed the dark smoke puffing out from where he threw in the grenade and on the other side of the berm.

He went over to one of the hootches and brought a 12 year old village girl over to the hedge-row and made her rake away the foliage in front of the spot where the blast had come out, on the other side of the berm. He continued to probe with his stick into the tunnel that was uncovered. Phou made an old man and old woman from the hootch help the girl dig out the tunnel. After the tunnel entrance was cleared, Phou threw in another grenade. When the dust settled, Phou told the three to continue digging. Soon, they hit the wooden top of an underground chamber. Phou made the girl tie a rope to one of the boards on the wooden top of the chamber. The other PRU's gathered around with their rifles ready. They formed a half circle while standing back, away from the top of the chamber. Phou yanked the board off the top of the room. Like everyone else, I stood with my assault rifle ready to fire, expecting an explosion or someone to jump out of the chamber and start to shoot at us. Neither happened. Phou came over to me and asked for a grenade since he had used all of his. I only had smoke grenades. I told one of Lt. Miller's men to give him a grenade. He gave Phou two grenades.

Phou threw one into the gap between the boards. After the explosion, he told the three villagers to dig out the debris and tie the rope to another board. This procedure was repeated until all the boards on the top of the underground chamber were pulled off. Four of the PRU's looked into the chamber with Phou. The hiding place was empty, except for some civilian clothing and some cooking utensils.

Phou was done with the digging, and sent the villagers to their hootch. He continued probing the brushes in the hedgerows. I went back to the company command post location and lay down for a nap. After an hour and a half nap, the PRU's returned to my location. The PRU's reported all they found was an 81 millimeter mortar round. I radioed battalion headquarters with the results of the search.

The villagers told the PRU's the VC had been there the night before but left during the night when they heard my infantry company coming. The old woman said the VC headed north, along the west side of the mountain where Sgt. Espinoza was located. The information we received was called into the battalion operations center.

Battalion ordered me to move the company to the south and west. We were to sweep both the saddle and the smaller hill mass to the south. I told them we would move out around 1330 hours, after we chowed down. They asked if we had enough food for the PRU's. I assured them I would see the PRU's got enough for lunch.

We were glad to get rid of the extra meal we were carrying. It lightened our load. We dug out all the cans of rations and gave the PRU's their choice of whatever they wanted to eat.

They seemed to like the crackers and cheese, along with the canned fruit and canned pound-cakes. Being rice and fish eaters, they weren't keen on the canned meals with meat. Most of all, they liked the little accessory packs that came with the

C-rations. They kept the toilet paper, small can openers, and the books of matches, as well as the cigarettes for later and rolled their own pungently peculiar smelling smokes.

As we ate, the ten PRU's shared my phrase book to communicate with each other and with us. We joked, using the phrase book, as we shared our sodas and beers with them.

After lunch, I gave the platoon leaders and the PRU leader our orders. Danh said there were no VC on the hill to the south and west of us. I told everyone we had our orders, and we would sweep the saddle and hill to the south-west of us.

Danh laughed at the idea of searching a place where he knew no VC would be hiding. He told his men to stay with me and my command group during the move to the south, as we moved away from the VC. His men answered Danh in both Vietnamese and broken English, repeating that the villagers said there were no VC south of us. The PRU's shook their heads in disbelief, but they joined me and my company command group for the move.

We all put our packs on, grabbed our rifles, and started the move south. The three rifle platoons started out, each abreast of the other, and the rest of us followed. Sgt. Espinoza and his squad continued to stay on the mountainside, due to the man with the sprained ankle. I ordered Sgt. Grimes to explode the mortar round we found, after we moved out. Then he and his Weapons Platoon caught up with us. Acting as the rear guard, they followed my command group. By 1400 hours we were all moving.

As we crossed the hill mass, it became obvious that the PRU's were right. The open sandy mound had no hedgerows or vegetation and the empty sandy terrain didn't provide the cover which the VC and North Vietnamese soldiers liked to use to conceal the entrances to their hiding places.

In spite of that we quickly continued to sweep south of the

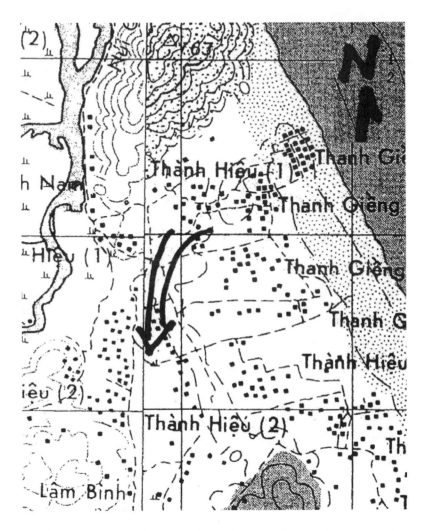

D Company moving south to the two hills at Lam Binh.

two hill masses until we were near the village where Lt. Claybaugh received fire several days before. I had the platoons cordon off the village and then the PRU's started their search. Suddenly, the PRU's started shouting in

Vietnamese and running for cover. I heard Phou shout, "Fire in hole."

We all ducked and hit the ground as fast as we could. After the Claymore mine Phou had thrown into the hedgerow exploded, Midge, Joe and I went over to see what was happening. Phou then exploded another Claymore mine, we all ducked for cover again. After the dust settled, we got up and moved closer to the hedgerow to see what the PRU's had found. One of the PRU's edged up next to me and said, "VC," as he pointed to the location where the smoke was billowing up from the shrubbery. Phou took a third Claymore mine from one of my men and threw it into the hedgerow.

After the blast, one of the PRU's went to a nearby hootch and got a boy who appeared to be about 12 years old. The boy protested but Phou roughly pushed him towards the area where he had been working. He told the boy to pull out the briar foliage, which exposed the entrance to a tunnel. Phou tied a rope around the boy and made him crawl into the tunnel. The boy had a look of both fear and pain on his face as he entered the hole, pulling a second rope with him as he crawled deeper into the tunnel. In a minute, he came crawling back out.

Phou, Midge and a few of the PRU's pulled the rope the boy had tied to something in the tunnel. The four pulled an almost headless NVA soldier out of the tunnel. The villagers took a quick look at the dead enemy, clothed in an NVA uniform, and quickly turned their heads away.

After searching the dead NVA soldier, Phou forced the boy back into the tunnel, with the extra rope again. After he came out the second time, they all pulled the second body half way out. The second dead NVA soldier got caught in the entrance. Joe Dodson and I grabbed the rope to help. As we pulled harder, we heard the sound of bones breaking. Finally we freed the dead soldier from the entrance. The rope had been tied around one of the dead man's ankles and his other leg had snapped when we pulled him out.

I got nauseated at the sight of the mangled body we pulled out, with one leg flapping along the side of the upper torso. I didn't watch as they pulled out the third body. Once again I saw firsthand that war was a gruesome business. I knew one thing for sure, no one could hate war more than those who had been in it - I mean those who really had been in the heat of combat, not a bunker soldier who was stationed in the rear. Infantrymen saw war differently from those who flew around observing from the air or those sitting on a track vehicle. I reasoned that only the grunts really knew what war was like. The rest just thought they knew. I wished that I hadn't seen what I did. It was different for me knowing I might go home when I'm finished. The boy would not have that option.

I told one of the men to search the bodies and bring the identification papers to me. The older one was 45. The other two were 30 years old. I called battalion with the information on the three enemy we had killed.

While I was on the radio with battalion, I got a call on the company frequency radio from the Second Platoon reporting they found what appeared to be another cave entrance. I told them to watch it, while I sent the PRU's over to join them.

I told Danh we found another cave. Danh answered, "No more VC." Then he asked that I radio for the helicopter to take them back to Duc Pho. I tried to convince him to stay and check out the new cave, but he stubbornly demanded to be flown back to our base-camp. I gave up and radioed for the chopper to return them to Duc Pho.

The PRU's were bounty hunters who were paid according to the number of VC and NVA soldiers they captured or killed. They were content with the 'piece work' they had completed that day. Evidently, they felt they had earned enough for the day, with the three dead NVA soldiers they killed. They didn't want to work anymore. They wanted to return and celebrate Tet with the sufficient financial gains they would receive for the day's work. If there were any more VC or NVA in the area, they didn't seem to care. Next week they could work, until they had enough money to stop working again. It appeared they were in no hurry to end the war. They were the ones who had fought on both sides. For now, they had a good job that paid them well, and it didn't require many hours of work if they could glean success quickly as they had that day.

The chopper soon landed and the bounty hunters boarded. With big smiles on their faces, they waived good-bye as they lifted off. They didn't like working with some American infantry companies, because they weren't treated well. Many of the other companies didn't allow them to operate in their own unique way, which delayed their finding enemy soldiers. Plus, a lot of American infantry company officers didn't study the Vietnamese language before coming to Vietnam, which made communicating difficult for them. I knew speaking their language was the best way to make friend with forengners.

We welcomed the PRU's and encouraged them to enjoy their stay with us. The results were good for both of us. Three enemy soldiers were eliminated, and they got their financial rewards. We treated them as friends, joking with them and sharing our food and drinks with them. They were good at what they did, and we appreciated it. They were the most efficient fighters I had ever met in Vietnam, and I was pleased with the results from the short period of time we had worked with them. The smiles on their face and their friendly waves as they departed showed their satisfaction with working with us.

The chopper crew unloaded some resupplies for us, but I didn't want to be caught in the open while redistributing the equipment. To establish as much protection as possible, I told Joe to instruct the platoons to logger in a secure area and send some men over to get their supplies. I also decided we would chow down for our evening meal within each of their defense positions. Then we would move out.

Once back in their defense positions, they cooked and ate their C-rations. Midge Anderson asked if I would like to try one of the LRRP meals. We received LRRP rations, (Long Range Reconnaissance Patrol) dehydrated meals along with our C-rations when they resupplied us. I had never eaten a LRRP meal before, so I accepted his offer. Midge handed me the pork and scalloped potatoes, since he didn't like pork. I used the C-Four which Jimmy Cumbee left burning after he had heated a half cup of water for his dehydrated meal. I heated some water in my canteen cup and poured the boiling water into the plastic bag until it made a hot, pasty meal. It tasted like the scalloped potatoes and pork that I had back home. It reminded me of the beef stroganoff dinners we could buy at most stateside grocery stores, except the meat was already included. Back then they were convenient for backpacking on trips with the Sierra Club. They were lightweight, easy to prepare, and they didn't taste too bad. We shared our canned and dehydrated meals with the kids from the village and gave an old woman some of our cigarettes.

- - - o - - -

Along with our resupplies, six new replacements arrived on Thursday, 3 April 1969. They were Privates First Class John M. Gilmore, Alan J. Cap, Ronald VanDuzer, Herbert T. Aue, and William B. Parker and Specialist Fourth Class Daniel M.

Butler. Herbert Aue was from California, so he and I chatted a little before I sent him to join the Second Platoon, along with Alan Cap and Ron VanDuzer. I sent John Gilmore, Bill Parker and Dan Butler to the First Platoon.

To my surprise, Lt. Larky Evans came out to join us on the second helicopter. I kidded Larky about arriving today instead of the day before, because he missed the long night's rock climb. Larky said he had been monitoring the company radio and was pissed that we had to move all night long, without any sleep. I told him he wasn't half as pissed as we were.

That's the way combat was, an ordeal some 10 to 20 hours earlier became something we joked about now. The day had been easy because the PRU's did all the work. We hadn't moved 1,000 meters after five that morning, compared to the 5,000 meters we moved earlier, before daybreak.

At 1800 hours, I ordered the company to move out, heading north. We were to relocate about 2,000 meters away and logger for the night. The next day we were to sweep to the north, covering the flat land between LZ Bronco and the hill mass that Sgt. Espinoza and his squad were still holding. We planned to meet with Sgt. Espinoza and the rest of his men in the morning. They would run out of food after their evening meal and we were carrying their rations, so they could have something for breakfast. I hoped their immobility had cut down their water consumption.

I knew that Sgt. Espinoza was resourceful enough to send someone down to one of the village wells if he needed water. Juan was a very proficient soldier, which was why he was promoted to sergeant in his short tour in the Army after being drafted.

Sgt. Espinoza was a beer drinker. While my men and I would get three beers he ordered a case of beer for himself. He strapped it to his backpack and continually drank beer instead of water or sodas in the field. Resupply clerks could forget his C-rations or LRRP bags, but they were in deep trouble if they forgot his case of beer. He wasn't with us when they resupplied us, so he missed the delivery of his case of beer. I was sure if they ran short of water, he would share some of his "cerveza" with his men.

-   -   -   o   -   -   -

At 1900 hours we moved over the saddle we had crossed earlier. After a short hike, dusk was setting in, so I ordered the company to hold up. Historically, the most vulnerable times for a surprise attack were just before dark and just before sunrise, and it was about a half an hour before dark. I had the platoons take a half-hour break in the lowlands and in the wash next to my position so they couldn't be readily seen. We had only killed three of the thousands of enemy soldiers who were operating around LZ Bronco, and I didn't know if the other enemy soldiers in the area were following our movement or not.

After making some entries under my poncho, I laid back and enjoyed the cooler surfside evening while we waited for darkness. We were just 1,000 meters from the beach and it was quite a bit cooler near the beach than nearly even 6,000 meters inland where we had been the week before. The sea breeze reminded me of home in Southern California during the summer.

When it was dark, I slid into my shoulder straps, put my canteen back into its holder on my cartridge belt, and stood up. Time to start moving. However, my pleasant lazy evening was quickly interrupted when I heard two explosions that originated about 15 meters to the east of me. I flattened myself on the ground, as did everyone else. We all waited to see if

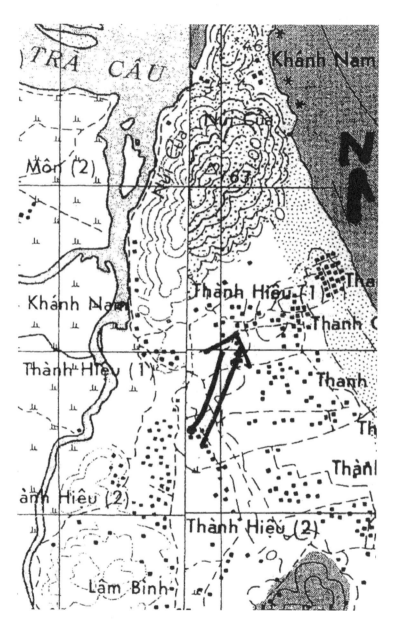

After the PRU's left, D Company moved north.

211

there was a third explosion. When that didn't occur, I told Joe to get on the air to see what had happened.

I told the men near us to move into the wash while Joe was checking with the platoons. Sgt. Grimes, who was right next to the company command group when the explosions erupted, moved into the wash behind us.

Using the radio to communicate allowed all elements, both those in LZ Bronco and in the field with us to hear how each platoon faired. All the platoons responded to Joe's radio call, except the First. No one in that platoon was in contact with us by radio. I told Cumbee to call in a report to battalion on their frequency. After he reported in, they wanted to know what was going on. I couldn't give them any specific information then, and they became upset and kept requesting more information. I ignored their requests and had both Joe and Cumbee try to contact the First Platoon by radio by switching Cumbee's radio to the First Platoon's frequency. Finally, someone from the First Platoon answered our calls and told us they had received what appeared to be two enemy rifle grenade rounds. We had found the enemy that day, but apparently we hadn't found them all. I asked for a casualty report and the radio operator reported, one man was hit by shrapnel and Lt. Evans was helping the wounded soldier.

I grabbed a couple of men and headed towards the First Platoon in the dark, which was about 20 meters away. When we arrived at the First Platoon's position, I asked some men to watch our rucksacks while we helped the wounded man. The injured man was moved into the wash where we left our backpacks. I couldn't see how badly he was wounded. It was too dark to see much.

I told Cumbee to switch back to the frequency and call battalion for a dust-off helicopter. Cumbee assured battalion we had secured a landing zone for the chopper when in fact we didn't. If battalion knew, they wouldn't come for our injured man.

While we were trying to assist the one squad of the First Platoon in the dark, Joe received a call from the First Platoon radio operator, who was at a different location. He reported they had another wounded man with them. I learned later the two wounded soldiers were new men, John Gilmore and Dan Butler. They had been with me such a short period of time, just half a day, I didn't even know where they were from.

I told the First Platoon radio operator to start moving the second wounded man to the wash and several men were on their way to help carry the man and their equipment. I instructed the First Platoon RTO to move fast, because the medevac chopper was on its way. I also ordered them to have the rest of the platoon consolidate and join us right away to get them out of the firing range of whoever shot at them.

The First Platoon operator reported they thought the enemy fire had come from the empty cane fields to the south of us. Next, Lt. Evans was on the radio and I told him to shoot some white phosphorus into the field to light it up while we lay a sheet of gunfire into the cane field. I had Joe let the platoons know what we were doing. Lt. Evans reported some of the First Platoon men had jumped into the cane field after the first incoming round went off. I ordered him to take charge of the First Platoon, get them together as soon as possible, and bring them into the wash where we were.

I headed for the wide portion of the wash to secure a landing zone and had the men in the recess spread out to leave a large enough space for the chopper to land. I had Cumbee change his radio frequency to the emergency air evacuation frequency so we could talk the chopper pilot down in the dark.

I took my flashlight out and asked the men around me for another one. One of the men took my flashlight and his and volunteered to guide the chopper into our position. After verifying all our men were accounted for, except for the First Platoon, I gave the men orders to shoot out from our position when the chopper started to land and when it departed. I thought everyone was in the wash, except for those in the cane field. When Lt. Evans arrived at my location, I wanted him to confirm all the First Platoon men were accounted for.

"Hell no!" he said. "There are still some men from the First Platoon that are unaccounted for,"

We both ran around the perimeter, telling everyone not to shoot when the chopper arrived. However, they were to keep down in case we got incoming fire during the dust-off.

As Cumbee talked down the chopper and one of the men guided the medevac dust-off down with the flashlights, I ducked into a recess at the edge of the wash. The sandstorm caused by the chopper blades whipped the sand, dirt, and dried vegetation against us. I couldn't figure out how the men carrying the wounded and their equipment could see where to take them in the swirl of blowing dust.

As the chopper took off with our wounded, two more rifle grenade rounds flew into the wash and exploded. The wash erupted with the ear-shattering explosions and bright flashes. The additional debris the bursts had thrown into the air filled the sky. I was hot, covered with dirt and dried vegetation, and anxiously waiting to hear if there was going to be a call for a medic. After what seemed like an eternity, but was just a few seconds, the silence told us we hadn't suffer any casualties from the last two blasts. While the platoon leaders were checking their men, I checked with Sgt. Grimes to see if he had all his members back yet. He didn't, since they had helped with the medical evacuation.

In the dark, I grabbed Lt. Evans by the arm and whispered as I asked if his men were still spread out or if they were all back with the First Platoon. He said he was checking, but didn't know yet. I rushed to Lt. Miller's location, and he told me his platoon was intact and everyone was accounted for. I told him to head east towards the beach and to start forming a logger perimeter when he found a good location. I told him to be sure to stay south of the village we had cordoned that morning.

I ordered Sgt. Wheelan to follow the Third Platoon to the beach and logger there. I told Sgt. Grimes to follow the Second Platoon to the beach and logger there when all his men were back. This gave Lt. Evans a little time for his squad leaders to account for all the First Platoon personnel. I told him when all his men were back together, he was to follow the Weapons Platoon to the beach. The VC knew where we were, and I wanted to get everyone out of the wash before more shells began falling into our position. Getting away without them noticing was the first thing on my mind.

While all this was going on, battalion repeatedly called to find out what our status was and what our night logger coordinates were so they could report them to the brigade operations center and to the artillery operations center. I let them know we had come under fire again, and we were moving out of the kill-zone. I told them we would inform them of our night logger position when we had reached it.

I checked the progress of the move. We were moving out, but not fast enough. The men were bunching up at the east end of the wash. I radioed Lt. Miller and told him to double-time his men in order to help us clear the area more quickly. I called Sgt. Wheelan on the radio and told him to move out right away, along side the last half of the Third Platoon, instead of following them. Sgt. Grimes had all his men accounted for and also followed the Third Platoon as we hurriedly emptied the kill-zone.

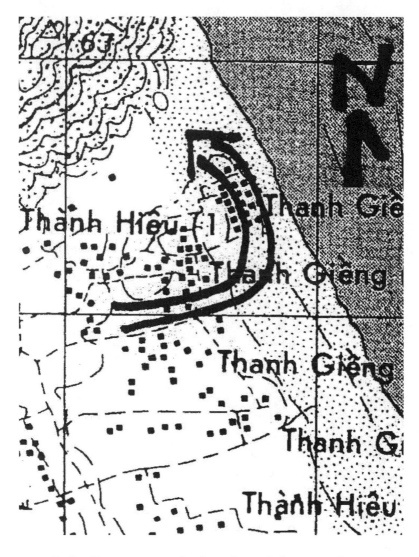

Delta Dogs run to the beach and then north.

Soon we were all running towards the beach. Lt. Evans and Sgt. Zartuche had collected all their men and ran after the other three platoons. The moon was just starting to rise. A full moon was expected, with one hundred percent visibility, so I wanted to get to a logger position as quickly as I could before the enemy saw us. We would be like sitting ducks if we didn't make it before the full moon illuminated the night.

When we got to the sand berm between the rice paddies and the beach, I ordered the First Platoon, the last one in our column, to stay behind as an ambush platoon, just in case any enemy followed us. After we crossed the sand berm and were on the China Sea side, I ordered the company to head north about 1,000 meters as fast as they could move. We were gasping for air and water after the second night in a row of making a forced march, moving as fast as our tired bodies would let us.

Some of the men were so dog-tired, they just dropped in the sand while their platoon continued to run on without them. I radioed Lt. Evans and asked if we were being followed. He reported, negative. I told him to have his platoon leave their position and move down towards the beach and then head north after us, picking up our stragglers on the way. We slowed down to a slow walk in the shifting sand in order to give the stragglers and the First Platoon time to catch up with us and for us to catch our breath.

Lt. Evans picked up the stragglers as he headed towards us. After another agonizing 15 minutes of shuffling through the sand with our heavy loads, I ordered the Third Platoon to find a good night logger position. When they radioed back they had one, I instructed them to start the logger.

They guided each of the other three platoons and the company command group into their positions as each caught up with the Third Platoon. As tired as we were, no one hesitated to dig in for the night. The moon was up and it was easy to see some distance from our logger position.

Keeping score in a macabre sort of way, we killed three communist soldiers and two of our men were wounded. In spite of that, there was no joy losing two more men, even if they were only wounded. Spc.4 Butler and Pfc. Gilmore had both been in Vietnam only two weeks and were wounded during their first day in the field as infantrymen. It was a short war for them. In a funny sort of way, they were lucky. They were going home. It would be a long war for other Delta Dogs. Some wouldn't be so lucky.

Once loggered, night watches were assigned. Those not on watch took advantage of the lull in activity to sleep. I'm sure some easily drifted off due to the hard trudge in the sand. I, and I would think others, shifted restlessly, reliving the day's events in our heads. *If I had ordered my men to move out ten minutes earlier, the two men wouldn't have been casualties. Why did I sit there and enjoy the pleasant evening breeze after I finished updating my journal?*

At 0600 we were awake and by 0630 we moved north, shuffling our feet in the soft, white sand as the sun rose from the sea. Before departing, I had called Sgt. Espinoza to tell him to move south and then to the beach until he met us. We moved north along the high sand dunes because I wanted to see any movement in the farmland or on the beach as we advanced north.

When we were about 300 meters south of the mountain where we had left Juan Espinoza, we stopped and loggered for breakfast. I figured our stopping would give Sgt. Espinoza and his men time to reach us.

Just as we were finishing our breakfast, someone shouted that Juan was coming. Sergeant Juan Espinoza was a colorful character who was always drinking, singing, and joking with everyone. He was everyone's friend. He was also one of the best sergeants I had. When he was given his morning rations,

Juan jokingly complained about us starving him. He kidded everyone around him about his beer. As he ate, he joyfully gestured that we had run off, deserting him on the mountaintop. He also bragged if he was with us, Charlie wouldn't have gotten away after they lobbed grenades into our position the night before. Most of the men in his platoon countered him by joking back with him. Everyone knew he was a kidder, but they also knew he missed being with us.

We kidded out loud, but underneath, everyone was sorry about the two new men who were wounded. The men hid their fears and sorrow as they kidded about seemingly senseless things. They all knew, as I did, it could have been any one of us who was hit the night before or the next time.

After Sgt. Espinoza and his men finished their breakfast, we started heading west towards the rice paddies just southeast of LZ Bronco, in the direction of the village where we had found the hidden room the day before. We were to sweep the deserted villages of An Lac (1), An Lac (2) and An Lac (3). We hugged the south side of the mountain on which Juan and his men had spent the last day and night.

The area we swept had thick vegetation in the hedgerows and in the uncultivated fields. About every third or fourth field was well cultivated and apparently attended to regularly. There were far too many family-type bunkers, but no families. Everywhere we looked, we saw growing or drying crops, yet no sign of human life. It appeared the government-protected hamlet farmers didn't tend to their crops during Tet.

We swept through about 20 fields of rice paddies, with elevated dirt islands, deserted farmer's bunkers and hootches, and heavily vegetated hedgerows that separated each rice paddy. I felt uncomfortable, since these were good ambush locations. The communists could catch us between elevated

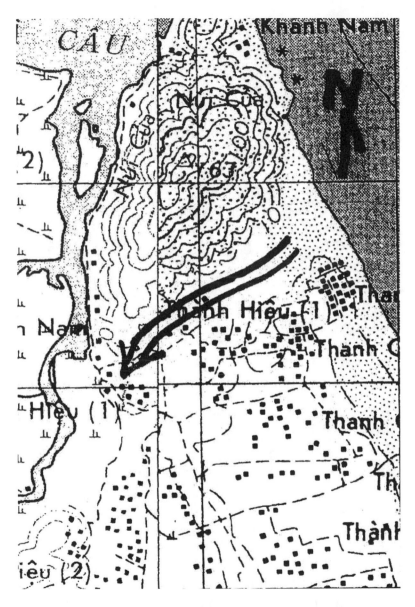

Delta Dogs sweeping towards the Suot Cau Mong River.

islands of soil and hedgerows. We were searching cautiously, since this was the area where Lt. Wilson had been killed. To assure we would not be attacked from the rear, I changed the sweep from three platoons abreast to two platoons abreast and the other two platoons acting as rear security. This spreading out of the company allowed us better maneuverability.

The First Platoon, which was sweeping westward on the north side, reported seeing someone move on the high ground to the right and just a little farther north of us. Our First Platoon's soldier who spotted the unknown man, raised his hand to signal everyone behind him to stop. He crouched to conceal himself, as he continued to observe.

He whispered to the men around him, "Enemy to our right, on the high ground."

The message was quickly relayed back. The platoon sergeant, Tuche, quietly joined him to observed the enemy.

When I heard the news, I sent Lt. Faust up to their position to determine the enemy's location. Once he confirmed the location, I let him use our battalion frequency radio. It was switched to the artillery frequency and the encrypted coordinates were sent to his artillery command post.

We all hugged the ground and waited for the artillery strike to begin. When the first round fell north of us, a man in the First Platoon noticed a flash of light to the south of our position indicating the enemy was on two sides of us. The man in the First Platoon who detected the light focused his attention in the direction of the light source and observed a North Vietnamese soldier in uniform, with a rifle on his shoulder. His brass belt buckle reflected the sun as he turned to observe the artillery round explosion.

Lt. Faust, our Artillery forward Observer ordered the firing of single artillery rounds as he incrementally walked the bursts down the mountain until one explosion hit at the first location where the enemy soldiers were sighted. Then he gave the artillery support unit the fire-for-effect order. We watched as dozens of artillery rounds slammed into the earth. Lt. Faust shifted the artillery impact to the second area to the south of us where the enemy with the shiny belt was seen.

-    -   -   o   -   -   -

Camouflage was one our best defenses, so our belt buckles were black, my Captain's bars on the front of my helmet and on my right lapel were sewn with black thread; my cross sabers were also made of black thread; each of the enlisted men's ranks were sewn on their uniforms with black thread. The only items I had that were silvery metallic was my mess kit, my eating utensils, and my canteen cup, which stayed in my olive drab canteen case, unless I was using it to heat water.

Blending with the landscape also meant keeping quiet. In the field we didn't sing or talk out loud, didn't smoke, or make any noise that was not necessary. There were several occasions when we were right next to the enemy, and they didn't know it. I'm certain there must have been times when the enemy was next to us, and we didn't know it either. The only time we chose to let them know we were present was when we started shooting or calling artillery strikes on their positions.

Obviously, we wanted to surprise the enemy, and didn't want them to surprise us, so I tried not to stay in one particular area for too many days or go back through an area we had just left. I tried to be unpredictable, so the enemy couldn't figure out where we were going to go next. I earned the reputation as the only commander in the brigade who would not make a night logger in the same place where the men cooked their evening meal. My unpredictability and refusal to unnecessarily expose my men to enemy fire made my unique field style known to many at both the battalion and brigade level.

I knew there were no South Vietnamese soldiers operating in this vicinity; therefore, the man with the shiny belt buckle had to be a North Vietnamese soldier. Plus his NVA uniform was so distinctly different from the South Vietnamese soldier's uniform, it could not have been mistaken. After saturating the second area with artillery fire, over 300 meters south of us, we ordered the artillery barrage to stop so we could sweep the area. I ordered the platoons to sweep south three platoons abreast with the command group and the Weapons Platoon following the riflemen.

While sweeping, one of the infantry men found a pair of telephone wires lying on the ground, running towards where we saw the soldier with the shiny belt. We cut the wires, one at a time to be sure they were deactivated. Then we followed the telephone line in both directions. They could have been communication lines or booby-trap detonation wires. At the north end, we found the two wires were stripped bare. The exposed metal strands were not corroded, but shiny, indicating they had been stripped recently. We followed the line to the south and found it led into a field, with a tree line at the south end of the open field. We found a string of concertina barbed-wire, un-coiled and spread across the open field. This was the first time I had seen concertina wire anyplace other then around our rear base-camps.

I had one of the other platoons cross the open area, while the three platoons spread out on the north side of the field to provide fire support if it was needed. After the platoon crossed the open field and had spread out along the tree line on the south side of the field, I had the men who were following the cable, follow the line across the open field.

I reported the finding of the two wires we were following to our battalion operations center. The battalion command chopper flew overhead and asked us to mark a landing zone for the battalion intelligence officer. The intelligence officer is responsible for collecting and disseminating information about the enemy to the company and battalion officers. The finding of the wire was an unusual occurrence and the S-2 officer wanted to see the lay of the wire. Captain Walters, the intelligence officer (S-2) and former commander of the Delta Dogs, wanted to see the wires.

I popped smoke near the company command group, north of the open field, and the chopper landed. When I arrived at the chopper's location, I asked the chopper crew for any smoke and hand grenades they might have since we had used so many the day before. We didn't get many, but received a couple from the command chopper door gunners. After dropping the S-2 off, the chopper took off and headed back to LZ Bronco, taking the wounded Butler and Gilmore's equipment and weapons back to our rear area personnel.

Capt. Walters and I joined the men following the wires. He asked what I thought of it. I shared that I thought it was either a communication line for the NVA who was following us, or it was a detonation line for an enemy sapper. A sapper was a soldier that specializes in demolitions.

"How long do you think it'll be before you find out what's at the other end of the wire?" Capt. Walters asked.

"I don't know; it's hard to tell," I said. "We're moving cautiously, since there may be a North Vietnamese battalion on the other end. And, we don't want to walk into an ambush."

"I agree," Capt. Walters said. "Let us know what it looks like when you get to the other end of the wire." Then, he went back to talk to his old Weapons Platoon sergeant while he waited for the return of the chopper. The S-2 had been very curt with me, as I was with him. In my mind we didn't get any troop support during our battle west of <u>Duc</u> <u>Pho</u> because of his inaccurate assessment of the enemy forces we were up against. Plus we were picked up by the tracked vehicles in the enemy's kill-zone because he failed to inform anyone about the enemy's disposition when we were transferred to the new battalion. The poor location where the tracks were sent to pick us up caused six additional Delta Dog casualties.

I ordered the men who were following the wires to return to their platoon on the north side of the clearing. It was near 1100 hours. I commanded the men located on the south side of the clearing and the two platoons still on the north side to take up defensive positions and break for lunch. I didn't want to move south again until after the chopper came back for the intelligence officer.

Soon the chopper landed, picked up Capt. Walters and also to drop off additional ammunition and smoke grenades for us. After the chopper departed and we had finished eating, I ordered the men on the north side of the clearing to follow the wires again, while the rest of the company maintained their fighting positions.

While the men were crossing the open field, an infantryman on the north side of the clearing spotted several North Vietnamese soldiers who appeared to be sneaking to our east. I was able to track the enemy with my binoculars. It appeared the NVA soldiers were following the same route we took that morning when we were heading north to meet with Juan and his men. I thought it was beginning to look like they had set up an ambush, but it also looked like we moved too far north and east for them to catch us.

I called Sgt. Grimes and had him join me. I pointed out the location of the enemy we observed and asked him, "Do you think you could drop a couple mortar rounds on them from here?"

"No problem, Sir," he replied, then moved back to his platoon's position. He set up the 60-mm mortar base plate, took a sighting on the enemy location, and adjusted what he thought was the proper angle of the mortar tube as he held it with both his hands. The enemy was well within his mortar range of up to 2,000 meters. He had one of his men drop a mortar round into the tube, lobbing a round towards the enemy position. It fell about 50 meters beyond their position, so he moved his hands to adjust the tube angle, and had one of his men drop another mortar round down the tube. The second time the round hit in the wooded area where he was aiming. Then, he had his men drop in several more rounds, one after another, to pepper the area with mortar round explosions.

While observing the area, I received a call from the men who were following the wire. They had found the south end of the wires and the wires were attached to a command-detonated mine. They asked if they could blow it in-place. I gave them the okay to detonate it with C-Four explosives.

I radioed battalion and let them know what we found at the south end of the wires and let them know we were detonating the explosive. They ordered me to continue our sweep to the north once we completed the destruction of the enemy ordinance. I instructed the platoon on the south side of the clearing to return and join the rest of us on the north side. Then we waited for the destruction of the mine. My men used two detonators in the C-Four explosives to assure detonation, in case one failed.

After the explosion, we continued north to where we had stopped the sweep to follow the wires. As we trudged north, I thought about the old woman who told us the VC had moved north of her village just before we arrived. She lied. It was probably part of their plan to have us think they were VC, when in reality they were North Vietnamese Army regular soldiers. It appeared they had set the mine to catch us when we advanced north from the village the day before. It also looked like the men to our east and north were part of the ambush they had prepared for us. Fortunately, I had my men move to the east and up the shoreline to meet Juan, instead of trying to follow the directions the old woman gave us. Her lying didn't surprise me. The North Vietnamese Army Commander-In-Chief was from this province. We were much like the British soldiers, during the American Revolutionary War, who would ask the farmers in George Washington's home town which way he and his men had gone. It was tough believing anything the local Vietnamese told us.

We had a lot of territory to cover before we could get back to LZ Bronco, and it was almost 1300 hours. The three An Lac villages we were going to sweep were on the west side of the Suot Cau Mong River. The river was probably going to be too deep to wade through, so we would have to find suitable crossing points.

We planned to resupply our canteens by dipping them into the river when we crossed it. However, tracking the wires delayed our getting to the river. By the time we reached the river, we were strung out about 300 meters wide. I checked with each platoon to be sure we were not being followed and then the first two platoons started across the river, side by side. I drank the last of my water before I reached the river. The 115-degree heat, walking in the sunlight instead of the shade, and all the liquid I had lost due to the physical exertion during the long day had dried me up and overheated my body. As I started dipping one of my canteens into the water, someone hollered that the river contained salt-water. I pulled the half full canteen out of the water. I was too hot and the water was

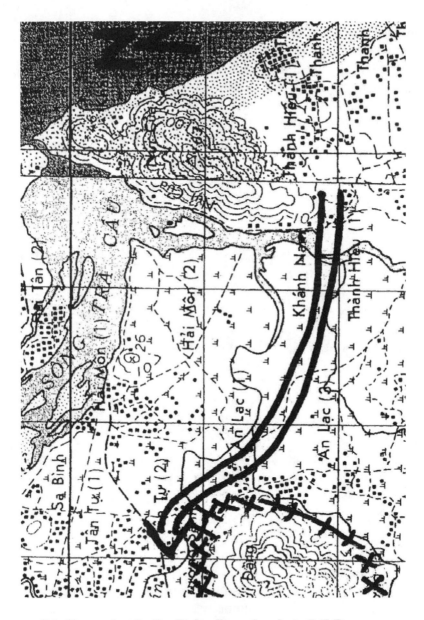

Lt. Evans leads the Delta Dogs back to LZ Bronco.

too cool to not use it. I couldn't drink it, so I poured it over myself to cool down. I dipped the canteen into the water again, poured another wash of cool salt-water over my head as I held my helmet under my arm and my weapon away from my body.

Not finding fresh water was a surprise that brought a different type of panic than I felt when we were ambushed. I radioed the rear and informed them we were completely out of water and couldn't continue our mission without a water resupply run. First Sergeant Arland Wheeler radioed me to assure us he would get some water to us right away.

After crossing the river, we continued our broad turn to the north. It was exceedingly hot. To stop would just delay our arrival at our base-camp, which offered us shade, ice cold drinks, and much needed rest. Wanting to get back as soon as possible, two platoons swept through An Lac (2) while the other two platoons continued on to An Lac (3) for a sweep of the abandoned villages. With concurrent sweeps we completed our mission faster. We were already behind schedule and I didn't want to spend another night in the field, unless absolutely necessary.

Lt. Evans had joined us for a one-night visit, but it was taking a little longer than planned to get back to LZ Bronco. We staggered forward, all dragging a little from the hard days and short nights we had experienced the last two days in the sweltering heat. Being out of water made thing worse and slowed us down even more. The human body sweats to cool itself off, but our sweat didn't evaporate much and didn't cool us because of the high humidity. We all suffered while crossing the dry rice paddies under the hot, humid afternoon sun. There were no trees and no shade, just the parched dusty, dry rice paddies. By then even the water in the leech infested, dung saturated rice paddy would have looked good, but we didn't even have that.

I received a call from LTC Pritchard saying he was bringing water to us. A few minutes later, the chopper landed at the LZ we had quickly secured for the chopper. He ordered me into the chopper, while the men were unloading the plastic containers of fresh water. I jumped on the chopper, and we took off. LTC Pritchard, Capt. Walters, Capt. Blanks, and the battalion Fire Support Coordinator, Capt. Jerry Simpson were already on board. No one was carrying a canteen, except the Fire Support Coordinator. When I asked for water, Jerry Simpson handed me his partially filled canteen, and I quickly gulped down what little water he had. I smiled with my parched and cracked lips, and gave him back his empty canteen.

I took off my backpack and set it on the floor. I was the only one on the chopper with a rucksack. Capt. Blanks and I sat on the front side, opposite the other three officers. The S-2, Capt. Walters briefed us as we headed west towards the mountains that lined the rice bowl we were leaving. We left the Duc Pho district and entered the Ba To district of the northern part of South Vietnam. We changed direction and went north into the Nghia Hanh district of Quang Ngai providence. We were quite a distance away from my company's location. I asked if they could contact Lt. Evans and have him take the men the rest of the way back to our base-camp. They sent the message as we crossed into the Minh Long district. We had traveled 52,000 meters to the west and 13,000 meters to the north, before the company objective for the next day was pointed out to me.

The chopper flew over what was thought to be the Third North Vietnamese Army Division Headquarters. We couldn't circle the area or fly low to get a good look at it without

230

tipping our hand. Instead the pilot flew a course that made it look like a normal run from of the mountain fire-base-camp south of us to <u>Chu Lai</u>. Capt. John H. (Boots) Blanks, my poker playing buddy from our in-country infantryman's training at <u>Chu Lai</u>., the Company C Commander and I were to observe as much as we could. We were both going to be air lifted into the North Vietnamese Division Headquarters the next day after a B-52 bomb drop was made on the area.

The battalion commander pointed out our landing zones and each of our areas of responsibility. The after-operations pick-up points were identified and the contingency plans discussed in case we got into trouble on the ground. Prominent terrain features were pointed out so we could determine our locations once we were on the ground. The next day, both companies C and D would be conducting an air assault within one hour after the B-52 bomb drop of 500 pound bombs was made on the target. The day we flew the reconnaissance flight was Good Friday, 4 April 1969. Easter Sunday was just another day for us. We didn't get weekends or holidays off. Each day was just another day in the field. It appeared that we would be spending Easter Sunday in a North Vietnamese Division base-camp.

-    -   -   o   -   -   -

Specialist Fourth Class Jimmy D. Cumbee was 19 years old when he was drafted on 14 May 1968. Jimmy was the oldest of three boys. The three boys and their sister lived in a small town, Twin City, Georgia. When he entered Vietnam 12 October 1968, then Private First Class Cumbee was assigned as an infantryman in the Third Platoon. While assigned as a point man, he cut such a wide trail through the jungle that he picked up the nickname of 'Highway Cumbee.' Before being promoted to Spc.4 he took the position as a radio telephone operator (RTO) in the Third Platoon. When Spc.4 Wayne McBurnett left the field at the end of March 1969, Jimmy was transferred to the headquarters Group to replace 'Mac' as my battalion net RTO.

Jimmy Cumbee was a half-full glass kind of guy, instead of a half-empty outlook person. When his younger brother, Tommy, wrecked the new car Jimmy bought before coming to Vietnam, he was happy, not mad. He said he was pleased that his younger brother wasn't hurt. He could always get another car. That was the kind of person 21-year-old Jimmy Cumbee was.

-    -   -   o   -   -   -

This is a list of those Delta Dog's heroes who were identified in this chapter.

Private First Class John M. Gilmore ** Wounded in action by a rifle grenade

Specialist Fourth Class Daniel M. Butler ** Wounded in action by a rifle grenade

Sergeant Robert C. Reed, from Lathrup Village, Michigan

Specialist Fourth Class Jimmy D. Cumbee, from Twin City, Georgia

Private First Class Alan J. Cap, from Niagara Falls, New York

Private First Class Ronald VanDuzer, from Wadsworth, Ohio

Private First Class William B. Parker, from Lorain, Ohio

Private First Class Herbert T. Aue, from Lone Pine, California

Chapter Eight

Specialist Fourth Class George M. Cato

I knew our next mission; to mop up an NVA division headquarters was going to be a touchy one. Being air-dropped into the enemy's headquarters could get pretty hairy even with the B-52's bomb run. We knew an NVA division normally contained between 15,000 to 20,000 men. We had no way of telling how many would be around the division headquarters, but I figured it would be hundreds. If the bombs didn't get them, our 200 infantrymen would be greatly out numbered. *What if the bomb drop was off by just one hill? Then we could be dropped into a fully intact and completely functional NVA division headquarters.* This mission was one assignment I wasn't looking forward to.

A forward artillery fire-base had been set up to the east of the target area to provide artillery support during the operation. That was helpful. We also had helicopter gun-ships available to cover us once we were on the ground. However, we were going in there with only two companies of American infantrymen. The prior experience I had when we needed additional infantry support resounded again in my mind. Plans are just plans. What happens during the execution of those plans was often quite different.

The pilot flew north for a while longer before we circled around and headed towards fire-base Cork, where Company D operated prior to my arrival with the Delta Dogs. To speed up the operation and to minimize chopper flights before the B-52 bomb drop, the Delta Dogs were to be air lifted to Cork by Chinook Medium Lift Helicopters (Hooks). The actual helicopter assault would be on HUID (Huey) helicopters.

233

Our helicopter landed at LZ Cork where we were met by Capt. Williams, the Company A commander who was stationed there. His infantry company shared the fire-base-camp with an artillery battery. It was this artillery battery, which would move to LZ Cam to support our assault.

I was still dehydrated and was desperate for anything to drink. Capt. Simpson asked Platoon Sergeant Fierros, the Company A 81-millimeter mortar sergeant to find something cold for me to drink. The sergeant left and soon came back with an ice-cold cola. I didn't care if he brought me water, soda or beer. Any drinkable liquid was acceptable. I wasn't just thirsty I was seriously dehydrated. I popped the ice-cold can open and drank the contents immediately. The drink was so cold it gave me a headache. But it was a good headache - one that I hadn't experienced for some time.

After a meeting with the artillery commander and Sgt. Fierros, Capt. Blanks and I sat in the shade of the sandbagged bunker, talking with the artillery and mortar commanders about the next day's operation. Someone brought some cold Kool-Aid out for us. I felt like a glutton, drinking so much soda and Kool-Aid, but my body needed it. My temperature was too high, and I was too dehydrated to be shy about how much I was drinking. Even after four cups of the cold Kool-aid, I hadn't quenched my thirst. By then, however, it was time to load up on the helicopter and head back to my men. I have to say the helicopter flight was great. It was like being under a big fan. The constant flow of air was a welcomed relief from the sweltering hot rice patties where we had been operating.

We landed at LZ Bronco at 1630 hours just as my company was entering the back gate. Lt. Evans, who was leading the company, had already been instructed not to leave any ambush patrols out that night. While the company was snaking its way towards our company area, I started preparing the operation order for the next day. When the platoon leaders arrived at our company area, I had them send their men to chow and asked the leaders to join me in the company orderly room after they had eaten, showered, and changed clothes.

I informed the supply sergeant that I wanted every man supplied with plenty of ammunition and three-days worth of rations. Since we would be moving out early, I wanted to ensure the men were resupplied right away. I told Sgt. Curry to be sure they had C-rations and not LRRP rations, because we might not have a chance to boil water for the dehydrated LRRP's. I also ordered all radio operators to change their batteries, whether they thought they needed to or not. In addition, I ordered each radio operator to carry an extra radio battery this time. On this mission we would be so far from any base-camp, I wanted to be sure we didn't have to rely on anyone for resupplies for several days, if necessary. Then, I put out the word that everyone was restricted to the company area. Everyone was to clean their weapons. The men were told that each platoon was to have a meeting at 2100 hours where they would be told about our upcoming mission.

- - - o - - -

Walking across the compound, all I could think about was the mound of paperwork waiting for me at my desk. One of my men, who was part of our rear attachment, brought my evening meal, as I was busy getting ready for the next day's operation and completing the company operations order. While I ate, I sorted through the pile of paperwork. After that I signed supply records, transfer orders, missing supplies reports, and many other company documents. I didn't know when I was going to be back in the rear again, so I wanted to clean my small wooden desk as completely as possible before we went out again. I usually liked to clean my own weapon, just to be sure it was functioning correctly during the next operation, but with all the work I had to perform prior to moving out the next day, I had the armorer clean my weapon .

Most of the administrative chores were routine. Rarely was there something unique waiting for me. That day was different. I received a letter from congressman Jacob H. Gilbert.

Sgt. Dan Brings laughed as he handed me the congressional letter. The congressman from New York was requesting Private Harvey F. Rosenblum be reassigned as a dental technician, which was his secondary Military Occupation Specialty (MOS).

I chuckled as I read the letter out loud so everyone in the office could hear it. It stated, "As you will note, Private Rosenblum was to be counseled on the procedures and prerequisites for submitting a request for a change of duty assignment to his secondary MOS as a dental technician. I was wondering if private Rosenblum did submit his application for a change of MOS and what, if any action was taken. Your prompt attention to this request, and reply to me at my Washington office, will be greatly appreciated.
Jacob H. Gilbert, Member of Congress. JG:SMK "

Everyone in the office snickered when I finished reading the official letter. "Harvey's Mommy wants to know if her little boy couldn't be reassigned from an infantry job to a job as a dental technician," Sgt. Brings said.

Everyone in the office laughed again. We found it humorous because most of the men would like to have such an assignment, just to get out of harm's way.

"Yeah," I said, "after I reassign myself as a dental technician." We all laughed again, as we found this letter a pleasant diversion from our every day ordeals.

I looked at the poorly typed letter. It had four strike-overs, one transposed set of letters, and two O's in office. One O was a capital letter and one in lower case. I felt sorry for Congressman Gilbert. I imagined having SMK as a secretary must have cost him a lot of votes.

"What is the story with our armorer, Spec. Four Rosenblum?" I asked Sgt. Brings.

"He said, he was pleased with his assignment and would rather stay where he is, if that was okay with everyone."

"Good!" I said. "Type a letter to the congressman saying just that, and I'll sign it."

- - - o - - -

Before I had a chance to shower, it was 2000 hours and time to give the operations order to the platoon leaders and Lt. Faust. I asked Lt. Miller to have his platoon sergeant join us for the briefing on the next day's mission.

When everyone was present, I started my briefing. "Enemy forces consist of the Third NVA Division Headquarters. Friendly forces consist of Company C, who will be air-lifted in with us. As for attachments, we will have support from the Minh Long Special Forces Camp. Detachments will be our company Weapons Platoon, who will be at base-camp Cam, along with the Battalion Reconnaissance Platoon."

It was obvious by the looks on their faces this was going to be a major undertaking; all present were busy taking notes with great interest.

"We will engage any enemy left after a B-52 strike and destroy them. Company C will be airlifted in first, and we'll follow them. The execution of the mission will be as follows:

"Concept of operation: Phase I. At 0645 Company C and our Weapons Platoon will be picked up at the southwest landing pad. At 0700 hours our company will be assembled in the company street and be ready to move onto the landing pad as soon as Company C is completely lifted out. Sometime before 0800 hours we'll be picked up by two hooks and taken to the Minh Long Special Forces camp.

"Phase II. After the B-52 bomb strike, about 0930 hours, twelve slicks (the name we use for Huey helicopters) will pick up Company C from LZ Cork and land them in the eastern target area," I said, pointing to the location on the topographical map previously attached to the orderly room wall.

"Then we'll be picked up at Minh Long in the following order, First Platoon, Command Group, Second Platoon and then the Third Platoon. We will land in the same order that we were picked up. Only three choppers will be able to land at a time in our assigned area. We'll move south in the bomb lane with the First Platoon on the west, the Second Platoon in the middle, and the Third Platoon on the east. The supporting fires will be the helicopter gunships that will wait at Minh Long and Cork after our insertion. Tactical aircraft will be on call. Four 105-Howitzers from B Battery of the 6th Battalion of the 11th Artillery will also be available."

Then, I went over to the map and repeated each phase to be sure all the platoon leaders knew everything in every detail. The leaders copied what I was saying on their plastic-covered maps with their black grease pencils. I discussed how many men from each platoon would mount on each helicopter, both when boarding the hooks and when boarding the slicks. I went over what time we would get up, what time we would eat breakfast, what time we would assemble on the street, and what time we would move over to the helicopter pad. We discussed what we were to look for during the bomb assessment - - enemy weapons, documents, and count the number of enemy killed by the bombs. We discussed how we would keep records of what we found and who would report the finding to whom. Lt. Faust, who was present at my briefing, would be responsible for plotting a map of the damages we found.

The meeting broke up just a little before 2100 hours. The platoon leaders then left to join their men to go over the next day's mission with them.

Just when I thought I could finally get a shower and shave, I got a phone call from the battalion operations center. LTC Pritchard wanted to see me.

When I arrived at the operations center, I found the Company C commander in LTC Pritchard's office. The colonel gave me a beer and went over the operation with Capt. Blanks and me once more.

"Can you imagine how it would be in the NVA Headquarters?" LTC Pritchard asked. In a deep voice, imitating a North Vietnamese Commander, he said, "I suppose you're all wondering why I brought you here this morning........" Then he switched back to his own voice, "Their division commander would start speaking, but before he can give them his pitch, it will start raining these huge bombs."

We all laughed. But, I only gave a half-hearted laugh. In my civilian life, I had usually felt a little sad when I saw a dog or wild animal that had been run over by a car. I only shot targets as a sport, but I hadn't hunted any animals or birds. The only things I had willfully hurt, other than gnats, flies and spiders, were fish. Then, only a couple times. I didn't even like fishing. I stopped chuckling. I felt sad. This was war. People were killed or wounded in war. However, it didn't have to be enjoyed.

I finished my beer and said I still hadn't been able to shower or shave. Then I asked to be excused. I was the only one in dust covered and sweat stained fatigues. I needed to clean up before turning in for the night.

As I was returning to my company orderly room, I thought of LTC Pritchard. He was the one who wouldn't let anyone indiscriminately burn hootches, shoot civilians, or destroy crops. His attitude was that we were here to assist the South Vietnamese people, and he intended to do just that. I admired him for that, but felt a little alienated from him and Boots Blanks for laughing about killing NVA soldiers. I wondered how many other officers felt like I did. I wondered if I was the odd one, feeling sorry for the enemy who would be killed the next day.

I took a cool shower, which felt great since the normal temperature at night was around 90 degrees. I double-checked my clean weapon to be sure it was assembled properly and working correctly. Then I finally laid down. It had been a long, hard three days for me, and it looked like it was going to be another set of long, hard days coming up. I dozed off without even realizing it was Good Friday.

There should have been 98 percent illumination that night, but there wasn't. Around 0200 hours, it seemed as if the plug had been pulled out of a tank of water over my tent. It rained like I had never seen it rain before. I went back to sleep and slumbered until dawn. I got ready to move out. The choppers couldn't fly in the heavy rain, so we were on hold. In the afternoon it finally stopped raining. The bombs had been dropped by the high flying B-52's who flew well above the storm clouds, however the choppers couldn't fly into the bombed out area due to the rain and the afternoon fog that was created by the evaporating rain.

At 1500 hours, the operation was called off. I was relieved. That was one mission I didn't want to undertake. Instead, Major Vaughn ordered us to conduct a joint sweep with

Company C in the rice bowl about 5,000 meters south of <u>Duc Pho</u>.

- - - o - - -

Our experience over the past several weeks was typical for the battlefield. No matter how much we prepared, no matter how many things we did to be ready, the execution of the assigned mission never seemed to go exactly as planned. The American soldier was flexible and adjusted to the ever changing battlefield situation. The enemy rehearsed for a month and then executed the plan to the last detail, no matter how screwed up everything was going for them. We could adjust to any situation quickly. That was the American way. Be prepared, but be flexible. This was one of the reasons we came out ahead during every contact the Delta Dogs had with the enemy and the United States forces had with the NVA and VC. The communists lost over 4,000,000 men during the Vietnam War, far more than the 58,000 we lost.

- - - o - - -

At 1600 hours, all the platoon leaders were assembled in the company orderly room to get our new mission from me. I gave them their orders. We would conduct a joint sweep with Company C of the <u>My</u> <u>Trang</u> villages (1) through (4) the next day.

The platoon leaders quickly went off to have their meetings and let their men know what was going to happen. After the evening chow everyone turned in, it was going to be another long day ahead of us.

After the platoon leaders left, I went back to checking the latest incoming mail. We received a very nice letter from Mr.

E. C. Reilly, a representative of the Liggett and Myers Corporation, 630 Fifth Avenue, New York, New York. The letter went on to say that a shipment of donated cigarettes has been consigned to the men of D Company. These cigarettes were furnished by McGuire Lumber and Supply, in Wylliesburg, Virginia, in honor of Private First Class William A. Ferrell. They didn't know he had been wounded and thought Ferrell was still in our unit when they contacted the cigarette company for the donation. In any event, I felt it was a nice gesture from some Americans who seemed to appreciate what we were doing for them in Vietnam. I told Sgt. Brings to distribute the cigarettes to the platoons.

-   -   -   o   -   -   -

At 2300 hours everyone was up. The company was still not at full strength. We needed every man capable of moving out with us. Lt. Evans told me a man in the Second Platoon refused to move out with us. The infantryman was high on dope and didn't want to go out to the field with us. I went to the Second Platoon tent and witnessed Lt. Evans order Willie into the field. Willie told him he didn't want to go, so he wasn't going into the field. I was outraged and told Sgt. Brings to file charges and to start the Court Martial proceedings. As we left the orderly room, Lt. Evans told me something I had difficulty believing, "The papers wouldn't go through, Sir."

"Why not?" I asked.

"Willie is a Negro, Sir. The army won't process the Court Martial papers."

"And why is that?" I asked.

"The military is under so much pressure from our enemy's friends back in the states that the Army doesn't want another issue to be raised questioning if the army is prejudiced against Negroes."

My face was flushed and I used an explicative or two to express my feelings. We both witnessed Willie acting as if he was high and refusing to make a movement under battlefield conditions. This was a serious offense, punishable by death.

We stood there in the dark, a short distance away from the company, as Lt. Evans tried to explain, "The Army is bending over backwards to show the world they don't have a racial problem, even if it meant not processing a Court Martial like this."

I felt very depressed at the injustice of it all. "Is there anything else we can do about Willie?"

Lt. Evans assured me he would see about what could be done.

Before I left, I asked, "Do the other men know we're not prosecuting Negroes in the army for dereliction of duty?"

"I think they must know," Lt. Evans answered. "Otherwise, Willie wouldn't have done what he did."

I felt a new found respect for those black soldiers in Company D, like Donaldson, Smith, Sterling and those who could have taken the coward's way out like Willie, if they had wanted to. Donaldson's and Smith's way out of Vietnam was suffering serious wounds while serving honorably. Sterling's way out was completing his tour of duty.

There was something I learned early on in combat, each and every man has to decide who he is and to act accordingly. We had cowards and heroes in Company D. I was proud of those who were brave soldiers and ashamed of those who had used whatever loop-holes they could find to follow their cowardly ways. We all knew who they were and so did they.

-    -   -   o   -   -   -

243

We had coffee and breakfast rolls at 2330 hours in our mess hall (being Irish-American, it was tea and a breakfast roll for me). Then we lined up on the company street at 2400 hours and started to move towards the main entrance of LZ Bronco. Company C moved out at 2400 hours that night. We moved out behind them at 0100 hour. Both companies moved stealthily west until we hit the old railroad berm, then we headed southeast with the railroad berm on the west side of us and Highway-One on the east.

We moved through the rain soaked rice paddies. Each step was followed by the sucking sound of our boots being pulled out of the oozing mud. Morning Nautical Twilight for Easter Sunday, 6 April 1969, was to be at 0551 hours. Easter Sunday was just another day in the field for us infantrymen - no services and no time off.

With sunrise coming so early, we had to move fast to cover the 5,000 meters required by the operation. The moon was already up by the time we moved out, and the 87 percent moon light illumination helped us move quickly. But good visibility for us also meant good visibility for Charlie.

We moved south through ankle deep mud in the rice paddies. When we could, we walked on the berms in single file to keep out of the water. Our combat boots had steel bottoms and canvas sides to provide protection from spikes and to allow for water drainage. However, we still wanted to keep our feet out of water as much as we could. In a tropical climate, that wasn't an option all the time. When out of the rice paddies we made less noise walking on the berm, and we were able to move faster.

A small pup from the village had started following us when we left the base-camp, and was still with us. Our move south took us across two streams that were more than crotch deep.

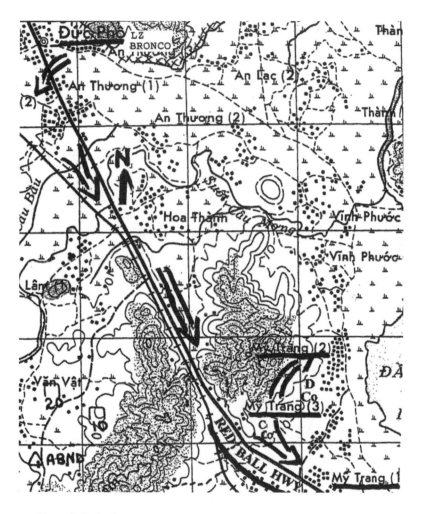

C and D infantry companies move south in the dark.

This was a problem, as we knew the polluted water would start giving some of us crotch rashes again. The small dog left us when we crossed the second stream. We kept going at a quick pace over the 5,000 meter journey as the illumination from the moon popped in and out of the scattered night clouds.

We reached the point where the railroad berm and Highway-One almost met. There we crossed the highway and proceeded southeast.

We trudged though the pass between the two hill masses until we were south of My Trang (3). The other unit, Company C, continued farther south, ahead of us, until they were adjacent to My Trang (1).

Just before Morning Nautical Twilight, at 0551 hours, we were in position and ready to sweep north through My Trang (2) and My Trang (3), the two villages we were assigned to search for enemy VC and NVA soldiers. At the same time, Company C would sweep through My Trang (1) and then west through My Trang (4). At 0600 hours we moved out and found what we expected in My Trang (3), women, children and old men.

As we were moving between My Trang (2) and My Trang (3), I saw something nearly half-a-foot long swimming away from us as I waded into the irrigation ditch we were crossing.

"What is that?" I asked one of the men who had been in-country the longest.

He looked at the fleeing swimmer, and laughed. "That's a leech, Sir."

I was surprised they got so big. After that I felt a bit uneasy while continuing to wad through the water. We stopped to take a break after crossing the stream, and the men checked themselves for leeches. One of the men found one on his leg. His buddy lit a cigarette and held the hot end near the leech's head. As I watched, the medic explained, "If you try pulling them off, their heads stay in the skin. That can cause a serious infection. By burning them a little, they back out themselves." The medic grabbed the over four inch long leech, threw it away, and applied some iodine and stuck a bandage over the wound.

After the quick break, we proceeded to the second hamlet and conducted the search. We found one house with an old 'PapaSan,' as Juan called him, who looked about 80 years old. There were also about a half a dozen women with him, young and old. Their ages appeared to be about 25 to 80 years old.

"You're an ugly old man, aren't you?" Sgt. Espinoza asked.

The old man nodded his head up and down, smiling with an almost toothless grin. Juan called everyone to gather around him and look at the old man.

Then he asked the old man, "Does your mother wear combat boots?" The old man nodded his head up and down again, still smiling. They all laughed, as some more of the men joined us.

"Do you eat pussy?" Juan asked the old man. The old man nodded his head again and everyone laughed, as the old man continued smiling. Juan moved forward and put one arm around the old man and gave him a hug. They both stood on the porch, smiling at the men who had gathered around the front of the hootch to watch Juan carry on, as he usually did. Juan Espinoza was not only a fine soldier and a compelling leader of men, he was also a comedian. He could always get the men to laugh about something.

The old man placed two of his fingers to his lips and nodded again towards Juan. Juan gave him a cigarette and lit it for him.

Juan looked out at the grunts, smiled and said, "This old, ugly son-of-a-bitch is my buddy. Anyone who eats pussy is all right."

He turned his head towards the old man and asked, "Isn't that right?'

The old man held the cigarette in front of his face and exhaled as he was nodding his head up and down while he continued to smile. It was obvious to everyone the almost toothless smiling old man didn't understand a thing that Juan was saying. We all continued to laugh.

"Are you VC?" Juan asked.

The old man nodded again, only this time he said, "VC" and pointed towards the mountain to our west. It was probably the only thing the man understood, besides cigarettes, since Juan started kidding with him.

Juan's comedy show broke up when we received a call from our orderly room at Bronco. They informed us they could fly out some hot coffee and freshly baked cookies, if we could find a safe landing area for them.

I told Joe to call the platoons to see who had a good LZ for the chopper. The First Platoon reported they had a dry rice paddy next to the hootch they were searching that would make a good LZ. I ordered them to set up security for a landing and to switch their radio to the battalion frequency to guide in the chopper. I told all the other platoons to set up security where they were and wait for the chopper to depart before they could share in the goodies being brought out to us.

All the kids from the hamlet gathered around when the chopper landed. After it left, I told the other platoons to converge on the First Platoon for their coffee and cookies. Then they all spread out to enjoy their morning break. We gave some cookies to the village kids. Juan also gave his new buddy some coffee and cookies.

After our break, we continued our sweep of the last village and the area around it. At noon we put out security and stopped for lunch in a grassy area, about 100 meters in diameter, with scattered trees and a couple of hedgerows running around and across it. Most of the men seemed a little nauseated due to the hard, rapid walking, the searching, and the moist heat. Consequently, most of them only nibbled at the C-rations. I had some fruit cocktail, cheese and crackers, and

A couple of the hootches the Delta Dogs searched.

a warm soda for lunch. Even though the soda was about 85 degrees, the cola tasted good in the over 120 degrees climate.

Sometimes I would take a swig of water even though it was 90-degree water. I swallowed it because it was wet, and I needed the moisture to replace the water lost due to my profuse sweating. That was a cardinal rule in the field, hydrate constantly.

Because we completed our sweep so early, I let the men take an hour-and-a-half lunch break and I used the down time to bring my journal up to date. I knew if I survived this ordeal, I wanted someday to write about what it was like to be an infantryman in Vietnam. I wanted the people back home to know what it was really like.

During our sweep we had found a 20-year-old male. He didn't have any identification papers. He also had a different kind of haircut. The North Vietnamese soldiers were usually pretty easy to identify, compared to the Viet Cong soldier. The Vietnamese northerners spoke with a different accent, much as the US Southerner and the US New Englander could be easily differentiated from one another. The North Vietnamese also wore a different style hair cut. The fillings in the NVA teeth were steel instead of the gold or silver used by the South Vietnamese. The VC and NVA were also very light skinned, because they hid all day. The South Vietnamese were out in the sun all day, and had a ruddy look.

Once the command and control helicopter picked up the detainee, we headed south again. We were west of the northern end of the <u>Xuan</u> <u>Thanh</u> village, butted against the mountains to the west side of the rice bowl. From there I could see the empty terraced side of the mountain. I also saw some trails leading to the tiered empty farmland. We had plenty of daylight left, and we were almost at the end of our area of operation.

The large bore single-shot shotgun type rifle grenade launcher fired a grenade that looked like a giant bullet. While it might have looked like a shotgun, it didn't fire like one. It could be fired at a high trajectory to let the grenade rounds drop in from above a target. The grenade launcher was cocked open in the middle, like a shotgun, and a rifle grenade round pushed into the back end of the barrel. Then, the weapon folded shut and is ready to fire. A new rifle grenade round was loaded each time a shot was fired. The weapon had a very long back sight that folded down when not in use. The sight allowed the round to be lobbed into the air, like a football being thrown.

The LAW (Light Antitank Weapon) was a shoulder-launched rocket we used against enemy bunkers. The back tube was extended when preparing to fire. The front and back caps were removed, the back extended, and the front and back sites folded up. The LAW was a single use weapon. Once it was fired, it could not be reloaded and fired again.

Since we finished the sweep ahead of schedule, I took the opportunity to see who was really good with these weapons. To better prepare for the next battle, I ordered all the rifle grenade launcher carriers to fire a few rounds into the mountainside. We shot at one of the vacant terraces on the side of the hill. I made it a competition to see who was the best rifle grenade launcher and LAW marksman. I only let the LAW carriers shoot half of their LAW's that day.

When the competition was over, it was apparent the grenade launcher shooters were more accurate than the LAW users. The grenade launcher carriers were the only ones to hit in the vacant tiered mountainside.

Company C radioed us when they heard the explosions to see if we were in contact with the enemy. My radio operator let them know we were just expending some of our damaged LAW's and taking target practice with our grenade launchers. They rogered our message and continued their sweep.

251

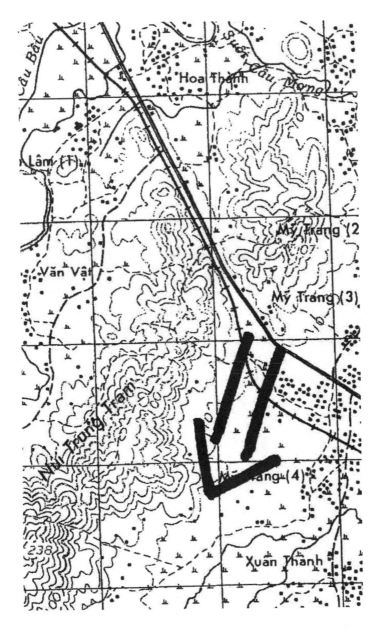

Delta Dogs sweep south and conduct target practice.

252

Later that afternoon we received a call from battalion, which told us to meet with Company C and co-logger with them for the night. They also directed each of us to put out four ambush sites and to coordinate where the eight twiggies were located. As we were walking to the east to join Company C, I mused to myself, *Well, I guess this is one way for battalion to get our night logger coordinates before sundown.*

By 1800 hours we had moved 2,000 meters to the east and were deployed next to Company C. No C-rations today. The choppers had flown out food for both companies while we were moving towards Company C's position. While I was catching my breath, one of the men who had brought the food out from the rear brought me a plate of hot chow and some ice cream.

I usually didn't get my meals served to me when in the field, but I guess the rear mess personnel must have felt sorry for an old guy of 36 humping with these young men all day long. I took little solace in the fact that most of the 18, 19, and 20 year olds were gasping for breath too.

After chow I joined Capt. Blanks, and we went over the locations our men would use for the loggers, and the routes they would take to set up the twiggies. We each enjoyed an ice cold beer brought out with the evening meal, as we plotted on our maps with grease pencils, identifying every location and path to be used. We didn't want to ambush each other by mistake. We both knew friendly-fire kills were the worst kills a unit could suffer. So far, we hadn't had any, and I didn't intend to start now. The only thing worse than writing a letter home to a dead soldier's family, was if his death was caused by friendly fire.

When I returned to my company command group, I gathered the platoon and squad leaders together and went over who was going to go where that night. I told them to plot both the Company C and D logger locations as well as the locations of all the eight twiggies. I wanted to be sure everyone knew where everyone else was, so we would only be looking for enemy infiltraters at night. The men on the twiggies left their rucksacks and extra gear with the squads that were staying in the company logger position.

It was still light out as the men conducting the twiggies started down the small hill on which we were loggered. Lt. Faust adjusted the firing of several artillery rounds into the rice bowl, so if he needed to direct any fire in the middle of the night, both the artillery support group and we would have a reference point from which to adjust fires. It provided quick artillery fire support if needed.

That night we all dug our fox-holes a little deeper than usual. I felt very uncomfortable about the logger position. If the enemy had been watching us, they would know exactly where we were sleeping. I only hoped if they were watching, they would think we would be moving after dark.

I kept waking up during the night. I had hurt my back before being shipped to Vietnam, and the heavy load I carried each day didn't give it a chance to heal. That was both a bad and a good thing for me. I couldn't get a good night's sleep, however, I did continually check on the radio watch.

Moonrise was at 2230 Hours, with an 80 percent illumination. The moon didn't set until 0900 hours the next day, which meant those on watch in our two company loggers, as well as those on watch in the eight twiggies, would have good visibility during the night.

The night was uneventful, and when the sun rose the next morning, all our ambush patrols started returning to our logger location. As they made their way back, we got a coded message from battalion directing both companies to move up into the mountain range to our southwest and search for VC and NVA base-camp locations.

With no clouds in sight, I knew it was going to be another hot one. We moved up the mountain as fast as we could throughout the morning to complete as much climbing as possible before the afternoon heat really slowed us down.

The climb up the nearly bare face of the mountain was really tough on me. I took off my helmet and hung it on my cartridge belt. I also took off my fatigue jacket and put on my olive-drab T-shirt. I slung my rifle over my shoulder and then took the olive drab face towel I usually wrapped around my neck to catch my sweat and trudged forward with my two arms raised and the hand towel stretched between my hands. It provided a little shade and relief from the blistering sun on my head. It wasn't much shade, but it was better than the hot sun-rays burning into my steel helmet or onto my bare head. I knew I wouldn't want much food for lunch, but the warm soda was going to taste good when we stopped to rest.

We finally broke into the high mountain jungle. I was thankful the canopy of the rain forest was shading us from the sun. I wrapped the towel around my neck again. In the shade it appeared to be at least 10 degrees cooler.

As we climbed, we searched each side of the canyon and stopped when we were two-thirds of the way up to the mountaintop. We were ahead of schedule because we hurried so fast before the heat of the day had set in. That allowed us to take a much-needed two hour lunch break.

At 1600 hours on Monday, 7 April, we reached our objective, Hill 258. No rain forest here. The hilltop had been burned off some time earlier. The vegetation growth was little more than low bushes and knee-high grass. Much of Vietnam was scarred as a result of the years of war.

255

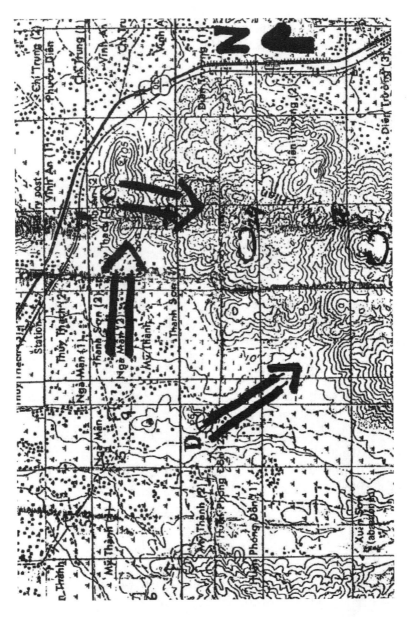

C Company moves east and D Company southeast.

After we put out our security, and before evening chow time, we saw a swarm of choppers moving toward a mountaintop south of us. One dipped out of sight for a moment and then rose to join the others in the air. One after another, they all dropped low out of sight into the jungle at different locations and then rose back up. They did this repeatedly for over a half an hour, covering about 3,000 meters of terrain. I found out later they were inserting a Long Range Reconnaissance Patrol (LRRP). Dropping into the jungle at widely dispersed locations prevented the VC or NVA from knowing where the LRRP's were. Actually only one of the helicopters carried the team. For us it was just a sideshow because they were too far away for us to run into each other.

After we settled down for chow, one of the men reported troop movement on a hilltop about 2,000 meters to our north. I ordered my battalion radio operator to call Company C, and ask them to encode and send the coordinates of their location. Something just didn't feel right. To me the troops we saw had to be Company C men, because the enemy seldom moved in broad daylight. If we were going to call in an artillery strike on someone, I wanted to be sure we were looking at enemy troops, not Company C. In the mean time, I had all my men move under cover so no one could see us, just in case they were enemy soldiers.

The coordinates we received back from Company C placed them some distance from the mountainside we were watching. That would indicate we caught an NVA company out in the open. If they weren't Company C, they had to be NVA, since they were in the olive drab uniforms that only the NVA, South Vietnamese Army and the US Army soldiers wore. The VC were outfitted in the black pajamas, not olive drab uniforms.

I got on the radio and requested battalion to verify no South Vietnamese troops were operating in the area. They confirmed that none were anywhere near us. Not satisfied, I requested they verify the information again with the South Vietnamese Army liaison officer in <u>Duc</u> <u>Pho</u>. I reminded them when we were operating off Snoopy, we bumped into friendly Vietnamese troops when none were supposed to be there.

After fifteen minutes, battalion radioed back and confirmed the original report. There were no South Vietnamese troops in our area of operation.

My years of experience kept telling me something wasn't right, and I was not yet ready to call in an artillery strike on the troops we were observing. It just didn't feel right to me that NVA troops would be meandering around in broad daylight like these soldiers were.

I asked to speak to the commander of Company C and Capt. Boots Blanks got on the radio. I asked him if he was certain they were at the coordinates previously reported to us. He personally gave me the same coded coordinates his RTO reported. I checked my map again and if he was correct, it was not Company C we were looking at.

There are times in combat when we have to follow doctrine and times when our gut feeling tell us more than any textbook. "Can you pop a smoke to mark your location?" I asked.

A cloud of purple smoke appeared in the middle of the troops I was watching, as Boots reported, "Goofy grape."

I breathed a sigh of relief. I was only moments away from calling in a deadly artillery strike that would have killed dozens of our own troops.

"Buddy, you're not where you think you are," I said. "You're off by over one click," (a click is 1,000 meters).

"Baloney. You guys don't know where you are," Boots answered. Lt. Faust, who had been with me throughout this ordeal, suggested that the fire-base artillery observers settle this for us.

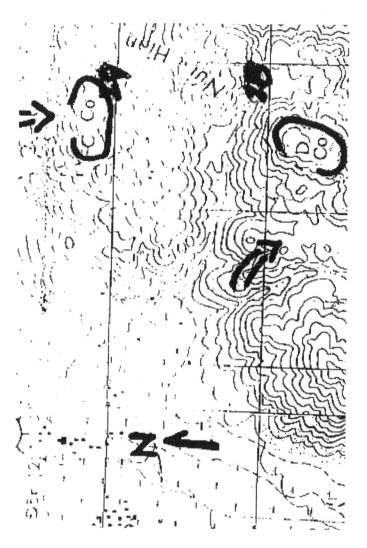

Logger locations of Company C and Company D.

"I will bet you a case of beer you are not where you think you are."

"You're on, but how are we going to prove who's right?" Boots asked.

"Let's call the fire-base and after we pop smoke, let them trisect our location. Then they can encrypt our coordinates and send them back to us," I offered.

"Agreed. Shall I go first?"

"Let's switch over to the red-leg channel and then you can go first."

We switched our radios over to the artillery (which we called red-legs) frequency channel. After we both checked in with the artillery unit, Boots popped a couple of white phosphorus grenades to mark his location.

The base-camp artillery unit plotted his location, encrypted the coordinated and sent them phonetically back over the radio. We both listened intently and decoded the coordinates after receiving them. Company C was not where they thought they were. Boots owed me a case of beer, but in truth, he owed me a whole lot more.

I felt pretty good that night, knowing that those in the rear who had been monitoring our conversation over the battalion radio frequency recognized what I was doing in the battlefield. That day I had prevented a terrible disaster, and saved many lives. I wondered if it would have been different with a less experienced company commander.

-   -   -   o   -   -   -

After sunset, we moved to another logger position. We had been in one location too long, and after popping the mellow-yellow smoke grenade to let the base-camp artillery plot our location, we had also pin-pointed our position to any enemy troops in the area. Battalion had already let us know we were to logger in our present position and continue the saturation patrolling the next day. Staying there would have been risky, so we moved. As usual I didn't let Cumbee call in our position until we had settled into the new night logger position.

We didn't put out any twiggies that night. Ambushes required a flat killing-zone, and the tropical forest we were in didn't offer any such terrain. I still had each platoon put out listening posts to alert the rest of us if we had any infiltraters.

The following day, 8 April, two days after Easter, the company headquarters group and the Weapons Platoon stayed in our position, and the three rifle platoons searched the adjoining area for any signs of VC or NVA activity.

We spent that night in the rain forest. Wednesday, 9 April, we moved down to the bottom of the mountain to take up a blocking position for some Republic of South Vietnam (RVN) soldiers. The RVN troops were sweeping the rice bowl that day. After we moved down to the flat land below, we spent a very relaxing hot day waiting for any enemy who might flee in our direction. This was turning out to be one of the easiest missions we had been assigned for some time.

The following day, Thursday, 10 April, we received orders to move back to our base-camp. We started heading north into the rice bowl, and while moving in a column formation, we received machine-gun fire from a group of hootches on our left.

Spc.4 George Cato of the Second Platoon was hit in the chest. We dropped our rucksacks, maneuvered around, and assaulted the farmhouse from where the shooting originated. As the platoon medic attended to Cato, we converged on the hootch. There was no one there. We looked for spider-holes but found none. Whoever shot at Spc.4 Cato escaped.

I had a platoon secure a landing zone for the medical evacuation dust-off while the rest of us searched for the shooter. Cato was evacuated within 15 minutes after he was shot. Survival depended on how quickly the casualty could be attended to in a field hospital. I hoped the quick response by the dust-off helicopter would give Cato a good chance to make it.

After his evacuation, we assaulted the hill behind the hootch with mortars, LAW's, rifle grenades and machine-gun fire in hopes of killing the Gook who attacked us. It was the same hill we had practice fired our LAW's and rifle grenades into earlier. We swept up the hill in scrimmage formation and found several large tunnels near the top. We searched the area to determine how many tunnels there were and tried to see if the enemy was still in the area. This was a very slow and painstaking process. We didn't want to be ambushed again, and we didn't want to trip any booby-traps.

When we called battalion to tell them of our find, they told us no engineers were available to come out and destroy the tunnels. They ordered us to logger for the night and put out twiggies to catch any NVA who might be trying to enter or leave the tunnels.

I set out our security, set up two ambush sites, and then set up a company defense position down in the rice bowl, away from the tunnels. Battalion said they would make a note about the tunnels and would destroy them at a later date when engineers were available. I was relieved we didn't have to wait for the engineers. We were glad we could just get away from the tunnels.

That night I moved the company a little farther into the rice bowl and set up our night logger position. I didn't sleep well that night, remembering what happened the last time we stayed around enemy tunnels too long.

The next morning, Friday, 11 April, we moved away from the tunnels and swept the rice bowl to the north as we moved closer towards LZ Bronco. At 1500 hours we stopped sweeping and marched up Highway-One towards our base-camp.

As we walked up the road, an older man on a bicycle approached us from behind. He had a doctor's bag strapped to the rack on the rear fender. When my men saw the bag, they stopped him and asked where he had been. He was coming from the direction where Cato had been shot. The old man said he had been delivering a baby at a farm to the south of us. My men let him proceed. When he got close to Sgt. Espinoza, Juan pushed him and his bike over. I quickly rushed to the location of the group of smiling soldiers and had them back off while the doctor got back on his bike and headed north. I figured Juan wanted retribution for Cato's being shot, and he let his frustration get the better of him. Plus, it was hard to tell who was the enemy and who wasn't. I believed in Juan's mind, the doctor was part of the enemy forces.

As I watched him ride away I thought, *Yes, you probably did provide medical aid to the wounded NVA soldiers that we've been fighting. But, you probably don't have much choice. I know this province is the home of the Commander and Chief of the North Vietnamese Army, General Giap. I guess just about every family probably has relatives fighting on both sides. If you take sides, then the other side will probably punish you. In order to be available to aid one side as a doctor, you most likely have to help the other side also.* I felt sorry for him.

The next day, 12 April, we were scheduled for a long overdue, three-day stand-down. We would be flown up to Chu Lai, check in all our weapons, store our rucksacks, canteens and ammo belts, and enjoy time off. The men could go to one of the hamburger stands or bars, and even swim on the beach, if they wanted to. In Chu Lai we could attend a USO show, visit friends (if we had any there), and go to the Post Exchange to buy tax-free souvenirs and presents to send home. I was planning to buy china, silverware, a slide projector, and other presents for my family at the tax-free and shipping-free Post Exchange. This was going to be free time at a large base-camp, and we could do whatever we wanted for the three days without concern about being called back into the field.

We all stepped a little livelier on our way back into LZ Bronco. We arrived around 1700 hours, just in time for a good supper. The men headed for the chow hall, anxious to eat something other than C-rations or LRRP's.

Unfortunately, I still had work to do and headed for the orderly room. One of the rear echelon men brought me a good hot meal, as I took care of all the paperwork which had once again piled up while I was out in the field. I signed company correspondence and records, read directives, memorandums, and orders. Best of all was a memorandum that said we were to be picked up by chopper the next morning at 0800 hours. I completed everything I had to do and turned in about 2230 hours. I was exhausted. This was the first good night's sleep I enjoyed for almost a week, and I needed it.

-    -   -   o   -   -   -

Specialist Fourth Class Vaughn J. Vandermeer was 19 years old when he was drafted from Grand Rapids, Michigan. Five months later Vaughn arrived in Vietnam as a medic in Company D. He served as a rifle platoon medic for almost six months before transferring to become the company command group medic in March 1969. Vaughn was promoted to Spc.4 on 23 January 1969. He moved to Phoenix, Arizona some time after returning home.

-    -   -   o   -   -   -

The following is a list of those Delta Dog's heroes who were identified in this chapter.

Specialist Fourth Class George M. Cato ** Wounded with a bullet wound in the chest
First Lieutenant James G. (Greg) Miller, from Newark, Ohio
Sergeant Dan M. Brings, from Belleview, Washington
Specialist Fourth Class Harvey F. Rosenblum, from Bronx, New York
Specialist Fourth Class Richard Sterling, from Plainfield, NJ

Infantry Company Organization

A fire team consists of five riflemen, one being the team leader. The fire team leader is a corporal or a sergeant.

A rifle squad consists of two fire teams. The squad leader is a sergeant or staff sergeant.

A rifle platoon consists of three rifle squads and a weapons squad. The platoon leader is a Lieutenant and the platoon sergeant is a sergeant first class.

A rifle platoon's weapons squad consists of two machine gun crews, with team leaders and a squad leader with ranks equivalent to the rifle squad.

An infantry company has three rifle platoons and one Weapons Platoon.

The Weapons Platoon has two machine gun teams and a mortar squad.

An infantry battalion usually has three rifle companies and a support company. The infantry companies in a light infantry brigade, like the 11th Light Infantry Brigade which we belonged to, had four infantry companies.

Each company was commanded by a Captain.

The infantry battalion was commanded by a Lieutenant Colonel.

A battalion headquarters company provided support for the battalion commander, his staff, and the four infantry companies.

There were four infantry battalions in the 11th Light Infantry Brigade. The brigade commander was a Colonel. Attached to the brigade were a dog platoon, chemical detachment, engineer battalion, signal company, helicopter company, field hospital, military police unit, ordinance company, cavalry troop, artillery battalion, maintenance company, transportation company, quartermaster unit, military intelligence unit, and other supporting units capable of running a small city consisting of five to ten thousand residents.

In the field in Vietnam our platoon sizes were usually about 25-30 men. Our infantry company strength in the field was between 73-105 men.

Chapter Nine

Lieutenant Colonel Walter L. Pritchard, Junior

I was awakened at 0600 hours by the company orderly so I could eat, pack, and assemble the men for the move on Saturday, 12 April 1969. After breakfast, I checked again to make sure all the paperwork in the company orderly room was reviewed and those items needing my signature were signed. Then I checked with the platoon leaders to verify that all the men were ready to move out. At 0800 hours we were at the LZ Bronco helicopter pads, waiting for our air-lift to Chu Lai, the Americal Division base-camp to the north of us. While we were sitting there with our rucksacks and weapons waiting for the medium lift Hooks to pick us up, I was monitoring the communications between Company B and the command and control chopper on the battalion frequency radio with Cumbee. We were still across from the heli-pad when the Huey landed to pick up LTC Walter L. Pritchard, Junior.

The Huey was on its way to the location of the company conducting a sweep in area we had swept on Good Friday. We heard their radio broadcasts as the battalion chopper flew away from Company B, to observe the hill from where the enemy fire had come when Privates Butler and Gilmore had been wounded during their first day in the field with us. The chopper was flying a circular flight about two hundred meters above the surface while the occupants were observing the concertina wire strung on the ground. The command and control chopper started receiving gunfire from the hill. They circled the area, as the chopper's machine-gunners were spraying the ground with M-60 machine-gun fire. Then, we heard, "My God, he's been hit! The Colonel has been hit! He's bleeding all over. My God, he's been hit in the head!"

The chopper quickly headed back to the medical helicopter pad at LZ Bronco to get medical help from our field hospital. Major Virgil W. Oglesby, the battalion Executive Officer was in the LZ Bronco operations center and got on the battalion command radio to try to find out how seriously LTC Pritchard was wounded. He checked to see how Company B was doing. He started checking on the other companies in the battalion as well. Major Oglesby was second in command and would assume responsibility if LTC Pritchard was incapacitated. A short time later we learned that LTC Pritchard was dead.

LTC Pritchard had been commissioned as an Army Officer after he had graduated from the US Military Academy, West Point in 1957. This was his first assignment as an infantry unit commander under combat conditions. He had been an army officer for almost twelve years. Not quite as long as I had been an officer.

I was commissioned a second lieutenant by the Army in 1955, after completing the Infantry Officer's Candidate School (OCS) at Fort Benning. Major Thomas B. Vaughn, the battalion operations officer who was on the helicopter with LTC Pritchard was commissioned after completing the infantry OCS school at Fort Benning, Georgia, as the top student in 1962, seven years after me. Army reserve officers, such as National Guard officers had to wait almost twice as long in each rank before being promoted.

The battalion commander's death had quite an impact on me. He had been the training unit commander in Chu Lai when I was the company commander of my two training companies. LTC Pritchard and I joined this infantry battalion on the same day. His death reminded me again how quickly any one of us could meet our maker.

Before this, the men had been joyful all morning at the prospect of the R & R in Chu Lai. They had been drinking sodas and joking while waiting for the Hook to fly us to the location for a little Rest and Recuperation.

"Thank God it wasn't me," I heard one man say.

Another added, "Boy, those new guys, Gilmore and Butler, they're the lucky ones. They got 'state-side' wounds. They'll be going home."

"Boy! If I go home after being hit, I hope it's like our guys and not like the Colonel," someone else added.

"This God damn war is lousy. Even a Colonel isn't safe in it," Midge said.

Midge, you are right. This war is lousy. Anyone who thinks that soldiers like war is nuts. A soldier has more to lose in it than anyone else, I thought.

We sat there in silence, waiting for the choppers pick up.

Company B was some distance away from the source of the ground fire which had hit the Colonel and weren't close enough to retaliate. That didn't mean the shooter was out of harms way, however. The battalion command and control chopper flew back out to the area with the battalion artillery fire control coordinator on board. He directed artillery strikes that blanketed the hill. Just to make sure the job was complete, an Air Force Bird-Dog (single engine, fixed-wing, air traffic controller airplane) arrived to direct air strikes. His arrival was followed by a number of tactical jet bombers making one bomb run after another over the hill.

For over an hour, we sat listening to the artillery and jets bombarding the enemy's location. From where we sat over four-thousand meters away, it felt like an earthquake occurring every few seconds as the large caliber artillery rounds and bombs exploded. We watched the gray smoke rise into the sky, as the attack finally ended. I had never seen so many planes drop so many bombs on one place at one time. I doubted that any person, animal, or plant was left alive for a square mile on the hill.

It would have been nice to receive that kind of support when we had been surrounded, I thought, as I watched the last plane pull away from the target area.

After the artillery fire and bombing stopped, the Hooks finally picked us up. Many of the men feared our stand-down would be canceled because of the colonel's death, and I think we were all relieved when the helicopters arrived. Our departure was only delayed until the bombers cleared out of the area.

I was on the last of the three Chinooks that ferried us to Chu Lai. I was still monitoring the battalion radio frequency and learned that our battalion intended to follow up the bombardment with additional white phosphorus and fire-cracker artillery barrages. They were firing 105 Howitzers, 155 Howitzers, and eight-inch cannons into the enemy area.

Then we turned the radio off. I wanted to put the incident out of my mind as we flew out of radio communications range.

- - - o - - -

Our First Sergeant, Arland Wheeler, Supply Sergeant, David Curry and our armorer, Specialist Fourth Class Harvey Rosenblum, arrived the day before to ensure everything was ready for us when we showed up. When we got to the stand-down area, we passed through a reception line that was organized to take care of the men so they could take full advantage of their stay. Spc.4 Rosenblum kept the armament records, as each man checked in his weapon. Members of the division ordinance team cleaned and checked each weapon during the next two days.

Sergeant Curry took each man's field uniforms and checked them for replacement with new gear if needed. The quartermaster personnel checked out all our field gear to ensure we had no jungle-rot or tattered equipment when we returned from our stand-down. They also took all our dirty clothes and laundered them.

First Sgt. Wheeler gave each person bedding and assigned a bunk for the next two nights. He also gave everyone a schedule of what was available during the stand-down. When the three days were over, we would have new or almost-new weapons and equipment. We would also be refreshed enough to return to LZ Bronco and the field.

We got through the administrative and logistical tasks as quickly as we could. Then, everyone went to the chow hall and started our stand-down with an exquisite meal. Fresh fruit was available 24 hours a day. We had access to food we never saw in the field such as bananas, apples, peaches, plums, strawberries, oranges, pears, and Lord knows what other exotic fruit. There were melons, tomatoes, celery, carrots, radishes, cauliflower and many other fresh vegetables we hadn't been able to enjoy for a long time. This was a rare spread of luxurious provisions, and we all overindulged, taking more than we could possibly eat. We acted like kids scrambling for the goodies that fell out of a shattered piñata.

After a diet of canned C-rations and dehydrated LRRP's, we felt like we were in heaven. The company fund paid for cases of ice-cold beer and sodas. Before Juan Espinoza got into the chow line, he headed for the cold beer. After he took two cans, he entered the chow line and drank while he was waiting to be served. Joe Dodson and I each grabbed an ice-cold carton of milk before we got into the chow line.

When we finished our meals, some men stayed in the combination mess hall and recreation room the rest of the day.

They drank, played cards, wrote home, and sat in the air-conditioned room watching the only English language television station.

After lunch, Lt. Evans and Sgt. Wheeler escorted me around the stand-down compound so I was assured every pleasure and assistance we could provide the men was available. Lt.'s Evans and Faust bunked with me in one room. Our room was the same as the others used by the men. We had screened windows with wooden flaps. During the day and evening, the flaps would be open to allow light and fresh air to enter. After dark, when ready to sleep, we would close the flaps to keep the room dark. The room had a single 100-watt bulb hanging from a wooden rafter, three army steel beds and three wall lockers for securing our valuables. Compared to sleeping on the ground and wondering if we were going to be mortared during the night, these accommodations were luxurious.

Satisfied that everything was in place for the men, I went back to my room and unpacked some of my personal items. I placed my toothbrush, shaving gear, journal and other personal items in my wall locker. In the field I had to re-pack my toothbrush and shaving gear immediately after using them, but now I could leave them out between uses. It was a small thing but a luxury in itself. In the field I carried a small bar of soap to lather my face before shaving. During stand-down, I could use shaving cream again. I also had a washcloth and clean towels. In the field, I used my olive-drab towel as a washcloth, a towel and a scarf. I also used the same towel after washing and shaving. It was the only towel I had for as long as thirty days at a time. To have clean towels every day during stand-down was another luxury. This would seem unimportant to those who had not been out in the field, but it was a big deal for my men and me.

Everything is relative, I thought. *Back home clean washcloths, towels, shaving cream and a clean change of clothes were taken for granted. Here, it is a true luxury to be cherished, if only for a few days.*

I took a long, hot shower to completely wash away the jungle grime. It was the first hot shower I had in over a month. Then I changed into a fresh set of jungle fatigues. They were nothing more than olive drab fatigues, not the camouflaged uniforms portrayed in the movies.

When I returned to the mess hall, some of the men were still there. They were drinking and playing cards. Most of the men, however, had gone off to take showers and change into clean, dry fatigues. I sat down with Joe Dodson, Willie, and some of the other guys. Yes, Willie, the pot-smoker, was still with us. After talking it over with Lt. Evans, Larky recommended and I agreed not to make an issue of his dope use. Taking punitive action would be doing exactly what Willie wanted. By letting it slide, Willie had to re-join us in the field. He had tried the scam, and it didn't work, so he was once again one of the grunts. After an hour of playing cards, I lost the ten bucks I had set as my limit, and I left the card table.

-    -   -   o   -   -   -

Later in the day, just before dark, I called my California buddy, Hugh Hollingsworth, who was a civilian contractor working at the base. We had worked together for a company making inertial guidance systems for aircraft. He had been sent to <u>Chu</u> <u>Lai</u> as a civilian company representative to repair aircraft guidance systems. We had skied together on the slopes of several California resorts and had attended some parties together before he took the position as a field representative,

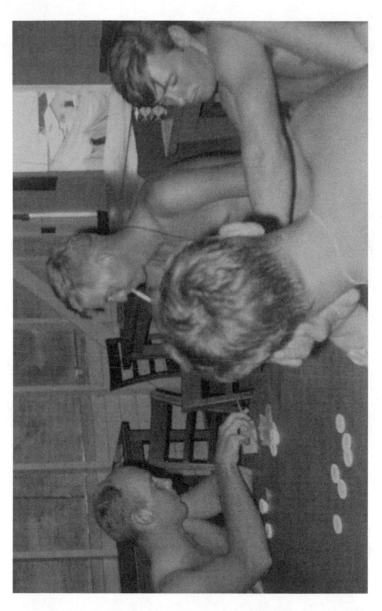

Lt. Evans on the left and Joe Dodson in the middle smoking while playing cards.

and I was called to active duty. When I first arrived at <u>Chu Lai</u>, I ran into him at the Post Exchange. I was as surprised to see him as he was to see me. I didn't know he had been assigned to <u>Chu Lai,</u> and he didn't know that I was in the Army.

Sergeant Brings, our personnel Sergeant, gave me a ride to the main officer's club where I met Hugh for dinner. In the field, officer's meals were furnished at no cost to the individual. In the rear, except at the stand-down chow hall, officers paid for their meals. Instead of eating free in the stand-down area, I wanted to have dinner with Hugh.

Hugh was waiting for me when I arrived. We greeted each other, and I jumped on the back of his motorcycle. He took me over to the MAG 52 (Marine Air Group) officer's mess hall for dinner. Since he was stationed there, he had tried all of the mess halls at <u>Chu Lai</u>, and he felt that this particular Marine facility was the best one available. After dinner, we had several drinks while waiting for the evening movie to start.

After watching the opening scenes, we decided we didn't care about the movie they were showing. We went out onto the patio with our drinks where we sat, reminiscing about our skiing excursions, parties we had attended, and the people we both knew back home. We talked very little about my combat experiences or his work.

Around eleven, Hugh took me back to the stand-down area. I was beat and needed some shut-eye. I think Hugh could have stayed up half the night talking if I had let him. However, it was my first night in the rear, and I needed a good night's sleep. I slept until about ten o'clock the next morning. It felt great to sleep in. This was the first day I had off since arriving in Vietnam. After eating a late breakfast, I chatted with some of the men who were playing cards and then hitched a ride to see the Americal Division recruitment officer, Captain Domingo (Dom) Molinelli. We were friends, and we chatted

From left, Spc-4's James Baillie, who was called "pops" as he was 25 years old, Jack Calmia (Killed In Action), and squad leader Ronald Isenhour during stand-down.

about how long it had been since we last saw each other. Then, he drove me over to the main post hospital, so I could see one of my men. Lt. Evans had been checking on Spc.4 George Cato, the last soldier who was wounded in the field. He was the only Delta Dog in the <u>Chu Lai</u> hospital, and I wanted to see him.

The hospital ward was a quonset-hut with beds on each side and an aisle down the middle. The hospital beds were separated by wooden wall-lockers containing the patients' equipment. Each area had a hospital-type bedside table, a chair, and a suspended cloth enclosure on the aisle side of the patient's cubicle.

I visited with Cato for a little while. He couldn't talk because he was covered with bandages and had tubes sticking out of his mouth, and more tubes running out of his chest, stomach, and arms. I did all the talking. Even though he was heavily sedated and probably couldn't remember much of what I said, I assured him we all missed him and that he was a lucky guy because he was going home. I let him know both Lt. Evans and First Sgt. Wheeler had been keeping me up to date on his progress. I informed him I checked to be sure the USO ladies were writing letters home for him and letting his family know he was getting better every day. I had also checked to be sure his mail, which had been sent to the hospital instead of our company, was getting to him. He confirmed it with a nod of his head.

Life is not easy and I thought it would be nice for Cato to have a friend with him during the hard part. It was difficult carrying on even a one-sided conversation with him, but I did the best I could under the circumstances. He seemed to appreciate my company, and maybe I stayed too long with him. He was one of us grunts, and I wanted to be sure that everything he needed had been taken care of.

When a combat buddy, like Cato, was wounded, it was not the infantry Captain's duty to see how he was doing. It was an emotional bond that tied us grunts together, and I wanted to be sure that he was receiving everything he needed. The feeling of pity, sorrow, respect, and empathy for a fellow combatant made us go to the extreme to assure that he had been really well cared for. We all knew that, except for the grace of God, the man lying in that bed could easily have been one of us.

After I finished visiting with Cato, Dom showed me the bed in the next cubicle. It was occupied by Lt. Loise Hamer, the glamour queen of our first training class. Dom was one of my officers during the first new-arrivals training company class in LTC Pritchard's program at <u>Chu</u> <u>Lai</u>. The nurse in the bed next to Cato was the one we all fantasized about when we were in the two-week course at <u>Chu</u> <u>Lai</u>. She was young and beautiful.

Most of the young officers in my training company had tried to get closer to her and sit next to her at mealtime or play cards with her in the evening. Most of the time they lost out because she had preferred to spend time with Dom, Boots Blanks, and me. Maybe she just felt safer with us than she did with the younger, more aggressive officers who were buzzing about her like bees around honey. Loise was hospitalized for Infectious Mononucleosis, called the kissing disease. I had to laugh to myself. There was absolutely no doubt in my mind that many of my Delta Dogs would have gladly risked Mono to have the opportunity to kiss her.

Dom and I visited with Loise for a little while, and then we left the hospital for our lunch. As the Division Recruiting officer, Dom visited most areas in the base-camp and ate in most of the mess halls. That day Dom joined me in the stand-down mess hall for lunch. He knew it was one of the best places to eat at the <u>Chu</u> <u>Lai</u> base-camp.

After lunch I was told the enlisted men's club next to the stand-down area had presented my men with an interesting proposition. The club's proprietor had contracted a Filipino band with three hot-looking singers to play at their club in the evening. He said if our men chipped in enough money, Company D could have the group play for us in the afternoon. The decision was not really up to me, and besides, I hadn't even been in the stand-down area most of the morning. By the time I got there, the men had already taken up a collection and had one-hundred and fifty dollars, enough to hire the band.

The afternoon show was in the enlisted men's club. Before the show started, the club's representative told my men it was an open club. That meant they couldn't prevent other soldiers from coming in to watch the show we paid for. However, that wasn't really important because most of the enlisted men at Chu Lai had to work during the day. That meant the performance was almost exclusively for the Delta Dogs.

Before the show started, Hugh showed up to spend some more time with me. I told him about the show, and he joined Dom and me at a back table. The three of us were sitting next to the smaller of the two bars. We had to pay for our drinks at the enlisted men's club, but the drinks were cheap. For the price of a couple of drinks, we got to see a really good show.

In the one corner of the building, next to the stage, the tables were filled with Company D infantrymen. Most of the men had been drinking all morning and were feeling no pain. The company's rear echelon personnel were supposed to stay sober, so they could drive and take care of the field soldiers during their three days of being in the rear, but that did not happen. First Sgt. Wheeler, Supply Sgt. Curry, Armorer Spc.4 Rosenblum, Company Clerk Sgt. Brings, Mail Clerk Spc.4 Michael B. Fusillo, Motor Sgt. Jerry D. Koontz, Commo-man

Spc.4 Reginald E. Steele, and Supply Clerk Pfc. Andrew Bracy all joined in the fun.

Delta Dogs enjoying a stand-down show at Chu Lai.

Sgt. Curry and First Sgt. Wheeler were completely smashed when the show began, and they had a lot of company.

In 1969 a soldier didn't have to be 21 to drink on an Army base.

The band was good. After being out in the field for quite a while, the three female Filipino singers looked beautiful in their mini-skirts and tight blouses. They sang and danced, jumped off the stage, danced in the isles and on the tables to the complete joy of the men. It was like a road-house show with all the drunken men, most under 21 years old, who were too drunk to do anything but watch, cheer, and continue to drink away a month's worth of bad times.

Eighteen-year old Midge Anderson was almost completely saturated and shouted for the singer to come down from the stage and sing for him. The lead female singer noticed the infantrymen seemed to like the suggestions Midge was hollering, and she started following whatever he said. She danced for Midge, first in front of him, then on his table, and then she gave him a lap dance. The drunken crowd went wild. Midge hammed it up even more, enjoying the personal attention he was receiving from the most beautiful girl any of them had seen in months. When she returned to the stage, Midge's buddies had to hold him back. He tried to get up on the stage with her. In the meantime, all the other guys at the front row of tables were shouting and gesturing for the three girls to come down and dance for them.

The lead singer came down once more. She headed right for Midge. She stepped on his chair, right between his legs, and then stepped up over his head, onto his table.

Unintentionally, or maybe intentionally, I'm not sure, she kicked Midge in the crouch while climbing up onto the table. While she was dancing on the table and singing, Midge was doing his own dance next to the table, while grabbing his private parts. The crowd seemed to think it was funny watching him and the look on his face. Clearly, he was in pain, but at the same time he was smiling, having been touched there by a beautiful girl. Everyone laughed at her and Midge, each doing their own unique steps and vocal presentations - one to the music and one to his own joyful, yet painful involuntary beat. She gyrated and he kept bending over and straightening up as they both screamed their hearts out in order to be heard above the laughter and hooting of the audience. We thought Midge could have been faking it, except for the purple color in his face and the tears rolling down his cheeks. Ironically, this made the men laugh even harder.

At the completion of the song, the singer stepped down on Midge's empty chair and joined him on the floor. She gave him a big hug and asked if he was okay. He nodded his head with a painful smile. She gave him a big, long kiss on the lips and then told him she was sorry before jumping back up on the stage. Everyone was still laughing, as the performers started another song. Midge eased over to his chair as the whole room joined the band, singing, "I want to get out of this place." That song had been a very popular tune for those in-country in Vietnam during 1969.

Although still smiling, Midge appeared to be completely sloshed. It was as if he had overcompensated for his prior continued state of dehydration. He was in a safe place where he could over indulge without fear of losing his life or worst yet, the lives of his buddies due to his inebriated condition. Midge was safe, at ease, and unrestricted. He could let himself go as wild as he wanted for these couple of days before returning to the hot, grueling task of jungle warfare.

After an hour and a half, the band packed up and started storing their instruments for the evening show. Most of the men headed back to the stand-down area, where the beers were free. I heard Midge and a couple of the other men hung around and talked to the girls in the band. Maybe they were trying to get lucky.

Hugh gave me a ride back up to the MAG 52 officers' club

Spc-4 James (Mac) McConnel and Pfc. (Doc) Bernard Kelly, both celebrating stand-down.

on his motorcycle for our evening meal. After we finished eating, we went over to the Medical Hospital's Officer's club. We thought it would be a nice to have a drink with some of the nurses, who were all officers. That way Hugh could meet some of the ladies at his base-camp. The plan was good, but the commander of the Hospital Group had other ideas. He restricted their officers club to members of the Hospital Group only. Unable to get into their club, we went to the division headquarters officer's club instead and spent my last night in the rear base-camp drinking and reminiscing.

Hugh was an avid surfer, and he offered to teach my eight-year old son how to surf when he got back home to the San Fernando Valley, where we all lived. I only played volleyball when we went to the beach. No water for me, except to drink or shower.

-    -   -   o   -   -   -

The three days of rest and recuperation (R & R) was really only forty-eight hours, with two half-days traveling to and from our base-camp. The last day at Chu Lai, I slept late again, made a Post Exchange run for things I wanted to take back to the field with me, such as chapstick, sun block, and razor blades. I also purchased presents to send home. We weren't allowed to drink liquor on our last day. At noon we had our last good meal, then we received our equipment and weapons. We packed up, mailed our letters and were ready to head back to Duc Pho.

At 1350 hours, Tuesday, 15 April, we boarded our choppers for our flight back to LZ Bronco. We all had a good time in Chu Lai, but we knew all along it was only temporary.

We were returning to combat and the dangers of patrolling in no-man's land again. It had been fun, but it was over.

-　-　-　o　-　-　-

We didn't have to wait long for something to happen. The day after we returned, on Wednesday, 16 April we were ordered back into the field. In fact, we were returning to the 29 March battlefield site. We were to look for spider-holes and NVA positions located in that area. Lieutenant Terry T. Hodgkinson joined the Delta Dogs as the First Platoon Leader. With his arrival, I now had two officers as platoon leaders and two non-commissioned officers as platoon leaders. One platoon sergeant was a draftee and Sgt. Grimes was a regular army NCO.

We marched past Duc Pho and started searching the old battlefield where we had lost many of our comrades. We loggered there for the night and were scheduled to continue the search the next day. The next morning, I received a radio message telling me one of our helicopters had just been shot down. The crash site was just about 5,000 meters to our northwest. Both Company C and the Delta Dogs were to move to that location as soon as possible, secure the area, and rescue the helicopter crewmembers.

We moved out in two columns as quickly as we could. Company C was closer to the crash site than we were when we got the call for help, and like us they moved to get there as quickly as possible.

After humping for about an hour, we saw some North Vietnamese soldiers running from a hootch just northeast of us. That stopped our march toward the crash site as we started exchanging fire with them. I contacted battalion to let them know we had an engagement with the NVA. Fortunately Company C continued towards the crash site.

After plastering the hootch with machine-gun and rifle fire, the enemy fire stopped. We surrounded the hootch and threw a

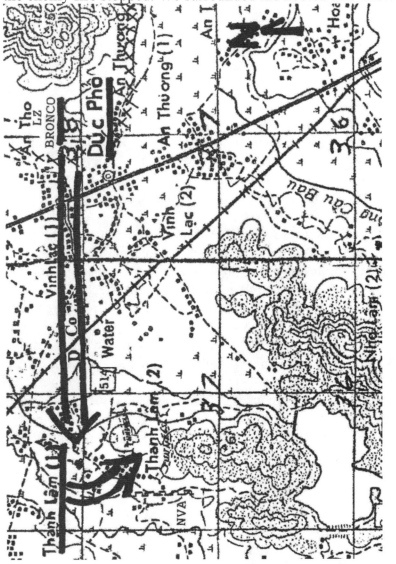

Delta Company visited the battlefield of 29 March.

couple of hand grenades inside. After the explosions, we entered the hootch and found several NVA-uniformed bodies lying on the floor. We also had found a number of dead NVA soldiers outside the hootch.

While searching the area, we heard noise coming from under the elevated hootch. I ordered one of my men to holler, "Den day!" which was Vietnamese for "come out." We waited a bit and after repeating the command, no one responded. I told the man to throw a couple of grenades under the hut.

After the grenades exploded, we checked underneath the wooden floor of the hootch and found a dead NVA soldier, a woman, and a baby. It appeared we killed the enemy soldier and his family. I felt sick to my stomach. I had to remind myself that we were fighting communism in Vietnam instead going through this back home.

We collected the papers from inside the hootch and the documents we found on the nine NVA soldiers we killed. When the rear interpreters looked over the papers, they reported we had broken up an NVA and VC infrastructure meeting.

I was monitoring the battalion radio frequency and knew Company C had engaged an enemy force that was apparently heading for the downed helicopter. In the end, Company C spent a couple of hours fighting the enemy before recovering the downed crewmen. The helicopter crewmembers were okay and later were picked up by another helicopter when the enemy withdrew and they could secure a landing zone.

After another chopper picked up the recovered documents, we were ordered to move west and pursue the fleeing enemy Company C had been fighting.

We were feeling pretty cocky about killing nine NVA and not suffering any casualties. *Yeah, we walked through the valley of death, and we feared no evil for we were the meanest fighting force there,* I thought.

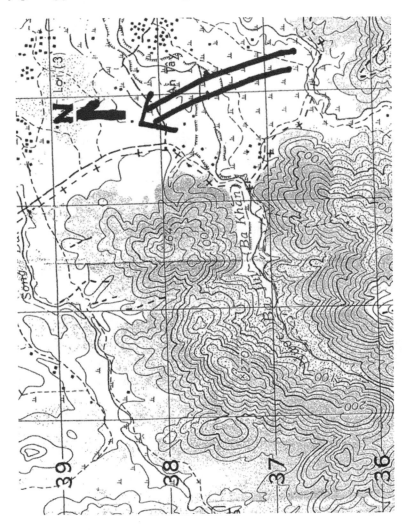

Delta Dogs moving towards the helicopter crash site.

No one felt good about killing the baby and the woman. We certainly weren't there to kill women and children. There is a lot of ugliness in war, and this was a tragic example.

We continued our march under the hot summer sun towards the downed chopper site. When we reached the far edge of the rice paddies, we headed up into the mountains. It was tough going at first, moving up-hill through the trees and thick underbrush. We had to cut a path into the dense vegetation with our machetes to make multiple trails into the high mountain forest. Since our orders were to sweep, we had to cut a dozen paths through the jungle. Once we were in the heavy forest, the solid canopy over us prevented undergrowth from growing on the forest floor. This made our ascent a lot easier. Plus, without the sunlight bearing down on us, it was not as hot. We continued working our way up the mountain throughout the day without making contact with the enemy. I had the men logger for our evening meal. After dark, I ordered the men to move farther ahead to a night logger position. As usual, battalion once again was upset with our delay in reporting our NLP (night logger position) until well after dark.

I knew what every infantryman should have known -- don't show the enemy where you are going to spend the night. The preventative actions we took were validated several months later when I received an intelligence report from the Third Battalion, First Infantry. It reported that between 25 May 1969, and 14 June 1969, the battalion had five nights that defensive positions were attacked by grenades, mortars or enemy fire. These night attacks resulted in six US soldiers being killed and thirteen wounded. Having battalion get upset with me every night was a price I was willing to pay to prevent a disaster. During the time I commanded the Delta Dogs, we were never attacked after we loggered into our night position. This was the direct result of not showing the enemy where we loggered at night.

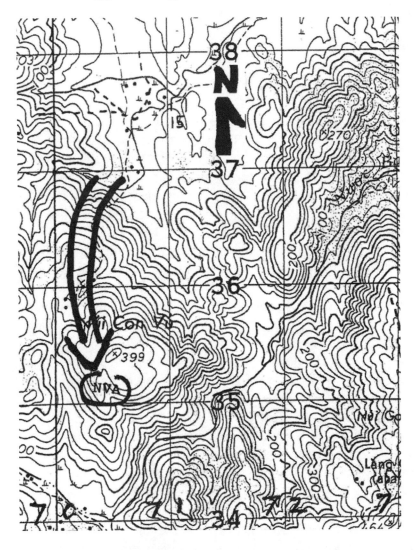

D Company followed the enemy to the south.

- - - o - - -

We spent Friday the 18th of April searching the mountain area for signs of the VC or NVA soldiers. It was hard and tedious climbing and cautious searching, even without the undergrowth. We were on the constant lookout for spike-pits, booby-traps, and ambushes. We found none of them during our search.

The following morning, Saturday, 19 April, we made contact with the enemy. We spread out and engaged them in a running battle. They fired at us while they retreated. We returned fire as we pursued them. Because we were fighting them on their terrain, they were able to move more quickly and didn't have to worry about booby-traps or ambushes. Before the engagement was over, some of my men ran out of 60-mm machine-gun ammunition. After two firefights our ammo supplies were almost depleted.

I had told my RTO to radio battalion when enemy contact was first made. The battalion command and control helicopter was in our area supporting Company A. They flew over us, but the forest was so dense, support could not be provided.

Once we no longer received fire from the fleeing enemy, we cautiously searched the area and found a large enemy complex. The enemy compound was protected by multiple rows of bamboo spikes pointing away from the ten-foot high bamboo fence behind them.

The tall bamboo fence was thick. It was difficult for us to see through it. We didn't know what we would find behind the barrier. When we got inside we were surprised when we found the bamboo wall surrounded half a football-field-size enemy encampment. Inside I counted nine bamboo and thatched buildings. Outside the compound, we found four other similar buildings.

Down the hill, three of the four buildings were connected by a 90-foot long entrenchment. The four hootches located outside the encampment appeared to be fighting positions and sleeping quarters combined. One hootch at each end straddled the trench. A third hootch over the ditch was located about half way between of the other two. The excavation was cut

The bamboo prison wall with spikes pointing outward.

three to four feet wide and at some points came to the forest floor level, presumably to allow a path, which provided a guarded access to the compound. Beside the roadway, the cut dipped to as much as five feet deep.

The main buildings inside the compound consisted of three VC and NVA sleeping hootches, plus two more for prisoners. There was a chicken coop, a kitchen and two workshops. Inside the compound there were two classrooms and a latrine.

Underground tunnels connected the NVA sleeping quarters. The complex also had underground storage rooms in the prisoner's hootches. The size of the buildings ran from 10 by 20 feet for the NVA sleeping quarters to 15 by 25 feet for the prisoner's barracks. The NVA sleeping buildings contained double-decked sleeping bunks.

The prisoner buildings had a single matted surface, elevated three feet above the floor, with two wooden boards running the length of the sleeping area. The boards had a half circle cut out of both the lower and upper boards. When pressed together and locked at one end, they resembled the old New England type head and hand stocks I had seen in history books. Apparently a prisoner had to lie down on his back before they locked his ankles in for the night, and he had to sleep on his back all night long.

It was obvious to all of us the compound was a combination NVA camp and prison camp. The difference between the NVA sleeping huts and the prisoners sleeping quarters were the wooden leg-irons and there were no other furnishings in the prisoner's facility. The NVA buildings had running water through bamboo pipes and the NVA soldiers' hootches had escape tunnels underneath them.

The buildings provided enough room to sleep about 150 soldiers and a couple dozen prisoners. Since the entire camp was empty when we searched it after the gunfight, we

1st Lt. Roger Faust mapping the prison camp, with Pfc. Millard (Midge) Anderson, his RTO, sitting on ground smoking while guarding him.

speculated the prisoners had been working and not locked down when we hit the camp. If they were lucky, they used the opportunity to escape when their captors fled.

In the concealed rooms under the prisoner's hootches, we found 3,000 pounds of bagged rice, 1,000 pounds of bagged salt, 2,000 pounds of dried potato slices, five cans containing 25 gallons of cooking oil, fish, and about 1,000 pounds of fire wood (chopped and bundled), plus other supplies.

Before being sent to Vietnam, I was made aware of the NVA practice of using prisoners as slave laborers. The existence of this camp supported that belief, as it looked to be a broom, hat, basket, and a tool factory. It also seemed like a supply depot for the NVA troops in the area. The prisoners appeared to have made the several dozen Vietnamese type machetes, bamboo canteens and camouflage wheels that we found in the complex.

The camouflage wheel was a double circle of wicker, with two loops of string. Fresh foliage was pushed between the two circles of wicker. An NVA soldier could then stick his arms in the two loops and look like a walking bush.

We also found a large number of spears, crossbows, long-bows and arrows. There were stacks of woven buckets for carrying rice, thatched fans, hats and farming hoes, which must have been made by the prisoners. We found quite a supply of ammunition and uniforms as well. Apparently they took their weapons with them when they fled, but left everything else behind.

Battalion ordered us to map the layout of the complex and destroy everything we couldn't carry out with us. I took a Vietnamese machete, a cross bow, a bamboo canteen, a camouflage wheel, and an NVA uniform as souvenirs. Other men took whatever they felt like carrying. Then we burned the rice, oil, wood, and hootches. As we left, we blew the tunnels

Bamboo Canteen and Camouflage Wheel

shut with C-Four explosives. After setting the compound on fire and detonating the explosives, we moved away from the prison camp. A couple hours later, we found a secure location for our evening meal.

- - - o - - -

My men had become accustomed to not having the night logger position in the same place as where we ate our evening meal. When new men came into the outfit, it would be explained to them why we kept moving after dark and I could see from the reaction on their faces that they recognized its importance. We would try to pick an area that would provide good fields of fire for us and could provide protection from enemy fire. After dark that night, we moved into our night logger position. Once again, battalion was upset with our late location report. In particular, the new commander of the battalion, LTC Elliott, was not pleased with our being late in reporting our night logger position and let me know.

The next morning, we were ordered to move to Company A's location. They were near a clearing where the choppers could pick us up. We were to give the maps and the information we had recorded about the prison camp to the command and control chopper personnel. Then we were to be airlifted along with Company A into an enemy base-camp about 12,000 meters to the west and 17,000 meters to the north of us.

This mission sounded to me like the B-52 bomb assessment mission that was scrubbed because of rain. I was given the encrypted map coordinates so I could check the lay of the land while we were waiting for the helicopters to lift us out of the forest.

I requested that the slicks bring 30-caliber machine-gun ammo and C-rations when they came to pick us up. We had enough water, which we got from the prison camp.

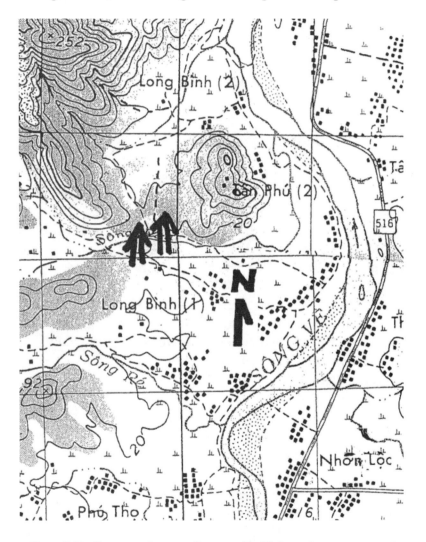

C and D Companies perform a B-52 bomb assessment.

The Huey slicks picked us up and dropped us off into a field of deep elephant grass, thirty men at a time, with ten per helicopter. As we flew into the area, I could not help but wonder if I would land on bamboo spikes hidden in the tall grass. I also wondered if there were enemy soldiers in the mountains on either side of the valley. The choppers hovered about eight feet off the ground, while we jumped out into the four to six-foot-deep grass.

Dropping into the valley didn't make much sense to me, since the enemy placed their base-camps on the hillside, like the prison camp we had just found. The enemy liked to have their base-camps at least one-third the way up the mountain and not closer than one-third from the top. This allowed them to get water from above and left room for the water to flow down and away from their base-camp.

Unfortunately, the army seemed to use on-the-job-training for its command officers. LTC Pritchard hadn't served as an infantry officer in combat before he took command of our battalion, and I don't think LTC Elliott had either. Military officers could read all the strategy books in the world and attend as many practice combat exercises as they could, but the best teacher was combat experience when it came to understanding the enemy. I had begun to see that some officers, if not most in the chain of command, didn't know our enemy very well. This case proved my belief to be true.

After all our men were airlifted into the valley, we spent a hot Sunday searching the valley, but found no base-camp. We did find a lot of big holes in the ground. The huge craters left by our 500 pound bombs were large enough to hold a small house.

I ordered my men to search up the side of the hill, where I knew the base-camp should have been. We found footprints on the side of the mountain around the area where the enemy had run away after the B-52 attack. We didn't find any indication that the strike killed anyone, but I was certain it had at least caused hearing problems for them. When the bombs fell, I could hear the bursts and feel the ground shake even though I was over ten miles away from ground zero. When the mission was declared complete, all of us piled into the choppers, eager to get back to the relatively safety of base-camp LZ Bronco.

-    -   -   o   -   -   -

There were two different types of Field Packs. When in the field, we received one of the cardboard boxes once a month. They had different contents. The following is a list of what the two Field Packs contained.

FIRST BOX: 10 cartons of cigarettes (both filtered and un-filtered), 2 packs of cigars, 2 packs of cigarillos (small cigars with wooden lip holders), 4 plugs of chewing tobacco, 3 packages of pipe tobacco, 2 boxes of match books, 2 packs of flint, and 1 package of pipe cleaners

SECOND BOX: Packages of Chuckles, soft caramels, Charms, Hershey's (with and without nuts), tropical bars, Abba-zabas, M&Ms, writing paper pads, envelopes and pencils.

When we were in the rear area, we had to buy these items at the Post Exchange. However, in the field, we usually received them less than about once a month. We gave some of them to the supply personnel to trade for 60-mm mortar rounds. Ammunition was more useful than candy and tobacco when we were in the field.

-    -   -   o   -   -   -

My company frequency RTO, Specialist Fourth Class Joe W. Dodson, was twenty-four years old when he was drafted on 14 May 1968. He was from a small town in western Kentucky with a population of less than 3,000. Before he was even eighteen, he married his high school sweetheart and worked at the General Tire Company plant in western Kentucky. The early draft didn't include married men, but as the war drug on, married men started getting drafted.

He lived a pleasant yet simple life in the rural heartland of America. Joe was a likable fellow who seemed to have gotten along with everyone in our infantry company. He was also very concerned about the well-being of his fellow infantrymen. He constantly went that extra mile to help those he could. I didn't think Joe could possibly have an enemy in world, except those we were fighting. I thought Joe was the kind of guy we would all want as a best friend back home. Joe was twenty-five when he arrived in Vietnam, he was older than some of the platoon leaders and sergeants. Most of the men in Company D were between 18 and 22. Those who were 24, 25, or 26 were considered old men. Some of the men gave them nicknames, such as 'Pops.' Since I was 36, I was called the 'old man' when I wasn't around.

-   -   -   o   -   -   -

This is a list of those Delta Dog heroes who were identified in this chapter.

Lieutenant Colonel Walter L. Pritchard, Junior, West Point Military Academy 1957

Second Lieutenant Terry T. Hodgkinson, from River Rouge, Michigan

Sergeant Jerry D. Koontz, from Mocksville, North Carolina

Specialist Fourth Class Michael B. Fusillo, from Canastota, New York

Specialist Fourth Class Reginald E. Steele, from Charlotte, North Carolina

Private First Class Andrew L. Bracy, from Mobile, Alabama

Chapter Ten

Sergeant Juan Espinoza
Sergeant David E. Curry

The sweep of the valley found no evidence of a destroyed NVA base-camp, but I never expected to find one on the valley floor where the bombs had been dropped. Once we had completed the sweep of the valley, we returned to LZ Bronco to be resupplied. For the next three weeks we were assigned to be the palace-guards of the Navy Base, called "Gilligan's Island." Gilligan's Island was the supply depot about ten miles southeast of Duc Pho. It was a small facility where most of the supplies used in our sector were brought into the country and stored until they were needed. Guarding this base was a soft job. The grunts of Delta Company were overjoyed with the assignment. We knew hot meals and ice cold drinks would be available 24 hours a day and we wouldn't have heavy packs to carry around the countryside.

Moving into the already-constructed bunkers, foxholes, and fortified barracks for the three-week assignment meant an opportunity to rest and relax. Everyone was in a festive mood as we prepared for the ten-mile march to "Charlie Brown," the nickname for the army compound next to Gilligan's Island.

Early Monday morning, 21 April 1969, everyone was up at 0600 hours, chowed down, and on the Red Ball Highway by 0730 hours. We marched southeast on Vietnam's main highway. Even though it was the country's main highway, it was little more than a two-lane dirt road that ran the full length of both South and North Vietnam. We moved along the dusty road in the early morning heat, one column on each side of the road. It was daylight and we were on a friendly highway so we didn't expect enemy activity, but walking on the sides of the dirt road would give us the opportunity to dive off the road for cover, it needed. We still had to be alert for possible enemy attacks or booby-traps at all times.

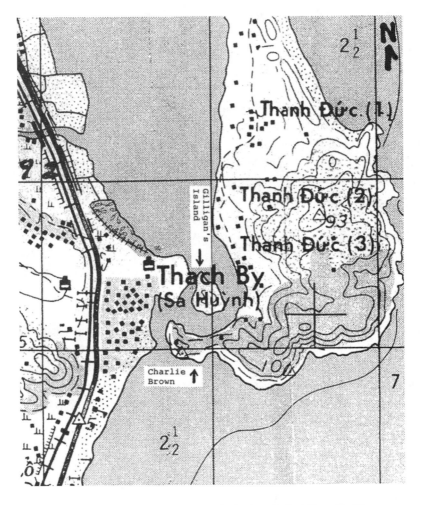

HWY #1, Thach By, Gilligan's Island & Charlie Brown.

It was mid-day when we marched past the barricade and across the bridge that led to Charlie Brown. We continued around the Navy Base and toward the Army's fortified position and continued up the hill and entered the compound. The Army Base-Camp, Charlie Brown, overlooked the entrance to the bay, the Navy Base and <u>Thach By</u>, the local fishing village. My executive officer, supply sergeant, and mess sergeant had arrived at Charlie Brown before us to coordinate everything with the departing company.

My platoon leaders and I were given a tour of the base-camp while the rest of the men sat down to a meal in the mess hall. I made sector assignments that called for two of the four platoons to guard the base-camp. That left one platoon available to patrol and one in bunkers near the mess hall and my command bunker.

The First Platoon, with Lt. Hodgkinson, Sgt.'s Wampler, Scribner, and Taylor, moved out on patrol the following morning. Lt. Hodgkinson left one squad to guard the bridge to Charlie Brown and Gilligan's Island. The other two rifle squads patrolled the valley, the Red Ball Highway, and the hills surrounding the seashore village. Pfc. Vaughn McClendon was the new medic we received for the First Platoon. I had deployed the remainder of Company D in the bunkers around the base-camp the night before.

Located on a peninsula, Charlie Brown was not very large. It consisted of an army signal relay station on the hilltop, a mess hall, a command bunker, and a couple dozen defense bunkers. Other then the narrow entrance at the back of the compound, the entire parameter was protected by high cliffs, barbed-wire and water. The base-camp overlooked the Navy supply depot that lay to the north. The Navy provided their own security.

The Vietnamese hamlet across the harbor from us was a fishing village. The 60-foot long junks moored in the harbor were used for open ocean fishing in the South China Sea. Each junk had a lantern hanging on the front. If they were going to go out for night fishing, the boats were required to be out to sea before 1800 hours and were not allowed to return before 0600 hours the next morning. While at sea during the night, they had to have their running lights on, which for them were nothing more than lanterns, for identification by the US Coast Guard. The Coast Guard boats patrolled the waters and any junks sighted without lanterns to identify themselves were sunk. This seaport, Thach By, was the main supply point for fish in the area, one of the main food staples for the Vietnamese people.

- - - o - - -

I was bringing my journal up to date after the evening meal, when one of the NCO's ran into the company command bunker. "Sir, a bunch of whores are being ferried over from the village," he reported excitedly.

I put my notes aside, grabbed my helmet and rifle, and followed him out of the bunker. We walked towards the harbor side of the base-camp where some of my men had pulled back the concertina barbed-wire making a gateway to a trail that followed a zigzag path down the cliffs to a flat area at the water's edge which was used as an unloading platform.

When I looked over the edge of the cliff, I saw village boys paddling half dozen large circular basket-type boats across the inlet. Aside from the boys doing the rowing, each small boat contained a couple of nicely dressed Vietnamese girls.

When my men saw me, they rushed over and pleaded for me to allow the girls to stay in the compound over night, pointing out the men in the company which just departed had been allowed to have girls stay overnight with them. They all seemed to know about this luxury long before we had ever

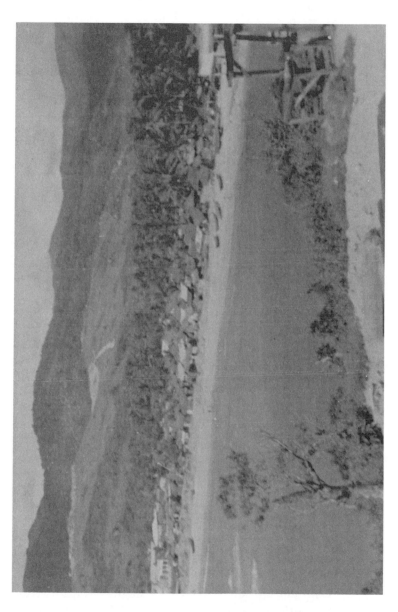

**A view of the fishing village Thach By from
the U. S. Army base-camp Charlie Brown.**

reached the compound. When I look back now, I'm sure that was the main reason most of them were so happy when they heard we would pull a stint as supply guards at Charlie Brown.

I looked at the pleading young faces and considered their plight. As their commander I was responsible for their safety and welfare, and that meant I was sometimes forced to make unfavorable decisions. I was aware that condoms were issued free to the men for their protection. I also realized it was likely some of these young men would not live long enough to enjoy a sexual encounter with a woman back home. These thoughts weighed heavily on me while deciding what to do.

There was also the likelihood that some of these women were VC. After all, this was Quang Nagi Province, just south of the demilitarized zone separating North and South Vietnam. Almost every family had someone on both sides of this war.

I finally made my decision. I yelled down to the boys paddling the boats, and told them not to return to the village until I instructed them to do so. I told all the women to come up the trail and to gather where I waited. I had all my men who were present stand to one side, away from the women because I didn't want anyone mingling until everyone understood the rules.

I sent the men on watch that night back to their assigned positions. Then I said, "Anyone who wants one of these women to spend the night with them, come to some agreement with them after I have finished speaking."

Before I could even finish what I was saying, eye and hand signals were being exchanged between the soldiers and the twelve women. In spite of that I continued, "No woman is allowed in the command bunker or in the perimeter bunkers. No woman is allowed to leave your bunker between now and 0600 hours. Any woman found in the open before 0600 hours will be shot. That's an order. Does everyone understand?"

The whores whispered among themselves first, and then my men and the girls all nodded or answered in the affirmative. Then I added, "Any woman not selected tonight will go back to the village immediately. Now select those who will stay and those who have to return to the mainland. Carry on."

I moved up the hill a short distance and watched the bartering. One of my command group men came over and asked, "Sir. Does that mean none of us can have a woman?"

"No," I said, "it means if you select a lady, you can not sleep in the command bunker."

He smiled and ran down to where the women were bartering with the men. After the selection process was quickly completed, two of the girls were not selected and returned to the boats for their trip back. The boat boys waited eagerly for my command to return to the mainland. The Vietnamese boys knew the boat curfew of 1800 hours was drawing near, and they appeared to be anxious to be back in the village by then. I signaled for them to leave, and they paddled off with the two unsolicited women. Ten of the men retired to their bunkers, each with a woman.

Joe, Cumbee, and I chose to sleep alone. Being married certainly was the factor in that decision. I thought being so close to meeting our maker and not wanting to break one of the Ten Commandments might have also factored into our decision.

-    -   -   o   -   -   -

Before my shipment overseas, I had studied the South Vietnamese culture and learned a good deal about their heritage and customs. One custom, which caught my attention, was the one in which men living in rural areas seldom married beautiful women.

The rural Vietnamese lifestyle was both austere and hard in 1969. Women worked in the rice fields ten or more hours a day. At the end of the day, they returned to their one or two-room dirt-floored, thatched-covered huts where they cooked the evening meals for the extended family. There were no stores, malls, frozen foods, refrigerators, and in most cases, no iceboxes. They didn't have natural gas for cooking or heating water, and in most cases had no electricity. If they had electricity, it was only used for light bulbs. They didn't have radios, television sets, or appliances. In the farm villages, there were no cars or motor scooters and only a few bicycles.

For all those reasons, choosing a wife was a practical matter. The Vietnamese farmer wanted a hard-working woman who would stay around to raise their children. They didn't want a pretty wife who might be tempted to leave for indoor toilets, a bicycle, an icebox, or pleasant working conditions.

Because of the hope for a better life and with little prospect of finding a husband most of the pretty girls gravitated towards the big cities and military bases, where their beauty would be appreciated for the right price. Their goals were simple. They wanted nothing more than to earn as much money as they could and as fast as they could so they were able to provide for their families and themselves. For these girls, prostitution was considered an accepted way of life, and when their beauty faded so would their livelihood.

-    -   -   o   -   -   -

Each day I rotated the platoons' assignments and each night after the evening meal, whores were paddled over, selections made and a few men spent the night cloistered in bunkers with their new temporary companion.

On Thursday, 24 April, the third day in camp, the battalion command chopper flew over our base-camp and reported that one of my bridge guards was observed having sex under the bridge, and that eight kids were on the bridge talking to the other guards. I radioed the platoon sergeant and let him know what had been reported. "I want the situation corrected," I said. "You can let them relax a bit, but don't get stupid."

The following day, Friday, 25 April, the battalion helicopter flew over the camp again and reported that some of my men were swimming in the river. They also reported that a soldier alongside the river had his shirt off and was sunbathing. Once again I was on the radio with a different platoon sergeant ordering that the problem be corrected.

A few weeks before when Colonel Treadwell saw I was giving my men a break to take a swim he didn't complain, because he knew we were in a relatively secure area. My current problem was with the prior battalion intelligence officer (who had become the battalion operations officer the week before) and the new battalion commander. They didn't seem to want the men to enjoy themselves, even when they had plenty of security deployed around them. Consequently, they continued to fly over the area, and the soldiers continued to get me in trouble. The water was just too inviting, and as the different platoons were sent to patrol and guard the bridge, there seemed to be someone who couldn't resist taking a dip during the over 100-degrees day.

Saturday was a repeat of Friday and once again I radioed the platoon to correct the situation. It seemed to me, considering what all these men had been through and would experience in the days to come, someone taking a swim was

311

hardly worth all the attention battalion was giving the incidents.

For the past week I had eaten well, been housed inside a cool bunker during the hot days and had ice-cold sodas available all day long. I loved playing chess and successfully took on a new opponent each day. The best opponent was the Third Platoon 'tunnel-rat,' David Giles. He had been promoted to Sergeant the week before and was now a rifle squad leader in the Third Platoon. David was from Saint Paul, and I was born in Minneapolis. As both our families were from eastern Minnesota, we had a lot to talk about during our chess games.

The following Sunday, 27 April, the US Coast Guard personnel invited the platoon leaders and me out to their boat for a barbecue. A small fifteen-foot long skiff picked us up, three at a time, and took us out to the small US Coast Guard boat used to patrol the harbor and adjacent seaways. They had a hibachi set up on the fantail for barbecuing steaks and corn on the cob. There also was a large, chilled potato salad tray with celery, radishes, and pickles garnishing it. We drank ice-cold beer, ate heartily, and shared our stories with the Coast Guardsmen. These sailors had provided gunfire support in the field for us earlier with their 3-inch gun's high explosive rounds. They had done a good job in supporting us when we were operating in the hills south of the <u>Duc</u> <u>Pho</u> rice bowl.

After we were there for a while, the sea started to get choppy, and we experienced some of the downside of shipboard life. None of the sailors seemed to agree that the violent rocking of the boat was a problem. As the boat rolled, Sgt. Grimes lost his footing and fell, with his foot landing on the half empty potato salad tray. We all laughed, as we looked at the imprint of a size 13 in the middle of what remained of our lunch. It was a good thing we had all eaten already, or we might have thrown Sgt. Grimes overboard.

Because of my fear of water and the sea getting rough, I requested to be taken back to Charlie Brown under pretense of paperwork that was awaiting me. One of the crew volunteered to take me back, while the rest continued to drink and share

**The US Coast Guard boat that patrolled the Thach
By fishing village harbor and the South China Sea.**

what the Coast Guard guys called "sea stories." On the way back, the skiff was almost swamped by a big wave. It might be hard to believe, but I was more fearful on the return trip then I had been during the battle we fought on the 29th of March.

I learned later that when the rest of my men started back on the skiff, it was swamped by a wave that capsized them. Everyone onboard had to swim around the boat while they righted the skiff and bailed the water out. Then, they proceeded back to Charlie Brown, soaking wet. I was very happy I had left when I did. I don't know how I would have survived if I found myself in the South China Sea. That thought alone horrified me.

The next day, Monday, 28 April, Capt. Benson, the brigade Chaplain, came down to conduct worship services. Since he was the only Chaplain in the brigade, he couldn't conduct worship everywhere on Sundays, so we had our worship service on Monday. Benson was a Protestant minister, so some of the Catholic soldiers and I didn't attend the services. He kept his services non-denominational, but I preferred the traditional Latin Mass.

After completion of the services, Capt. Benson asked if the two of us could talk in private. I didn't know what he had in mind, but I hoped it wasn't about the prostitutes. I was in enough trouble with battalion already, and that was not something I wanted them to know about. Since they had made a big deal about the men taking a swim when they had plenty of security around them, I could only imagine how they would react to Vietnamese girls spending the night in the compound with my men.

We walked a short distance up the hill until we were well away from everyone to allow the Chaplain the privacy he had requested. We sat on the hillside and marveled at the beauty of the seaside village below us. We enjoyed the view and talked about insignificant things until the Chaplain felt comfortable enough to discuss what he really wanted to talk about.

Then he hit me with what he wanted to discuss. He asked, "Captain, are you aware that one of your men has requested that his entire pay check and his death insurance go to the Vietnamese girl he fell in love with over the past few days here at Charlie Brown?"

I couldn't believe what he was saying at first. Then, when I thought about our past and possible future situations in the field, it made sense to me.

Capt. Benson had discussed it with the soldier earlier, but he felt like he had been unable to dissuade him. The Chaplain thought I might be able to talk more directly to him and show him the folly in his plan.

I knew when a young man first enjoyed sex, he could think that the powerful feeling he experienced was true love, and certainly these professional girls could be experts in pulling that feeling out of the men.

I assured the Chaplain I would talk to the man. Then Capt. Benson filled me in on the details. The attractive young girl convinced the soldier that the village chief was holding her parents prisoner, and would not release them until she paid him an outrageous amount of money. She told the young man she became a prostitute in order to rescue her parents. If she could get enough money to free them, she wouldn't have to sell herself anymore.

With my assurance that I would try to intercede, Capt. Benson felt better about the situation, and we walked down to the mess hall where the helicopter would pick him up later in the afternoon for the short ride back to LZ Bronco.

That afternoon after the Chaplain left, I took a squad of men with me and visited Thach By. I told the village chief what the prostitute had said. He laughed and told me these

315

girls were not even from his village. They were from <u>Saigon</u> and <u>Quang Ngai</u>. Their parents were never within a hundred miles of his village. No, he was not holding her parents prisoners. He had no prison in which to hold anyone. He pointed out that all arrested Vietnamese were sent to <u>Duc Pho</u> or <u>Quang Ngai</u>. What he said confirmed what I had already suspected. She was conning the young man, and he was naive enough to fall for it completely.

The next afternoon, Tuesday, 29 April, I had a talk with the young soldier. "Have you ever studied European history?" I asked him.

"No Sir," he replied.

"Well, I've studied European military history. I found that a long time ago, before medieval times, the city of Paris, France, was threatened by an approaching horde of barbarians. The Paris nobility and their army fled the city. Only the beggars and paupers were left in the city. They had nowhere to go and no way to get there. So, they assembled at the gate to the city with their pitchforks, hoes, and clubs."

He listened with a wide-eyed look on his face.

I continued, "When the barbarians found there was no army to fight, they withdrew. After defeating an army, they would loot the nobles and collect the weapons of the conquered army. With no nobility or army opposing them, they didn't see much of a payoff for fighting paupers and beggars even though the victory was assured."

The look on his face said, 'So why are you having this discussion with me?'

"Since then, begging has been a respected profession to the Parisians," I said. "When they say 'a fool and his money are soon parted,' they believed this was not a dishonest thing. The beggars believe if you are dumb enough to fall for their con-job, then they justly earn every penny they conned from you."

316

I watched the quizzical look on the young soldier's face turn to a startled look.

"The French colonized Vietnam, and called it French Indo-China. During this time the Vietnamese picked up the concept that if you are dumb enough to give them your money, for any reason, then they deserve the money. You don't deserve to keep your money because you are stupid."

His startled look changed to shock as he finally started to make sense of the connection.

I then aimed at the heart of the matter, "This is the first time you've slept with a woman, isn't it?"

He nodded his head yes.

"Well the first time is quite an emotional experience, isn't it?" I asked.

He nodded again.

"I talked to the Chaplain after he talked to you. We both agree that this experienced woman is trying to take advantage of you. The village chief and I discussed what you had told Captain Benson. The chief keeps no prisoners. The chief and I both think she is a good con artist. Why don't you get her name and address. When you get back home, if you still want to be with her, you can write her. Don't do anything with your money now. Please wait, just in case the village chief, the Chaplain and I are right. Wait until you are home and all your emotions have had a chance to settle down. Then do whatever you think is right, okay?"

He nodded his agreement and then stared off into space. He appeared to be trying to make sense of the world he knew, which had just been turned upside down.

After a minute, I asked, "Do you have any questions about what we just covered?"

He shook his head from side to side, with a blank expression on his teen-age face.

I stood up. "Why don't we head back to the bunkers and join the rest of the men?"

He gave me a faint smile, then we went back to the bunker area and from there we went our separate ways. I don't know how he took our conversation, but there were no more requests for giving his pay or death benefits to any of the ladies-of-the-night.

-    -   -   o   -   -   -

That afternoon, the battalion chopper flew over Charlie Brown. Again I had to listen to complaints about the bridge guards talking to the Vietnamese children from the village. Battalion let me know they didn't want bridge guards talking to the villagers. Battalion wanted the guards to chase the villagers away. I relayed the orders to the platoon leader who had furnished the bridge guards that day and had them chase the kids away.

In spite of battalion not wanting us to talk to the villagers, I felt pretty good that evening, until 2300 hours. My tranquil evening was interrupted by the sound of shouting and screaming coming from outside the bunker. I grabbed my boots, helmet and weapon and left the command bunker. I moved down to where a group of soldiers and girls were gathered.

When I arrived I found a dozen soldiers and half a dozen Vietnamese girls standing around a soldier and a woman, each screaming at the other.

I shouted, "Everyone, shut up! One girl only, tell me what is going on here?"

A Vietnamese girl who spoke English explained, "GI said his woman stole his money when he sleep."

I asked the infantryman who had been screaming at the girl, if that was what really happened?

"That's exactly what happened, Captain," the soldier answered.

Then I asked the accused woman what she had to say. She answered in Vietnamese, and the one who was interpreting told me what she said. "She said, she no take any money."

I told the interpreter I was going to have the soldier search her. She relayed that message to the suspect. The accused girl boldly stepped forward, held her head high and nodded her head, consenting. I nodded towards the soldier, and he proceeded to search her while we all watched. He didn't find the missing money.

I told everyone, "Okay. Here is what is going to happen. I'm going to lock her up for the night and assign a guard to watch over her. In the morning I am going to take her to the village chief and let him handle this. Everyone must return to their bunkers. If any woman leaves their bunker before morning, she'll be shot. Any questions?"

When no questions were raised, I pointed to two soldiers without women and told them, "Apprehend this woman. Everyone else, return to your bunkers." Then I pointed to the girl that was interpreting. "Tell her that I'm imprisoning her for the night and I will turn her over to the village chief tomorrow."

She did and then she returned to her bunker with her soldier. I ordered the two men to place her into a six-foot long storage locker and nail boards across the open side. Then the men took turns standing guard over the captive for the remainder of the night.

In the morning the whores were ferried back to the village. I took the accused woman to the village chief, told him what had happened, and left her for him to punish her as he saw fit.

I knew at this point I would never find out if she did take the money or not. If she did take the money, she could easily have hidden it. When the next infantry company took over Charlie Brown, she could return and collect it. However, the problem wasn't mine any longer. *When one sleeps with dogs, you may wake up with fleas,* I thought.

The platoons rotated assignments again, and I took the opportunity to visit the Navy Supply Depot on Gilligan's Island for lunch. The platoon leaders and I received a tour of

Spc.4's Fred Haney and David Giles (with a Rifle) in front of a Charlie Brown bunker.

the island and had a few beers with the sailors on the island.

Wednesday, 30 April, was an uneventful day. No problems with the prostitutes; no problems with any of my men; no fly-over by battalion, so no complaints about swimming, sunbathing, or talking to the villagers. Wednesday was a peaceful day for a change.

However, Thursday, May Day, was different. Once again, I thought we had caught enemy soldiers in the open, but after double-checking, it turned out that the First Platoon thought they were in a different location than they actually were.

On Friday, 2 May, I had a more serious incident. The Second Platoon made contact with enemy troops. I sent the First Platoon out to reinforce the Second Platoon. The Third Platoon, the Weapons Platoon, and my command group stayed on Charlie Brown. I kept the compound personnel on high alert, because I was concerned the enemy contact might have been a ploy to weaken the defense of Charlie Brown and Gilligan's Island.

After a brief firefight, the enemy withdrew. Apparently, we hadn't caused any enemy casualties, at least not to our knowledge. We also had no injuries inflicted on our men.

Friday afternoon I lost one of my most valuable and experienced NCO's. I stood at the gate saying good-bye to Sgt. Juan Espinoza as he climbed aboard a truck and headed back to LZ Bronco. Espinoza was being transferred to our company rear area because he would be leaving Vietnam on the 7th of June. After spending almost a year in the field, we traditionally let a grunt spend the last month of their tour in the rear. That way they were safe and so were all his buddies. When a soldier becomes a 'short-timer,' he tended to be a little more cautious. Being overly cautious could delay reactions in combat situations and that could get the soldier or one of his buddies hurt.

Friday evening, I stopped the visits by the prostitutes. With the increase in enemy activity in the area, I thought it would be far too easy for a VC woman to infiltrate our compound as a whore. The benefit was no longer worth the risk.

The following evening, on Saturday evening, 3 May, at 2030 hours, the Second Platoon came in contact with enemy soldiers. The firefight ended with none of my men being injured. We didn't find any signs of the enemy being wounded or killed.

I slept lightly that night. There seemed to have been too many enemy contacts around Charlie Brown and <u>Thach By</u>. I felt the enemy might be planning something. It seemed to me to be far too much of a coincidence to have just bumped into them so frequently. Fish and rice were the two food staples of the Vietnamese people. The fishing village provided a fresh supply of fish for our troops, the South Vietnamese Army and probably for the VC and North Vietnamese soldiers operating in the area as well. The enemy soldiers may just have been on a shopping trip when my men bumped into them. For whatever reason, the enemy was more active in our area, and it made me uncomfortable.

Sunday, 4 May, the metal bridge barrier fell apart from corrosion. It was used to block the road that led to Gilligan's Island and Charlie Brown. I requested a welder be sent down from LZ Bronco to repair the steel barricade. The request was refused by battalion. This was just one more example of the lack of support that our battalion provided our company. I knew there were plenty of welders in the battalion maintenance section, the helicopter support company, or in the engineering company at LZ Bronco.

I sent one platoon down to repair the barricade as best they could and had the platoon that was patrolling and guarding the area to provide the security for the repair job. No contact was made with the enemy on Sunday.

On Monday, 5 May, the platoon leaders and I were invited to a luncheon with the village chief. They knew it was getting near the end of our tour at Charlie Brown and the village elders wanted to show us their appreciation for patrolling the area around their village. I knew the Vietnamese used human waste for fertilizer, had no indoor plumbing, and did not have dishwashers to steam clean their dishes. I didn't want to share a meal with them in the village, but it was expected of me.

In the field when I ate from my aluminum mess kit, I performed a quick cleaning process that most of us used while in the field. I rubbed my eating utensils in the dirt, or sand, to remove the food particles. Then I rinsed them with some of my canteen water. Sometimes I heated the water before rinsing the utensils. I knew that my eating utensils were not sanitized, but that is a condition we had to live with in the field. Most of the time, I just ate out of the C-ration tin can or the LRRP plastic bag. Consequently, only the spoon I used needed to be cleaned.

Both my rudimentary cleansing and the Vietnamese villagers' lack of cleanliness were continued concerns of mine. At the luncheon, I ate a little chicken, rice, and cooked vegetables. I didn't eat any of the cabbage salad covered with vinegar and oil. Lt. Faust did and got a serious stomach ailment, which didn't become noticeable until a week later.

- - - o - - -

On Tuesday, 6 May, we all left Charlie Brown for the last time and headed towards the hills to the west of Thach By. After we left, an infantry company from a different battalion took over the Charlie Brown complex. We trudged along the dikes of the fertile rice paddies just outside the fishing village. Then we started the climb up the mountains to the west. Our mission was to move west and look for enemy base-camps.

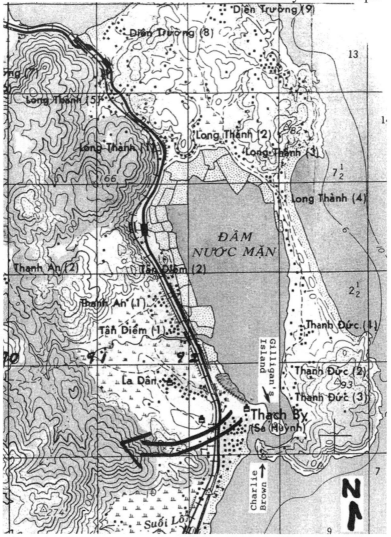

Delta Dogs move into the mountains west of Thach By.

It started getting cooler once we were into the rain-tree forest. However, cutting our way through the dense underbrush required very strenuous effort. In order to search for base-camps, twelve point-men had to cut the dozen paths side-by-side through the jungle growth, each path about ten paces apart. As each of the point-men tired, another man in each squad rotated to the lead-man cutting task. Looking for base-camps on the side of the mountain was much harder than sweeping the flat lands.

Nightfall approached as did the old familiar power struggle. Battalion wanted to know why we hadn't settled in to our night logger position. I believed very much in the necessity to follow orders. I realized that battalion's strategy was to terrorize the enemy to prevent them from moving as soon as it turned dark. I realized I represented someone to them who was frustrating that effort, but I would not needlessly expose my men to danger just to allow battalion to fire off a few random and ineffectual rounds. The bottom line for me was history had shown that Charlie would maneuver at night regardless of what our actions were. Battalion's plan, I felt might have made sense on paper, but had no place in the field. Our men must come first in my mind. We loggered after dark and put out two twiggies to see if we could catch the enemy during their night movements. We did not encounter any of the enemy and the following morning, we continued our search of the mountains to no avail.

By the time Friday came around, we were exhausted and had to medevac four men because of heat stroke. They were Spc.4 Larry Busbee and the Third Platoon medic, Pfc. Bernard Kelly, and from the Weapons Platoon Spc.4 Gordon Gray and Pfc. Robert Murphy. The strain of climbing up the mountain, cutting through the underbrush, and the heat took its toll on everyone, especially right after three weeks of comparative leisure. We also had to call for a water drop along with our next three day's worth of rations. The last several days we had been able to find streams or springs to replenish our canteens, but Friday we hadn't been able to find any water. That may

**D Company searching for NVA base-camps
in the wooded mountains west of Thach By.**

have contributed to the rash of heat strokes we were experiencing.

On Saturday I had to call for another water drop. Before we got the water, the battalion command and control chopper flew over my company to check on why we were making such slow progress. They had us pop smoke grenades to identify our location. When they observed the smoke coming from about one-third the distance down the side of the mountain, LTC Elliott wanted to know why we were on the mountain side instead of the mountain top. I replied that we were searching for enemy base-camps. His voice was raised, almost shouting, as he ordered my company to the ridge top immediately. Once there he ordered me to deploy my men to provide a secure landing zone for his chopper.

I ordered my men to stop their search mission and move up to the treeless mountain ridge. It took us about a half an hour to cut our way up the side of the mountain. Once we were on the ridgeline, I told the platoon leaders to secure a landing zone for the helicopter. When the command and control chopper landed, LTC Elliott ordered me in and it took off.

LTC Elliott blurted out, "Captain, I am going to ruin your career. I am going to give you such a terrible efficiency report that you will never get promoted. No one will want you to serve with them. Captain, I am going to end your career in the Army."

I looked at him in disbelief. I was sure I had covered my back in everything that I did. I couldn't think of what had riled him up enough to reveal his intentions to me in front of witnesses.

"What was your mission, Captain?" LTC Elliott shouted.

"To look for enemy base-camps along the mountain ridge running to the west, Sir," I replied.

"If so, then why were you down on the side of that ridge instead of sweeping the ridge?"

It was clear to me he had no idea what was going on, but I had to be careful with what I said. I knew he had been passed over once and if he was passed over again, it would end his career prematurely. I also knew my reporting our night logger positions late each night made him look like he was not capable of commanding his subordinates when he failed to report his units' night logger coordinates on time.

"Sir, the enemy establishes their base-camps between one-third the way down the side of a mountain to about one-third up from the bottom. That way they can have running water from above that flows down and out of their base-camp. Isn't that right Captain Walters?" I asked the battalion operations officer.

Captain Walters had a pained look on his face as he agreed, "Yes, Sir. He is correct. Base-camps are usually on the hillside, not on the ridge or in the valley."

LTC Elliott's face was already red, but now it turned purple with rage. He hesitated a moment, then barked, "I want you to stop looking for enemy base-camps and start sweeping the ridge to the west. Understand, Captain?"

"Yes, Sir," I replied.

He ordered the chopper to circle back to my company's location. During the return trip, no one spoke to me. I had embarrassed the battalion commander in front of his operations officer and his artillery forward observer, and no one wanted to aggravate the situation further. I knew I had won this battle with the battalion commander, but in the end, I knew I was going to lose this war between us. I had always been on thin ice with the battalion operations officer and the battalion commander. Now it was out in the open. He had stated he wanted to ruin my career.

Little did he know the joke was on him. My career was in engineering, not the army. I had only stayed in the Army, the Army Reserve and the Army National Guard because my older brother had convinced me I was needed. He had said there were a lot of jerks in the world and if all the good guys like him and I got out of the service, then our country would be dependent on a bunch of jerks to keep us free. In the end, I pledged to my older brother I would only stay in the military only as long as I was needed. When I was no longer needed, I would end my avocation and focus on my vocation, engineering.

I gathered the platoon leaders together and gave them the new mission. I didn't share with them what had happened in the chopper.

The supply helicopter arrived with water, cold sodas, and our mail. As we ate and rested before moving on to our new mission, we read our letters from home. Midge let out a soft utterance, "Oh, crap!"

Jimmy Cumbee, Joe Dodson, Vaughn Vandermeer, Lt. Faust and I stopped what we were doing and looked to see what had happened. The six of us always maneuvered, ate, and slept near each other. Since we shared every moment awake or asleep, we would also read our mail to each other.

After a minute of silence, Midge said, "I got a 'Dear John' letter."

We all stopped what we were doing and sat there in silence. We were waiting to see what Midge was going to do or say next. He stood up beside his rucksack, radio, M-16 rifle and helmet that were lying on the ground and began reading the letter aloud.

"Dear Midge, Hope you are doing okay. It has been sometime now since we have left high school, and we have grown apart. I think it is time that we should start seeing other people. Your friend."

We sat there in silence as Midge took her picture out of his pocket. Tears trickled down his cheeks as he stared at the photograph lovingly. There would have been little any of us could do or say to make things better, so we just sat next to Midge, without saying a word. We were all thinking our own thoughts. I was sure the others felt as I did. I wanted to be missed. I wanted to be wanted. I would like to have been appreciated for giving up so much comfort and freedom while serving in Vietnam. Like most of us, Midge had three legs of support that he spoke about often. He relied on his family, his high school sweetheart, and his fellow soldiers. One leg of support had just been yanked out from under him. We were all concerned now about how he would react.

Midge kissed the photograph, then he tore it into little pieces and scattered them on the dusty, hot, barren mountain ridge. He was not yet nineteen years old when he was shot down in the jungles of Vietnam with a 'Dear John" bullet.

We all knew a year was a long time to spend each night, each weekend, and each holiday away from a loved one. There was no doubt it would test a relationship. We didn't have a great deal of temptation to turn our heads away from long term relationships and our loved ones. We were acutely aware, however, that around every corner there were guys back home pursuing our women. The 'Dear John' letter was a shock, but it was not completely unexpected, and we knew our own letter might come with the next mail call.

Midge finally regained his composure, smiled, and said, "A year is a long time to be alone. I don't blame her."

Although I didn't agree with Midge's assessment, I just answered, "Yeah, Midge, you're right." I couldn't think of anything else to say that would ease his pain.

We loggered for the night, after sweeping the ridge. Again we were late in reporting our night logger position. I could only make up so many excuses as to why we hadn't found our night logger position. It was easily justified to say we hadn't reached a defendable position, but battalion was on to my methods. I could justify delaying orders, but they knew what was really going on. I asked myself, *Why the hell didn't they fire rounds in other areas while my troops were moving in our area of operation. They had everyone else's coordinates and knew approximately where we were.* It just didn't make sense to me.

The next day, Sunday, 11 May, Mother's Day, we continued the sweep to the west. While we continued to sweep, Juan Espinoza was on a truck with Sgt. Curry and a truck driver bringing supplies from Gilligan's Island. While traveling north on the Red Ball Highway, a bunch of kids ran along side the two-and-a-half ton truck. They were waving and shouting for gum or candy. While Juan reached into his pack to get some candy to throw to the kids, one of the kids lit a fuse on the bottle bomb he was carrying and tossed it into the truck bed. The explosion caused glass to pepper one side of Juan's body and to hit Dave Curry. The kids scattered before the truck stopped. The streets were empty as the driver attended the two men.

Though I had given Juan a safe assignment, he probably would have been safer staying in the field with us. In Quang Ngai Province we didn't know which kids, which women, or which men were on which side. I suspected some families were on both sides. That way, they were on the winning side, no matter which side won.

We heard later from the rear that both Dave Curry and Juan Espinoza were going to be all right. His wounds meant that he would have to spend the rest of his tour of duty in Vietnam at the hospital in Chu Lai, instead of in our rear at LZ Bronco.

-    -   -   o   -   -   -

Private First Class Millard "Midge" Ray Anderson was from Wooster, Ohio. Midge loved his family, his country and his high school girlfriend. He thought so dearly of his country that he didn't wait to be drafted. He joined the Army before graduating from high school. He finished high school while in the Army. After six months of basic and advanced training, he arrived in Vietnam in February 1969. The 18-year old young soldier, Midge Anderson, was the Radio Telephone Operator for the company Artillery Forward Observer, Lt. Faust. Midge was a fireball of energy who volunteered without hesitation when someone was needed to help the next guy. He felt all the men in Company D were his family members. He joked with them, led them while cutting paths with his machete through the jungle when needed, and got along well with everyone. For a slight young man, not yet finished being a boy, he pulled his share of work as if he were a giant of a man.

-    -   -   o   -   -   -

This is a list of those Delta Dog's heroes who were identified in *this* chapter.
Platoon Sergeant Juan Espinoza, from Texas ** Wounded with glass shrapnel
Supply Sergeant David E. Curry, from Liberty Lake, WA ** Wounded with glass shrapnel
Sergeant Ronald Scribner
Sergeant Lee Taylor, from Muncie, IN
Private First Class Vaughn C. McClendon, from St. Luis, MO

Chapter Eleven

Private First Class John (Jack) Rozow

On Monday, 12 May, my men were up at 0530 hours with their gear packed and ready to move out to another location for our morning meal. It was a morning with no overcast, which meant it was going to be another hot day. We moved 200 meters up the ridgeline and loggered to provide security while we stopped for breakfast. A half an hour later we continued conducting our search for enemy soldiers on the mountain tops. I knew this was an easy assignment, as there wouldn't be any base-camps on the ridge. After we finished the sweep of the ridgeline, we were directed to sweep down the north side of the mountain.

Battalion received a report from the South Vietnamese Regional Force located at <u>Thuy Thach (2)</u> village that an NVA company had moved into the Rice Bowl between our location and Company C. They reported the NVA Company was armed with two 82-millimeter and two 61-millimeter mortars plus a heavy machine-gun and had joined a VC Battalion of over 300 men. We were also informed there was a mass exodus of the civilian population who lived and worked in the rice bowl. The enemy force was identified as the Ninety-Third MF Battalion.

North of our location, Company C was moving south from the Red Ball Highway to about 4,000 meters into the rice bowl and taking up a position as a blocking force 9,000 meters north of us. My orders were to push any VC or NVA soldiers down from the mountainside, up the valley, and out of the rice paddies. It was important for Company C to keep a low profile while waiting for the enemy. They were to engage the enemy forces fleeing our advance.

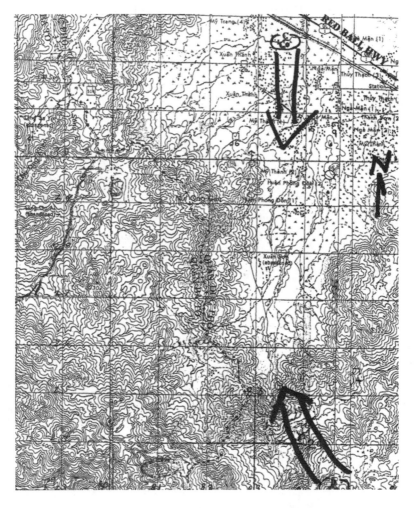

Company C moving into a blocking position in the north, as D Company sweeps down into the valley.

Our move down from the high mountain was slow and difficult as we cut twelve trails through the thick underbrush of the mountain forest. We were to meet Company C if we hadn't made contact with the enemy. Captain Boots Blanks was still the commander of Company C and I looked forward to seeing him again because he still owed me a case of beer.

The Third Platoon moved to the west and then started down the side of the mountain. The First Platoon headed east and then down toward the valley. The Second Platoon headed down the draw between the other two platoons. I had the Weapons Platoon and my company command group follow the Second Platoon.

By 0900 hours we had moved 2,000 meters and were near the last drop-off into the valley. We were ready to start the last leg of the steep decent into the valley by hacking with our machetes through the heavy brush that was under the double canopy of trees on the mountainside. Our hot and tiresome descent was interrupted by transmissions over the battalion radio frequency. Based on new information battalion had received, Company C was ordered to move out of their blocking position and to sweep north in the rice bowl away from us. Company C had complied but had not gone far before they made contact with the enemy.

I told Joe Dodson to inform the platoon leaders what was happening. When the platoon leaders heard what was happening with Company C, they stopped to take a break and consolidate their men in case we were needed to join Company C in the fight.

Before we finished our morning break at 0920 hours, Company C reported their first casualty. We started moving downhill again, still in our sweep formation. Twenty minutes later Company C reported their second casualty. By 1000 hours Company C had reported six wounded, and one soldier killed. While I monitored Company C's reports on the battalion frequency, we continued our descent cutting paths through the jungle. At 1035 hours Company C came under mortar attack, and by noon their situation was desperate. Despite heavy casualties, LTC Elliott ordered them to continue their attack. The count was now 33 wounded and seven killed. One of the wounded was Capt. Blanks. The radio transmission didn't specify how badly he was wounded.

As much as we wanted to help our fellow grunts, we couldn't just rush into the battle without our battalion ordering us to do so, because we might run into friendly fire from our artillery, helicopters or an aircraft bombing mission. I finally got the order to move north as quickly as possible to assist Company C. I got on the radio and gave the four platoon leaders my orders.

"Delta One, Two, Three, and Four, this is Delta Six. We know what it's like to be in a desperate situation. Charlie Company has been ambushed, and we need to do what we can to pull them out, and in order to do that, we have to get off this mountain fast. I want you to move into a column formation and race each other to coordinates Hotel, Whiskey, Mike, Uniform, Echo, X-ray and see which platoon can get there first. Hold at those coordinates while we reorganize. Then we'll move north together to assist Charlie Company. Over."

The four platoons rogered my transmission and got ready to run the rest of the way down the mountain and north in the valley as fast as they could. I was well aware of what I was asking them to do in the 120-degree heat with a full load of gear.

Lt. Hodgkinson requested that his men be allowed to complete their noon meal before heading north. I knew it wouldn't take them long to finish, so I okayed his request but told him to expedite things. The rest of us picked up our gear and raced north. Those of us who had gone through a similar ambush on 29 March wanted to get to Company C as fast as we could. I didn't worry about the First Platoon finishing their meal. I felt once they started moving, they would try to catch the rest of us as soon as they could. We all knew one platoon by themselves would not be enough men to successfully oppose a battalion of enemy soldiers. A full infantry company, like Company C, wasn't able to defend themselves. I knew the First Platoon would want to join us as fast as they could before they engaged the enemy.

Sgt. Grimes' Weapons Platoon was the first to move out. My command group followed him initially. The Second Platoon exited their trail and joined right behind the command group when they hit the flat valley floor. We ran down through a dry streambed that provided a fast, unobstructed path for us. Some of the new men started straggling behind a bit. Somehow, the experienced grunts found extra energy within themselves to keep going even though they were hot and low on water. I hoped the stragglers would catch up with us before we met the enemy.

Sgt. Kepler and his Second Platoon cut in front of us as we raced towards our assembly point. The Third Platoon radioed that they were out of water and asked for permission to stop at the stream we had just crossed to get some water. Since they were already behind the Second and Weapons platoon, I refused their request and ordered them to keep running. Once we reached our assembly point, we could look for a village well or a stream to get water. I pushed them hard because there was little choice.

Some of the Second Platoon men started dropping to the ground or stopping and bending over to catch their breath. As I passed them I shouted, "Keep going. I'm sick to my stomach too, but I am not going to let down those men lying on the battlefield. And, neither are you. Get going."

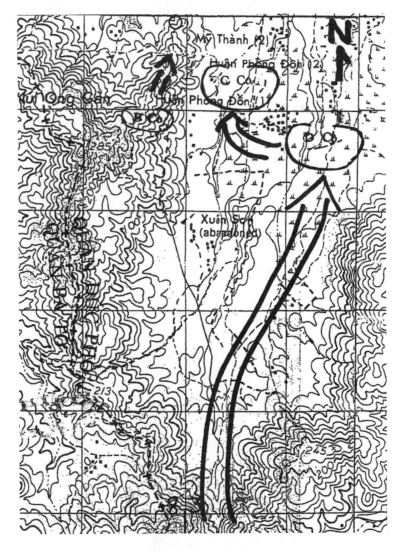

The Delta Dogs running north to assist Company C.

Even though they were hurting, they got up and ran. Those of us who had been under fire in the field could speak with a knowing tone that encouraged those who thought they couldn't move another step to dig down deep and find that added energy. We were running to save as many lives as we could. The memory of how it felt to be ambushed and wanting someone to come to our rescue was still strong. We ran as fast as we could to assist our fellow infantrymen in Company C.

Our command group was ahead of the Second Platoon because they had slowed down to gather their stragglers. At each step our muscles vibrated and our rucksacks slammed against our backs as we continued our five-mile run through the steep mountain trail down into and up the valley.

The cavalry armored vehicles arrived at Company C's location just as we were arriving at our assembly point. My command group succeeded in being the first group to arrive at the abandoned village, which I had selected as our rally point, and we found a water well. We started getting water and taking a break as the other platoons staggered in. While waiting for the rest of the men to arrive, we listened to the reports over the battalion frequency. Only one Company C platoon was still in radio contact, and they only had 15 men left in their platoon. Capt. Blanks had been wounded in the leg, arm, and chest. Company C men were running out of the kill-zone in groups of two and three. The cavalry was searching for survivors who could direct them to wounded men and those killed in the battle.

The battalion operations officer (S-3), Capt. Walters, instructed me to hold at our assembly point until Company B was dropped by helicopter onto the high ground to our northwest. The plan was for us to then sweep to the north in the flat rice paddies while Company B swept to the north along the ridge. Apparently LTC Elliott was only communicating with the B and C company commanders, but for some unknown reason the S-3 was communicating with me. After running full pace in the blistering sun, we were now ordered to sit and wait.

The Third Platoon called to identify their location and to determine where we were. After they transmitted their location, I told them to continue forward for about 500 meters and they would find us in the village. I ordered them to collect any of the stragglers they might find along the trail. They wanted to stop for water, but I instructed them they could only scoop up enough water to drink while they were running. They could get water after they joined us.

After all the men from the First and Third Platoons staggered in and everyone was accounted for, I let the platoon leaders know we were going to move north through the kill zone to help Company C. We would move out just as soon as Company B was air-lifted to their sweep position on the ridge west of the kill zone.

I had expected the Weapons Platoon to be the last unit to arrive, because they were carrying the heaviest load, but to my surprise, they were the third platoon to arrive.

I got a call from battalion. The one platoon from Company C that was still intact was receiving enemy fire while they were attempting to recover the bodies of their fallen men. In response, the tracked vehicles fired their machine-guns at the enemy but the bullets were starting to fall in our location. I called battalion and requested that they give our coordinates to the cavalry. In a few minutes the machine-gun fire stopped.

Lt. Miller's men reported observing enemy soldiers moving south along the ridgeline to our west. I called for artillery fire to saturate the area, but battalion negated the request. They had priority-of-fires and were using the artillery for a preparation bombardment on the ridge where Company B was going to be airlifted. After the preparatory fires were completed, they still would not grant our request because the artillery round's trajectory would interfere with the helicopters flight into the area. Consequently, we had to sit and watch the enemy move south along the ridgeline to our west. I requested fire from fire-base Debbie (named after Colonel Treadwell's daughter) or a fire-base whose trajectory wouldn't interfere with the air lift. Battalion again denied the request.

When the artillery bombardment stopped, helicopter gunships shot up the area where Company B would land. Still no fire was available for the fleeing NVA fighters. As Company B was being ferried in by helicopter, the gunships started shifting their fires to locations around the landing area. Their gunfire started landing close to our location. Once gain, I radioed battalion to instruct the gunships not to fire in our direction. It seemed like my company was receiving more friendly fire than the fleeing enemy. I informed battalion that we were popping smoke grenades so the gunships would know where we were located. Then I ordered the platoons to pop smoke.

LTC Elliott called and asked to speak to me. "Do you have your company in position to start your sweep north?" His question was more like an accusation than a query.

"I've been waiting for orders to move into the sweep position," I explained. "We're still in the assembly area."

"How do you expect to support Bravo Six from that location? I want you next to Bravo Company now!" His voice sounded hysterical.

"Roger that," I replied. "Now that I've received the order, we're on the way."

After I ended the radio contact, I told my RTO, Joe, to order the platoons to move into the sweeping position 500 meters to our west. Then I asked my two RTO's if they had received an order from battalion to move into the location for starting the sweep. Their responses were unanimous - - no one had received a call from Capt. Walters or LTC Elliott telling us to move out of our assembly point.

I thought, *Well you wouldn't talk to me up until now. So, you really don't know what your staff is doing. Well, well, well! What's new Colonel?*

As we were moving out, I came across one of my infantrymen lying on the ground in the shade of a deserted hootch. "What's going on?" I asked him.

He attempted to look as pained as possible. "I'm sick, Sir. I need a dust-off."

"Vandermeer, get over here," I shouted to our medic. "I want you to evaluate this soldier." When I looked at the man, he was sweating so I figured he didn't have heat stroke.

Vandermeer hurried to the soldier and looked him over. "He looks okay to me, Captain. He doesn't have a fever. I think he's just tired."

"Okay trooper, you've got two choices," I said. "You can wait here for the Gooks to find you or you can join your buddies in the sweep." Then, Vandermeer and I moved out to catch up with the rest of the company. The soldier picked up his weapon and followed us. When we caught up with the Second Platoon, he rejoined his squad.

We moved about 600 meters west to get into position to sweep north. My three rifle platoons were moving side-by-side, with each rifle squad in a column formation. It was just after 1500 hours when we started our sweep north. By the time we started the sweep, we had already moved over 7,000 meters (four and a half miles). The company moved forward toward the kill zone with the Weapons Platoon and company command group following the three rifle platoons. We were moving through flat, empty rice paddies, hedgerows, and empty water trenches. We were moving slowly because of our fatigue, and we were also looking for spider-holes, spike-holes, and enemy soldiers.

The gap between Company B and our company widened. When we had started the sweep, Company B was about 300 meters ahead of us. They were moving downhill through calf-high shrubbery. Their advantage of a head start and the downhill movement allowed them to proceed much faster than we were moving. Plus, they were fresh out of the base-camp and were not carrying their backpacks. The enemy was evading Company B's sweep and taking advantage of the gap between us.

We spotted some more enemy soldiers running south on the ridge to our west, behind and away from Company B. We were now within rifle-fire range of the fleeing enemy soldiers, so we maneuvered to the west and engaged them with rifle and machine-gun fire. I reported the contact to battalion. To my surprise, they ordered us to disengage the enemy and to continue sweeping north because there was a gap between the other company and us. By this time, Company B was close to 1,000 meters ahead of us.

What's new? I thought. *There was a gap between us when we started the sweep. They're moving down hill with clear vision, and we are sweeping the kill-zone. Either battalion has no idea what's going on, or this is a set-up to make my company look bad.*

Troop E of the cavalry unit was blocking to the north of us. Along with their normal compliment, they had picked up 35 men from Company C. The cavalry reported killing 17 enemy soldiers. I wondered how many weapons they had captured. If the captured weapons did not equal the number of enemy reported killed, the number killed would be in question. More kills than actually occurred were sometimes reported by officers who wanted to make a name for themselves. The count of equipment recovered was a reasonable way to verify the accuracy of kills reported.

Battalion reported that artillery was now available, and we could call in a bombardment on the ridgeline to our west if we still needed it. I replied, "Negative," because we had moved towards the west and we were too close to the ridge and the artillery barrage shrapnel could hit my men.

As we headed north, we made contact with enemy forces. After receiving AK-47 fire from the enemy, we returned fire. I called battalion and asked if Company B was moving. They replied affirmative. "Can we get them to hit the ground?" I asked. "We are taking fire and can't return fire without putting Company B in the line of fire."

"Negative, Delta Six. Fire only to the north," Capt. Walters said.

"Goddamn," I said. "How the hell are we supposed to shoot north? Did someone forget we are in a war here and we are being shot at? Return fire means we shoot at whoever is shooting at us."

I was glad the send button wasn't depressed: only those around me heard my outburst. We only had two compasses in each platoon. How were my men going to know when they are returning fire to the north?

I was frustrated with the incompetence of our leadership. How could army professionals flying over the battlefield be so blind to what was actually happening? The purpose of the sweep was to engage the enemy. We were engaged with the enemy and ordered to break contact. It seemed LTC Elliott thought the sweep itself was what was important, not what the sweep was suppose to achieve. I had no doubt the frustration could be heard in my voice.

"Look," I told Capt. Walters, "I'll have them maneuver around to the west so they can attack to the northeast."

"Sounds good. Roger that, out," he answered.

I ordered Lt. Hodgkinson to maneuver his platoon to the northwest, and fire into the cane field from where the enemy gunfire came. I also ordered the men in my command group to collect white phosphorus grenades in order to set the field on fire.

Midge Anderson thought throwing grenades was something he would like to do and asked if he could toss one. With my approval he dropped his radio and joined the First Platoon infantrymen. Midge was so excited that he threw his grenade too far and it landed on the other side of the cane field. However, the First Platoon grunts threw their grenades a little closer and ignited the cane field.

When we moved into the burned-out area we found only two enemy undetonated Chicom grenades. We detonated them with C-Four explosives and continued our move north.

Company B reported killing an NVA soldier and capturing one-hundred rounds of 30-caliber ammunition. They also found an abandoned thirty-caliber machine-gun and an extra barrel.

My First Platoon engaged an enemy position and killed an NVA soldier. In the process of searching for other NVA soldiers, as well as protecting our flanks each platoon came under fire from various positions. By the time this battle ended we had killed six enemy soldiers. These weren't easy kills. They involved time-consuming maneuvering and intense fighting.

While we were engaged with the enemy, battalion repeatedly called and ordered us to move to the north because we were not fulfilling their vision of a side-by-side sweep with Company B. I informed them that we were engaging the enemy. They still wanted us to move north along side the infantrymen on the ridge to our west.

As we attempted to comply with the order, we engaged yet another NVA soldier and killed him. Not long after that we fought another NVA soldier sitting behind a Type 54, 60-caliber heavy machine-gun at the entrance to a tunnel. The ten-foot-high and eight-foot wide tunnel was at the bottom of the 20-foot descending dirt ramp. When Pfc. Jack Rozow descended down the dirt ramp to check out the tunnel, he was killed by the enemy. The Third Platoon fired down the ramp and into the tunnel. They tossed grenades into the tunnel entrance. The NVA soldier in the tunnel entrance was killed.

Before recovering Rozow's body, members of the Third Platoon went over to the other platoons to get more grenades, because they had run out. They wanted to throw more grenades into the large tunnel entrance. The machine-gun was still sitting in the entrance to the tunnel on its wheel-based stand and protective front plate, menacingly pointing up the dirt ramp.

I was moving towards the ramp when battalion called again. LTC Elliott was still demanding we move north. I had Jimmy Cumbee tell him that we were in the process of recovering the body of one of our dead infantryman. He ordered us to leave one squad with the dead man and move forward immediately. I passed the word on to the Third Platoon, but they refused to leave their dead comrade.

I arrived at their location and asked who was going to retrieve his body. No one volunteered to go down the ramp with the enemy's 60-caliber machine-gun pointing at Rozow's body. We had seen in the past how deep these tunnels could run and how large the number of enemy soldiers a tunnel could hold. It was a dichotomy situation. They didn't want to leave Rozow's body on the battlefield, yet they didn't want to

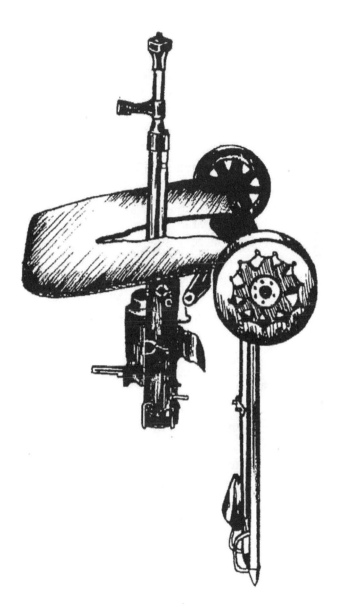

**Chinese Communist 12.7-mm
Heavy Machinegun Type 54.**

temp fate by crawling down an enemy ramp while being exposed to the deadly end of an enemy heavy machine-gun.

This was a decisive moment for me. I had to get them moving, yet I couldn't comply with battalion's order to leave a fallen comrade's body on the battlefield for the enemy to booby-trap again. I ordered the platoon to deploy around the edge of the ramp and above the cave entrance with all their rifles pointing at the tunnel entrance. I took off my backpack and moved towards the top of the ramp. One of the Third Platoon men gave me a rope to tie around Rozow's feet so we could pull the body back up the ramp. Before going down the ramp, I ordered several white phosphorus grenades to be thrown into the tunnel. If there were any more enemy soldiers in there, I thought the burning white phosphorus would get them, the lack of oxygen would suffocate them, or the thick smoke would prevent them from observing me trying to recover Rozow's body. At least I hoped so.

Crawling down a ramp in the face of a 60-caliber machine-gun was not the smartest thing I ever did, but I felt it was necessary. Most of us would go through hell and back to recover a fallen buddy's body. However, the machine-gun at the end of the ramp stopped Rozow's buddies from recovering his body that day.

When I started crawling, Sgt. Robert C. Reed, the rifle squad leader, and Pfc. Midge Anderson joined me. We crawled down the ramp, while Sgt. Kepler and his men kept the cave entrance covered. The three of us brought white phosphorous (WP) grenades with us. We did that because the grenades thrown from the sides didn't make it into the mouth of the tunnel very far.

Midge pulled the pin on his WP grenade and threw it deep into the tunnel. He did such a good job Sgt. Reed tossed him another grenade. He pulled the WP grenade pin and tossed the

Sgt. Reed on the left talking to Pfc. "Doc" Kelly.

second far into the tunnel. He was doing so well with his grenade tossing, we let him throw all our grenades for us.

As the dense white smoke belched out of the tunnel entrance, Midge crawled forward and tied the rope around Rozow's legs.

As he backed out, Reed and I kept our M-16 assault rifles pointed at the tunnel entrance. We edged back up the ramp and across to one side of the ramp. Some of the men joined us as we pulled Rozow's body up the dirt ramp. His squad members wrapped his remains in a poncho and carried the shrouded body, his weapon, and his rucksack away from the tunnel.

I had already ordered the First and Second Platoons to move north while we recovered Rozow's body. As they moved in that direction, they found a deep dry water-way trench that was filled with spider-holes and caches of enemy equipment. It proved to be a big find. Counting the weapons we took from the NVA soldiers we had killed and the equipment we found, we captured two AK-47 assault rifles, one Chinese Type-54 sixty-caliber machine-gun, three M-16 assault rifles, two M-79 grenade launchers, four M-72 Light Anti-tank Weapons (LAWS), one machete, one Bangalore torpedo (bamboo poles stuffed with explosives), four Claymore mines, four RPG rocket rounds, 18 rounds for the 61-millimeter mortar, 250 rounds of AK-47 ammunition, 65 rounds of machine-gun ammunition, 15 US rucksacks full of equipment, three US helmets, five NVA cleaned and neatly pressed uniforms, an NVA medical supply kit, an NVA officer's map case stuffed full with documents, plus other items such as ammunition magazines and shovels.

I joined the men in the trench, looked at all the supplies we had captured so far, and reported the large amount of enemy weapons and equipment we captured to battalion. As it had been throughout the day, LTC Elliott seemed irritated with the delay. He did not seem to care about enemy contact or the capture of enemy equipment. Battalion appeared to have but one interest -- to carry out the joint sweep, even to the extent of letting the enemy flee to the south along the ridgeline. I believed our kills that day would have been much greater without his interference.

Since what I believed to be stupid orders were becoming typical of battalion, it was no surprise when we were ordered to carry both Rozow's body and the equipment captured with us while we continue the sweep. I advised that it would slow our advance to a crawl. LTC Elliott ordered me to leave one platoon with the body and equipment and to move out immediately to continue the sweep.

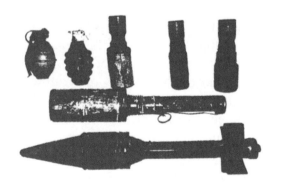

Some of the weapons captured.

One of the men (who had burned his hand on his hot machine-gun barrel) and Lt. Faust (who was running a 104 degree temperature) remained with Rozow's body and the captured equipment. Later, when the recovery of the captured weapons and the body were recovered by helicopter, both of the men were flown to the rear.

As we left the Weapons Platoon and moved forward, we saw many NVA sandal prints heading south and southwest. I saw little point reporting the find, but I radioed the information in anyway. As expected, we were ordered to continue sweeping north.

I received a radio transmission from the Tactical Air Controller who was flying over our battlefield in a L-19 Bird-dog (Piper Cub style light observation airplane). He reported that two Marine jets were coming in, and he wanted to know if I had any targets for them. Because we were so close to the enemy, I was concerned with the type of ordinance the jets were carrying. "Napalm," the Air Traffic controller said. "Each one is carrying napalm and two-hundred-fifty pound bombs."

I did a quick conversion of the map coordinates of the ridgeline south of us, which the NVA had been using as a get-away route. I sent the coded coordinates to the air controller. Company B was at the northern tip of the ridge-line to our west, and we were almost 1,000 meters up from where we had first observed the fleeing enemy soldiers.

The Phantom II jets screamed down and swooped up the ridgeline, dropping their napalm along the path the fleeing NVA had taken. They circled around and then made a second pass, dropping their bombs on the west slope of the ridge they had just napalmed. The ground shook under us, as they exploded to our southwest.

I ordered the men to move slowly, not only because of the battlefield condition, but also because time was still needed for the helicopter pickup of Rozow and the captured weapons and equipment. The Weapons Platoon stayed behind for the pick-up. I was moving slowly because I didn't want to leave one small platoon alone in the kill-zone.

A chopper landed and retrieved the body, captured equipment, and the two injured men. After the chopper left, the Weapons Platoon destroyed the Bangalore torpedo, mortar rounds, and RPG anti-tank rounds we had captured. I hoped the chopper would bring the water, rations, and radio batteries I requested from my supply personnel in the rear, but no supplies were brought out for us by the helicopter.

I radioed my company rear personnel and asked where our water and supplies were. I was informed that LTC Elliott's battalion command and control helicopter was bringing them out to us.

That's all I needed, I thought. *Haven't enough things gone wrong here today?*

It was pretty clear to me the battalion commander and his operations officer didn't want anything to slow down our sweep north. They didn't want us to fight the enemy if that would slow things up. They were even willing to abandon Rozow's body if it would speed up the sweep. I was sure they didn't want to resupply us with the much needed water, radio batteries, grenades, and rations because it might slow down our sweep. It reminded me of the English during the Revolutionary War who were more concerned with keeping ranks during battles. Our American Minutemen were more concerned with shooting their enemy, the English soldiers.

After we ran down from the mountain to assist Company C at noon, we were ordered to sweep with the infantrymen on the ridge just after 1500 hours. We battled for over four hours,

353

moving over 1,000 meters through the kill-zone. It was after 1900 hours, and it would soon be dark as we continued our sweep north.

A little later, about the same time the Weapons Platoon was about to join us, I received a radio call ordering us to move to the high ground to our west. We were to join Company B and set up joint night defensive positions on the northern tip of the ridgeline. As we snaked up hill towards the location of Company B, I monitored the battalion frequency. Company B hadn't ordered supplies, and they requested water, ammunition, rations and batteries be brought out for their unit. To my surprise, I heard the command and control helicopter report that LTC Elliott was en route to resupply them with the supplies they had on board.

I immediately got on the radio and told LTC Elliott that we were out of water, food, ammunition and batteries and we needed the supplies our rear echelon people had sent out for us.

"You'll be taken care of," he chided me over the radio. "Bravo Six is already in their defensive position, so I'm giving them the supplies we have on board. You'll be taken care of once you're in your defensive position and have secured your area."

We had been moving all day long, for over fourteen hours. After four hours of fighting, we had expended most of our ammunition and smoke grenades in our afternoon battle. We had run out of water and needed fresh batteries for our radios. We were starting to feel the weight of the long hard day. It was already getting dark and I knew when we reached our night defensive position there would still be a lot of digging and defense preparation to perform before we would be resupplied.

The sun had already set a little after 1900 hours, and the moonrise wasn't until 0358 hours. The moon cycle was in its last phase, so even if it had been up we would have very little light. The darkness made the trip slow and hazardous as we dragged ourselves up the steep side of the ridge, trying to watch for spike-holes, booby-traps, and possible enemy soldiers.

As we climbed up the steep hillside in the dark, I thought of the score for the day. Company B had killed three NVA and captured four enemy weapons, two machine-guns and two assault rifles. The cavalry E Troop and the platoon from Company C had no confirmed body count NVA kills and had captured no enemy weapons, although they had reported seventeen kills. The Delta Dogs had killed nine NVA soldiers, captured seven enemy weapons, destroyed three more enemy weapons, and captured a large quantity of enemy ammunition and supplies. In doing that, we had received only one casualty. We fought a tough four-hour battle from 1500 hours until 1900 hours and came out pretty clean. As a reward for our efforts, we couldn't logger until after dark, and our supplies were being given to another company.

As we continued up the hillside, I could see flares illuminating the command and control chopper resupplying of Company B. The company was not at the tip of the high ground like I had been told, but they were about 500 meters back up the ridge. Running almost west of their location was a thirty-foot-high earthen dam with a concrete bottom and spill ways. We trudged up the stream bed and then up the dirt dam berm in the dark. Behind the dam was the concrete basin that was not shown on the map. It ran about 100 meters west. The dam was 200 meters long, running north and south. It looked like we had a long hard route ahead of us, and it was already late.

I radioed battalion and asked if we had to make physical contact with Company B or if we could take up a defensive position where we were. I was told we had to make physical contact and form a defensive position with them. That was not good news. If we had to maintain contact with Company B, moving before or after meals would not be an option.

We continued our trek along the dry part of the concrete basin, beside the stagnant water until we finally reached Company B. They occupied the only piece of dirt in the cement filled basin, and were deployed in a half circle with the backside of their perimeter overlooking the hard surface of the basin.

As we moved into Company B's location, I radioed them to find out where our supplies were. They told me only their own supplies had been received, but they had nothing for us.

We had not taken our defensive positions yet. As we were standing on the cement, completely in the open, a parachute flare popped in the sky above us. The bright flare illuminated the sky and exposed all my men.

My men dropped to the concrete. The infantrymen in Company B had already positioned themselves behind the rubble of the broken terrain, and there was no place for my men to hide.

I lost my cool and grabbed the radio mike as I yelled, "Goddamn it! Stop dropping those flares over us. You are exposing my whole company."

LTC Elliott got on the radio and replied, "If we don't light up the area, the NVA in the area will get away in the dark."

I was shocked when I found out it was LTC Elliott's chopper which was dropping the flares. I replied, "The NVA are hiding in the brush. The flares are exposing my men because we don't have anywhere to hide."

He responded, "Have your men dig in, then they won't be exposed."

"This is a concrete dam we are in. We can't dig in. I need to move my people out of here. Can we move or do we have to maintain contact with Bravo?"

He changed our orders, "No," he said. "You can move to a location where you can dig in."

I rogered his message and quickly moved my company out of the dam's basin to the mountain ridge to the south. After we arrived at a defensible location, I ordered the platoons to spread out and form a night logger. The company was well versed at moving into a logger position in the dark. Some of the men wanted to dig in under the light of the flares, but I wouldn't let them. The men could see what they were doing, but so could the enemy. We lay on the ground, without water and with little ammunition, as the command and control chopper continued dropping parachute flares well into the night. No enemy was sighted.

I burned with rage at my incompetent leader. No one believed war was going to be a pleasant thing. However, for our own battalion officers deliberately making this war worse for the sake of their own careers was unconscionable. I had to protect my men as best I could and not let them know how their battalion commander and former company commander had treated them so poorly. I figured if my men knew, it would only increase the adverse relationship with battalion. I wasn't sure if LTC Elliott was acting in a punitive way towards D Company because we were continually late reporting the logger positions, which in turn made him late reporting to brigade, or the fact that I exposed his incompetence in front of his subordinates when he showed his lack of understand of enemy tactics the day he threatened to ruin my career when I had correctly been searching for enemy base-camps. There wasn't much I could do about it, except continue to use good tactical techniques.

I inflated my air mattress to keep the little creepy-crawlers off me. I took off my boots, changed socks, got on the air mattress and lay with my head against my rucksack watching the flares light up the night. Cumbee and Joe were under their ponchos coding our coordinates so they could report our night logger position.

I was dead tired after the five-mile run, the day-long maneuvering, the night trek to the basin, and then our move out of the basin to a more defensible position. I was also emotionally drained from the continued harping and, what I believed to be, incompetent leadership of our battalion command.

I was tired, confused, and angry as I watched the flares float down. I'm sure LTC Elliott felt what he was doing was important. That was the most disturbing thing of all. He had no clue about what was happening, and he was our leader.

As I lay there, I thought about how much I missed LTC Pritchard. He was a commander who cared about his men and the Vietnamese people. He knew how to succeed in killing the enemy, and capturing enemy weapons. He understood the enemy and how to deploy his troops. The difference between the two commanders was like night and day. All officers came out of similar officer training, but each was different in their preparation for combat, their knowledge of the enemy, and how to deploy forces. I found it hard to believe LTC Elliott underwent the same training that LTC Pritchard and I did.

-   -   -   o   -   -   -

The importance of capturing enemy weapons had been etched into my mind by a story a sergeant had shared with me during my jungle warrior training in Panama. He told me, "Many NVA and VC soldiers don't have rifles to carry. The Ho Chi Minh Trail jungle supply line was a long hard trek from North Vietnam, through Cambodia, and into South Vietnam. The enemy had to carry their weapons, ammunition, or military supplies up and down the mountains and through the jungle. It took a lot of ammunition to wage a year's worth of battles. Consequently, more ammunition was carried south than weapons."

He explained, "When the enemy attacked us, some enemy soldiers are weaponless. The NVA soldiers without weapons snatched the weapons of their fallen comrades or from our fallen US soldiers."

The sergeant told me about one of his missions along the Laotian border. "I was walking along a trail when our patrol was ambushed. When the enemy attacked, I was knocked to the ground by the rushing enemy. Most of my comrades were killed by the initial burst of gunfire. I lay still, as if dead. One of the enemy soldiers grabbed my rifle and ammunition belt, then ran off, thinking I was already dead. After the attack was over and the enemy was gone, I checked my buddies to see who could be saved. None of them had any of their weapons or ammunition belts. They had all been taken by the enemy."

I remembered his story and was determined to deprive the enemy of their weapons and stop them from capturing any of our weapons.

-    -   -   o   -   -   -

As I started dozing off to sleep, I heard the familiar sound of Spooky, the multi-machine-gun propeller-driven airplane that also had a searchlight mounted on it. They flew at night, when Charlie was on the move. They circled our area and sprayed it with a rain of bullets for long periods of time. I moved over to Cumbee's position and listened on the battalion radio frequency. Spooky was asking for the coordinates of the target upon which he could fire. I got on the radio and called battalion, offering to provide the coordinates.

"Negative," LTC Elliott said. "Bravo Six will direct the fire."

"I've worked with Spooky before and I'm familiar with their procedures," I said.

"Negative," LTC Elliott said. "I pointed out the target areas to Bravo Six when I resupplied them. They will direct Spooky."

Incompetence struck again! I thought as I tried to fall asleep. I was parched and thirsty. The unquenched thirst reminded me again that LTC Elliott had given our water to Company B. As the anger within me swelled, the men around me took turns sleeping and keeping watch as the flares popped and bullets rained down on the valley below us.

-    -   -   o   -   -   -

The next morning we were up and awake by 0600 hours on Tuesday, 13 May. Before breakfast I had each platoon select three strong men and asked them to join me. I thought if Company B had our supplies, they would be labeled 'Co. D.' My RTO's, twelve men and I climbed down the hill into the valley below to check the containers the other company had been supplied.

The night before, Joe had fallen down the trail when we were climbing up the ridge in the dark. He had hurt his pride more than anything else. During the early morning trek, Joe took extra care not to fall again as we slowly edged our way down the steep hillside. We followed the dry stream bed that led to the outer edge of the dam. When we reached the dam, we climbed up and over the outer dirt berm and onto the hard concrete. We walked along the dried basin, past the stagnant pool of water toward Company B's location.

Each company operated a little differently. We found the men of Company B eating their breakfast in the same location they had spent the night, and where they had eaten their supper the night before. They hadn't dug in since they hadn't brought their rucksacks and entrenching tools with them. I thought this was very dangerous, but I couldn't save the world. I could only save as many of my men as was possible.

When I got to the company commander, I asked where our supplies were which had been dropped off the night before. He said no supplies had been dropped off for Company D. He said LTC Elliott had only dropped supplies off for Company B.

I walked over to one of the partially filled water containers with "Co. D" marked on the side of it with an indelible marker. I had my men take the almost empty collapsible plastic container. We walked around to each of the platoon's positions and took all the water containers with "Co. D" marked on them. I also had my men collect all the C-rations boxes with "Co. D" marked on them that hadn't already been consumed. I had requested three meals for each of my men. Company B soldiers had already eaten two of the three meals. We took the remaining C-rations. I also found boxes of grenades, M-16 assault rifle ammunition and smoke grenades with "Co. D" marked on them. We took them also.

The Company B soldiers weren't happy that we took the supplies that were marked Co. D, but they didn't try to stop us. Nor did the fresh uniformed, clean shaven men dare question a dusty, grim-looking captain backed up by a number of pissed off jungle fighters.

We returned to our logger position with what we gathered. Of the fifty gallons of water we requested, all but six gallons had been consumed by Company B. Each of my men took about eight ounces of water so there would be enough for everyone. Having been out of water for over twelve hours, we were very thirsty, and we all drank the water right away. Now we were out of water, but we weren't quite as thirsty.

Battalion radioed us with the operation order for the day. We were to link up with Company B, sweep southeast, and then sweep south through the valley we had swept through the day before.

I called the battalion operations center and reminded them we were out of water because our water and rations had been delivered to Company B. Without water or rations, we were not going to get far sweeping in the hot sun.

Battalion informed me to get water out of the pond in the reservoir. I snickered derisively, because I knew Company B was loggered right next to the pond which battalion wanted us to use, yet they gave them our water so they wouldn't have to drink the polluted water. I replied that the water was stagnant and not fit for human use. The S-3, Cpt. Walters got on the radio and instructed me to use purification tablets and the water would be drinkable. I told him the scum in the pond was so thick purification tablets would never make it drinkable. Then I ordered my men to move out, knowing battalion wasn't going to bring us any drinking water.

We moved back down through the basin, almost gagging as we marched past the foul-smelling, polluted pond. We moved down to the valley where the cavalry troop and Company B were spread out and ready to sweep the valley. I knew we would soon come across a well or a stream where we could get some water. I also figured when we stopped for water, battalion would use it as an opportunity to get on our case again about not moving fast enough during a sweep. It was pay-back time for battalion. The Delta Dogs were operating with the sister company which had knowingly stolen our water and a battalion staff who knowingly wouldn't provide us with water. One might think we were all on the same side, and we should be helping each other, not using petty tricks to diminish the effectiveness of our own forces. I wasn't mad at the other infantry company. Battalion had supplied them in the darkness of the night. They were sent to the battlefield without their field gear and C-rations. What they did is probably what we would have done if our roles had been reversed. At least I told myself so.

-　　-　　-　　o　　-　　-　　-

As we moved on, I had a flash back to the year before. I was working in an air-conditioned building at a computer company in California. Several vending machines were scattered throughout the plant with ice cold sodas, ice cream bars, donuts, and cold milk available twenty-four hours a day. What a difference a year made. I was dehydrated, covered with grime, hadn't taken a shower for over a week, and my throat was parched raw by thirst.

My lips were cracked due to sunburn. So were my cheeks. I could look at the face of one of my men and see the light tan and red skin peeking out of the cracks in the dark tanned cheeks. These were not nice, evenly distributed beach tans. These were field-hand tans earned after being exposed to the hot blistering sun day after day. The faces of my men showed the harsh conditions they had been through. Life as an infantryman in Vietnam was the complete opposite of the life I had enjoyed just the year before.

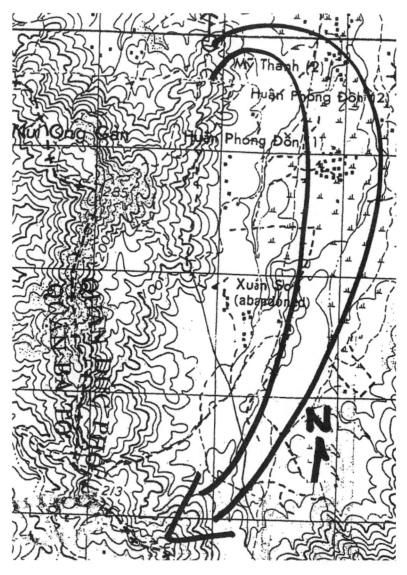

The Delta Dogs sweeping south to the mountains.

Delta Company was spread out on-line with four platoons abreast, covering a 900 meter front. Company B was next to us, intermingled with the tracked vehicles of E Troop. We swept about 600 meters when the command and control chopper flew overhead. The chopper radioed that they had some C-rations for us. However, they couldn't bring us out any water until we gave them the ten empty collapsible plastic blivits we had. The chopper landed and dropped off the C-rations and the smoke grenades we had ordered the day before. After they took off with the empty water containers, we found a stream. We greedily drank the stream water and filled our canteens. While the men were drinking from the stream, I had the C-rations distributed to all the men. I carried both a pint-size and a quart-size canteen, as did most of the men. Some preferred to carry two quart-size canteens. Juan Espinoza wasn't with us now, otherwise he would have been very happy with just a case of beer and a pint-size canteen of water. I missed the jolly sergeant already.

We moved out again, sweeping to the south. Some of the men commented they wished we were sweeping the area Company B was sweeping. That was the area we had swept the day before, and we knew where the tunnels and caves were located. However, battalion didn't take suggestions from the line companies well. We had to do things their way, no matter how much sense they didn't make. We knew there was a burned Chicom 60-caliber machine-gun and some burned AK-47 assault rifles in the cave where Rozow had been killed. After we had recovered his body, battalion ordered us to move out before we had a chance to recover the weapons we had damaged with our white phosphorus grenades.

While we were sweeping, we heard LTC Elliott ask why the tracked vehicles were moving in a column when they were supposed to be sweeping. The cavalry platoon commander replied they had swept the area while they were on their way to join Company B. I chuckled to myself as I heard LTC Elliott roger their message. While moving down from the high ground where we had spent the night, I had seen the cavalry moving in column formation en route to join Company B. I knew they hadn't swept the area earlier as reported, and were just placating the battalion commander who had been grounded during the initial movement.

For the remainder of the day, I listened on the battalion radio frequency for reports of enemy caves, tunnels or weapons being found. I figured the cavalry would probably sweep the battlefield the same way they swept on their way to join Company B - - not at all. I seriously doubted they would report finding the badly damaged weapons we left in their area during combat the day before.

We continued our sweep for the rest of the morning. When we came to the end of the valley, my low expectations for E Troop's performance proved well founded. They failed to find the caves, tunnels and destroyed weapons. Both units reported finding nothing.

Companies B and the Delta Dogs were ordered to continue the side-by-side sweep up the flank of the mountain at the southern end of the valley. We loaded up on water again from a valley stream before we started the hard climb up the mountainside on the hot, cloudless day. One of my men found a 250 pound bomb that was dropped the day before and which hadn't exploded. I reported the find to battalion. Both battalion and Company B wanted to know the exact location of the bomb we were going to detonate, so they would be sure that Company B and the cavalry were over 500 meters away from the explosion. I coded the coordinates and sent them to all the units.

From our location part way up the mountain, I could see where Company B was located. It appeared because they didn't bring their rucksacks and field gear with them the previous day, we were the only company moving up the

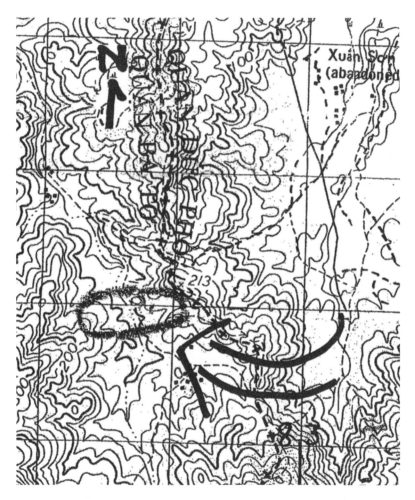

Delta Dogs moving into the mountains west of the battlefield of 12 May 1969.

mountain. They were ordered to continue up the mountain beside us and their field gear would be flown out to them. They reported they were advancing up the mountainside, however they did not advance as directed. Since there was no command and control chopper in the air, they waited in the valley for the resupply choppers to bring out their equipment.

I ordered some of my men to string primer and detonating cord a good distance from the bomb. C-Four explosives were attached to the bomb. We had both electrical and burning fuse activated blasting caps. We used the burning fuse so we wouldn't have to climb back down to recover the electrical wires. Once we were clear of the explosion impact area and the other two units had moved or taken cover, my men laid out the fuse and moved away from the detonation area.

We continued up the mountain to clear the area. When I looked back down into the valley, I saw that Company B hadn't moved in the last hour. I radioed them and asked if they were going to move before we exploded the bomb, and if so, in which direction.

Company B reported back over the battalion radio frequency that they were moving along with us on our flank. After arguing with them and battalion for a bit, I finally understood what they were doing. Company B was reporting they were moving with us when in fact they hadn't moved at all. It appeared that without their field gear they didn't want to move off the flat valley floor. If they did, they might not be able to be resupplied by helicopter, but they did not want LTC Elliott to know they had not obeyed orders. With the battalion helicopter on the ground in the rear, battalion couldn't verify any of our unit's location. I rogered their last report and told them to take cover, we were going to blow up the bomb.

My men lit the fuse and we took cover down in a draw on the side of the mountain. We heard the loud explosion of our demolitons and then we felt the vibrations of the louder explosion of the bomb. The earth and shrubbery shuddered, and debris fell as we braced ourselves along the side of a slow running mountain stream.

I told the men who detonated the bomb to join us in the draw where we had discovered a stream before the explosion. It was a hot day, with no wind blowing. I wanted to be sure everyone was watered down and had full canteens before we continued the climb up the side of the mountain. I put two purification tablets in each of my canteens, and shook them. After letting the canteen settle, I drank greedily. I was still dehydrated, and it seemed that I was sweating moisture out of my body as fast as I was taking water in.

As a rule, I put one purification tablet in the water if I was filling the canteen with fast-running water that we found in the field. If it was slow-running water, I used two halazone tablets. Three tablets if it was clear standing water. I added four if the water was still and cloudy. It made the water taste funny, but safe. If I used rice paddy water, I went overboard with the purification, adding five or six tablets and then let it settle before drinking from the canteen. Needless to say, the fresh water brought out to us from the rear was the best and safest.

Before the demo team could join us, they called and reported one of their team members, Pfc. Aue, was suffering from heat-stroke. I asked if he was sweating. They radioed back "Negative." I sent Spc.4 'Doc' Vandermeer back to join them and had Cumbee call battalion for a medical evacuation. Joe, Jimmy Cumbee and I were also feeling the heat. We had stomach cramps and felt nauseous.

The battalion radio operator wanted more information before dispatching the medevac helicopter. We called Vandermeer with the request. He reported Aue had passed out but was now conscious. He had a temperature of one-hundred and four. They had taken his equipment and jacket off and were watering him down. Vaughn Vandermeer confirmed that Aue wasn't sweating and required immediate evacuation.

Cumbee relayed the information to battalion. They rogered our request and told us to secure a landing zone for the chopper that was on the way. The chopper landed within ten minutes, and Aue was loaded aboard. They stuck an IV (intravenous infusion of liquid) in his arm to hydrate him. They iced him down as they took off to lower his body temperature. Ten minutes after the helicopter medics got to him, Herb Aue was at the infirmary at LZ Bronco.

It was 1130 hours so I told the company to take a lunch break. Joe and I were suffering from severe stomach pains. It was hot as hell and everyone was suffering from the heat, humidity and the tough mountain climb. Joe threw his poncho liner over a bush and crawled into the shade. I sat down and took off my equipment. It was too painful to sit so I got up and paced back and forth. When I stopped pacing, the pain seemed to increase. I didn't know if the pain increased when I stopped walking or if I just noticed the pain more when I stopped. While pacing I noticed that Company B was still in the same location where they had been two hours before. I didn't blame them. I wouldn't want to take my men into the mountain jungles without their field gear.

I finally sat down next to Joe who was still lying in the shade. I was too nauseous to eat. I crawled under part of Joe's poncho liner on the opposite side of the bush. Jimmy and Midge also crawled under poncho liners to get under some shade. I rummaged through my rucksack and took out a can of meatballs and beans. Even though I didn't feel like eating, I knew I had to if I was going to have enough energy to continue the mountain climb after our meal break.

I set the can in the direct sun light to heat it. I lay in the shade on my rucksack with my gear, helmet, and fatigue jacket off. I remained motionless for half an hour to prevent body motion from heating my body. As I lay there, I could feel the streams of sweat trickling down and off my body. *If only there was a slight breeze,* I wished.

After half an hour my stomach pains subsided, and I reached out to get my can of C-ration that was still sitting in the sun. It was so hot I couldn't hold it. I took my note pad out and knocked the can into the shade with it and let the can cool awhile. After another fifteen minutes I opened the can. I could only eat a little of the meatballs and beans. I was still too nauseous to finish the entire meal. I reached into my rucksack and fished out a can of pineapple chunks. I opened it and ate a few. The syrup was too heavy for me and the pineapple chunks were too warm. I discarded the uneaten meat and beans, as well as the rest of the pineapple chunks.

It was approaching 1300 hours. It was an hour and a half since we started our lunch break, and I alerted the platoons that we would be moving out shortly. The men took down their poncho liners, repacked their gear and gathered up all their equipment. When the sun shifted, it exposed my M-16 rifle to the direct sun light and when I tried to pick up my rifle, I burned my hand. I took my neck towel and covered my rifle when I picked it up. After I was able to sling my rifle over my shoulder and put on my helmet, I gave the order to move out.

We started moving up the side of the mountain in twelve columns, side-by-side continuing our search-and-destroy mission. 'Doc' Vandermeer joined us as we moved up the mountain. He had taken his lunch break with the demolition team. Joe got cramps again and moved up the mountain faster then the rest of us. He wanted to get as much of the climb over as quickly as possible so he could sit down and rest again. I also got cramps again.

We soon stopped to rest on the burned out mountain side. Joe sat down, then stood up again. No matter what he did, the pain did not decrease. I dropped my pack, weapon, helmet and took off my fatigue jacket. I stood there on the hot mountainside in my fatigue pants and olive drab T-shirt. There were no trees or shrubs. To escape the sun's rays, I held my neck towel over my head. I was trying to get just a little shade on my head. While walking in circles, I held the towel as high as I could, in case there was a slight breeze. I didn't want the towel to obstruct any breeze that might occur. However, there was no breeze to offer any relief. I didn't try fanning myself. It just took too much energy.

I kept walking around in circles with the towel raised above my head. As I walked, I shifted the towel to compensate for the angle to the sun. I stopped for a moment and gazed down into the valley and watched a shadow from a lone cloud that was edging across the valley floor.

I thought, *God, why doesn't a cloud pass over us?* Then I shouted, "God, where are the clouds?"

Joe was sitting on the ground with no bushes around on which to hang his poncho liner. He asked, "Captain, you've got to send me in. I can't stand this any more."

I looked at the perspiration cutting little trails down his dirty, agonized face. I knew he didn't have heat stroke. I answered, "Neither can most of the other guys, Joe. But, no one is going back unless they have heat stroke or a temperature of at least one-hundred-four."

Joe looked at me with a disappointed, harsh look on his face. I poured some of my precious water on my head to wash away the salt from my face. I tried drinking a little water, but it was luke warm, a nauseating luke warm. When we were resupplied earlier, it had been by the battalion command chopper instead of the normal resupply helicopter, so we didn't get our sodas and beers.

The First Platoon leader called. He reported Spc.4 Jarmus was a heat casualty who needed to be dusted off. I asked what his temperature was. Lt. Hodgkinson replied that he didn't know, because he didn't have a thermometer. I asked if the man was sweating profusely and he responded that he was. I told Hodgkinson I would send my 'Doc' Vandermeer to check him out.

I went over to where Spc.4 Vaughn Vandermeer was sitting and talked to him for a bit before I sent him to the First Platoon. I told him to assess whether the soldier had heat stroke or simply heat-exhaustion like the rest of us. I reminded him that if the soldier was not sweating, then it was heat-stroke and the soldier needed an immediate dust-off. Vaughn acknowledged that he understood.

I got back on the radio with Lt. Hodgkinson to let him know that my 'Doc' was on the way. I instructed the lieutenant to get the man under some shade, have him take off all of his equipment, boots and socks, loosen his belt and pants, and have the men pour water over his body to cool him down. By the time they finished, Vandermeer should be with them.

Soon Spc.4 Vandermeer radioed he had verified that the man didn't have heat stroke and his fever was not at the critical temperature which would have warranted calling for a medical evacuation. He was just suffering from heat exhaustion.

After the break was over and Vandermeer rejoined us, I ordered the company to continue the climb up the mountain on the west side of the valley. After several more hours of climbing and searching, we reached the ridgeline of the mountains that were on the west side of the valley below us. The Weapons Platoon called and reported Spc.4 Mark Ambler was suffering from heat stroke. I sent Vandermeer over to check him out. Ambler was not perspiring, I told Cumbee to call for a dust-off. We secured a landing zone on the ridgeline for the medevac helicopter. Several other men complained of having heat stroke and Vandermeer verified that Spc.4 Andrew Garcia was another heat stroke casualty. They were both dusted-off for treatment at LZ Bronco.

Being dehydrated from not being provided with water by LTC Elliott and Capt. Walters, the hot climate, and the tough climb up the mountainside had cost us a heavy toll. I had the men take up a secure logger position. Then we all tried to get some shade and much needed rest.

Tuesday, 13 May, the sun set at 1906 hours which brought a welcome relief from the relentless heat and humidity. I was enjoying the cooler evening just before twilight, when we observed the fiery trails of enemy rockets coming out of a valley about 5,000 meters away. The rockets were heading towards LZ Bronco. I got out my map and plotted the location of the origin of the rocket launches. I told Midge to call in the coded coordinates to his artillery battalion at LZ Bronco on his artillery net radio.

After we sent the rocket site coordinates in, I watched through my binoculars as a second set of rockets were launched towards LZ Bronco. As the trail of the new rockets traced across the sky I observed the friendly fired artillery strikes from our men at LZ Bronco. Our artillery strikes were hitting in a valley 1,000 meters beyond the target location.

Midge called to correct their target location. He was told the artillery computer tracked the trajectory of the incoming missiles and calculated a different missile launch site than the location we gave them.

I got on the radio and asked, "How in the hell can you guys not believe what we are seeing? You have to move your target area a thousand meters closer to us in order to hit the launch site."

They responded, "No can do. We have to fire where the computer tells us, based on the incoming trajectory calculations. We can't do anything else. Out"

I sat there shaking my head. I wondered what kind of crazy people would give orders to their men not to fire where a forward observer could see the enemy. We went to sleep, wondering why we had so many restrictions on effectively engaging the enemy. LTC Elliott and Capt. Walters wouldn't let us attack the fleeing enemy in the valley, and the artillery wouldn't adjust their fire to hit the enemy that was rocketing their base-camp. Sometimes we seemed to be fighting ourselves more than the enemy.

-   -   -   o   -   -   -

Sergeant Robert (Bob) C. Reed was twenty years old when he was drafted from Lathrup Village, Michigan. Eight months later, Bob was trained and promoted to Sergeant on 17 July 1968. Three months after becoming an Army Sergeant he was sent to join Company D in Vietnam. He was assigned as a rifle squad leader in the Third Platoon.

-   -   -   o   -   -   -

This is a list of those Delta Dog's heroes who were identified in this chapter.

Private First Class John (Jack) Rozow, from South Bend, IN ** Killed in hostile action.
Private First Class Herbert T. Aue, from Lone Pine, CA
Specialist Fourth Class Mark H. Ambler, from Homer, MI
Specialist Fourth Class Andrew Garcia
Specialist Fourth Class Vaughn S. Vander Meer, from Grand Rapids, MI

Grenades made by South Vietnamese prisoners and NVA soldiers.

Chapter Twelve

Lieutenant James G. (Greg) Miller
Sergeant Gerald D. Gerlach
Specialist Fourth Class Millard R. Anderson
Specialist Fourth Class Jimmy D. Cumbee
Specialist Fourth Class Frederick Givan
Specialist Fourth Class Charles Karpiak
Specialist Fourth Class Thomas P. Odea
Specialist Fourth Class David P. Robbins
Specialist Fourth Class Paul J. Spear
Private First Class Paul D. Brophy
Private First Class Denver L. Lewis
Private First Class Raymond Jackson

We started moving before stopping for breakfast. Then I received my orders for the day from LTC Elliott ordering me to move in tactical formation 8,000 meters or five miles north over mountainous terrain. This meant we had to sweep through the jungle. He wanted us to be at our destination by nightfall. Although not impossible, I knew it would be difficult to comply with his order. Moving over thickly vegetated mountains and valleys, while looking for enemy locations, meant we would have to move in four to twelve different parallel paths while we cut our way through the jungle foliage. The trek was going to be hard and slow over a great distance in the hot and humid jungle. I ordered the men to pack-up and move out right away in order to get a good start on our mission. I wanted to cover as much distance as possible before it got unbearably hot.

We moved northwest along the side of the mountain range that skirted the valley to our west. Whenever a platoon found a

377

Delta Dogs moving north through the valley.

stream, I had them radio the rest of the company so we could all get water. Cutting through the vegetation was hard work, but this time we were moving downhill or on level ground most of the morning, making the trek a little easier than the day before. In the afternoon when the temperature soared, we had three more heat-stroke casualties. My artillery RTO Midge Anderson suffered from heat stroke, as well as Spc.4 Michael Jarmus from the First Platoon and Spc.4 William Jasper from the Second Platoon. They were dusted-off.

We continued heading north, and by the time we entered the valley, we were less then halfway to our destination. Battalion flew over and chewed me out for moving into the valley in spite of their orders. I was ordered to move the company back up to the high ground to the east. With the intense heat and the climb, we tired quickly and our body temperatures soared.

When we were halfway towards our objective, we took a break on the ridgeline. One of the new men asked to see me. When he reached my command group's location, we were sitting in a draw just below the ridgeline. We had moved down the side of the mountain a little distance to take advantage of the shade in a gully. The new man said he had heat-stroke and complained his platoon leader wouldn't call a dust-off for him.

I looked at the man and observed he was perspiring. I asked Vandermeer to alcohol wipe his thermometer and shake it down. He did and put it in the new man's mouth. After a minute he took the thermometer out and read it. "One-hundred and two," he said. Then he showed the reading to the new man. The new man smiled. He must have thought the high temperature reading meant he was going to be taken back to the rear.

I asked Vandermeer to wipe the thermometer with alcohol and shake it down again. He did. I had him take my temperature. My reading was 103. Then, I had him take the two RTO's temperatures, and they were 102 or 103. I told the soldier, "We are all suffering from the heat. When you have a temperature of one-hundred-four or more, I'll send you back to the rear."

The man looked at me with disappointment on his face. "Yes, Sir." He returned to his platoon to suffer through the day with the rest of us.

During the break a spider bit me, and the bite area started to swell, causing a sharp pain in my arm. During the next break, Vandermeer put some ointment on it, covered it with a Band-Aid, and then gave me a Valium tablet for the pain. It was all he had for pain. We continued north for another hour and arrived at our destination at about 1800 hours.

A resupply chopper flew out water, C-rations, and supplies for us. By then I was too delirious to know what was going on around me. It seemed as if I was outside my body looking back at myself, instead of experiencing the hard, hot day. It was still bright at 1800 hours. One could see for miles from the ridge we were on. However, to me it appeared as if we were in a London fog. Everything was hazy and was moving in slow motion.

Vandermeer checked me and asked if I wanted to jump on the chopper and return to LZ Bronco. I refused to go back to the rear. In a sense, the spider bite was a blessing. I was feeling no pain and no ill effects from the spider bite. I felt no cramps from the hot march we had just completed, nor from the Gook-sores I had on both arms.

Gook-sores were a result of scratching our forearms when we hit the ground during combat. When the cuts got infected from the polluted streams and rice paddies, they festered and swelled. Most grunts had the raw oozing scabs on their forearms. The wet jungle climate prevented them from healing.

In addition to the Gook-sores, we all had the hard, red, crusty blotches from the heat rashes we developed. These were not the worst effects of jungle warfare. Some men had foot or crotch rot. I changed from one pair of socks to another each day and let my feet air out during the night. I also stayed

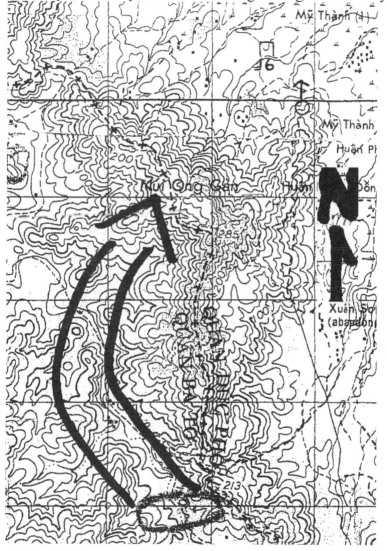

D Company ordered to move up the mountain side.

out of the water as much as I could to prevent crotch rot. I didn't have these two common jungle aliments, and I didn't want to get them. Far more common were cracked lips and cracked, tanned faces, but they were less painful.

The next morning, Friday, 16 May, we were under control of the First Battalion Twentieth Infantry. Our battalion had shifted command control for us the night before so they could concentrate on Company C. Even without their company commander, the seven men killed two days earlier, and the thirty-three wounded men who were no longer with them, battalion thought they were ready for more combat duty. The Company C men felt they weren't strong enough to go back out into the field.

My world was still a fog and I didn't remember much of the details. It appeared that battalion visited the unit and got them to move back out into the field. I was feeling no pain and didn't make much sense out of the communications I had heard between C Company and battalion. When the effect of the Valium finally wore off and I got the whole story. I knew how the Company C men felt.

For breakfast, I tried cookies and applesauce. It didn't turn out to be too appetizing. Even hard cookies, applesauce and a warm soda became loathsome after thirty days of the same breakfast. This day, canned ham and lima beans became a pleasant diversion from my usual breakfast.

I thought maybe having the same breakfast each day provided a comfortable familiarity, an anchor to brace ourselves against the coming day's heat, humidity, lack of water, and the fear of being attacked. It didn't.

After eating we moved out to continue our search and destroy mission. We soon came in contact with an NVA company and engaged them in a firefight. The engagement was not an ambush for either side. We just bumped into each other. Consequently, the enemy fought us only long enough to disengage and high-tail it out of the area before the choppers and jets could catch them out in the open where they had no spider-holes or tunnels to protect them.

During the firefight my wrist was injured, but I didn't let Vandermeer report it to the rear. The wound was not severe, but certainly enough to qualify me for a Purple Heart. After watching men lose feet, legs, and even their lives, I could not, in good conscience, justify a Purple Heart for my wound. I had it bandaged and continued the mission. I figured the men who would want a Purple Heart for a scratch would be those who wanted to get into politics or wanted to make the military their career. I didn't intend to do either, and I didn't want to diminish the importance of the award by receiving one for nothing.

My feelings about the significance of the Purple Heart were shared by others in the company as well. Less than a month later, Joe Dodson was scraped by a piece of shrapnel when an enemy rocket exploded near him. He refused to report it. He just bandaged it and went about his business. For us it was a code of honor that most people would not really understand.

Once the enemy broke contact and pulled out of the area, we searched the vicinity and found thirty-one dead enemy solders. We had suffered three wounded, all by a booby-trap. They were Sgt. Gerald Gerlach from the Second Platoon, Spc.4 Dave Spear and Pfc. Paul Brophy from the Third Platoon. They were medivac'ed to the rear base-camp.

We recovered several documents from the dead NVA soldiers, including a journal one of the men kept. I found it interesting because I was doing the same thing. A copy of the interpreted journal was given to me later. It read as follows:

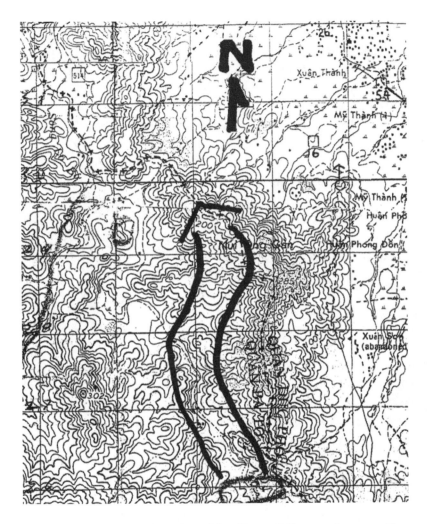

Delta Dogs sweeping the ridgeline while moving north.

"I started infiltrating to South Vietnam on 13 February 1969, with an infiltration battalion. We traveled by train through Ninh Binh Province, North Vietnam, to Vinh City in Nghe An Province, and took another train to Ha Tinh Province

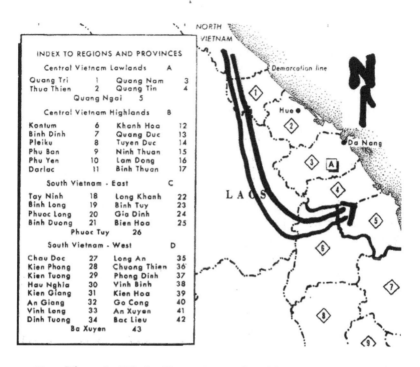

INDEX TO REGIONS AND PROVINCES

Central Vietnam Lowlands   A

Quang Tri	1	Quang Nam	3
Thua Thien	2	Quang Tin	4
		Quang Ngai	5

Central Vietnam Highlands   B

Kontum	6	Khanh Hoa	12
Binh Dinh	7	Quang Duc	13
Pleiku	8	Tuyen Duc	14
Phu Bon	9	Ninh Thuan	15
Phu Yen	10	Lam Dong	16
Darlac	11	Binh Thuan	17

South Vietnam - East   C

Tay Ninh	18	Long Khanh	22
Binh Long	19	Binh Tuy	23
Phuoc Long	20	Gia Dinh	24
Binh Duong	21	Bien Hoa	25
		Phuoc Tuy	26

South Vietnam - West   D

Chau Doc	27	Long An	35
Kien Phong	28	Chuong Thien	36
Kien Tuong	29	Phong Dinh	37
Hau Nghia	30	Vinh Binh	38
Kien Giang	31	Kien Hoa	39
An Giang	32	Go Cong	40
Vinh Long	33	An Xuyen	41
Dinh Tuong	34	Bac Lieu	42
		Ba Xuyen	43

at Ben Thuy in Vinh City. We arrived in Huong Khe District in Ha Tinh Province on 15 February.

The journey resumed on 18 February. We were transported by vehicles to Bo Trach District, Quang Binh Province, where we continued our trip on foot to Vinh Linh District, Quang Tri Providence. We crossed the Ben Hai River on 7 March. On 8 March the rear guard of the unit was hit by enemy aircraft. We entered Laos on 11 March. We crossed Route 9, Pon Po River on 13 March and Nguyen Chi. We crossed Thanh Slope on 14 March. On 24 March the advance guard sustained an air strike. We left Laos for the Western Highlands on 4 April and followed Corridor B 46. We reached Route Station 67, the last station controlled by North Vietnamese Soldiers in District 40, Kontom Providence, South Vietnam on 9 April. We arrived at our staging area which was Liberation Route Station 10 on 17 April after crossing the Rung Que woods.

Our daily rations consisted of only a half a can of rice (0.150 Kgm) and a half can of corn. The infiltration trip was very difficult, tiring and dangerous. Food supplies were scarce. Many a day we had to eat wild banana roots for meals. Members stole from each other. Many of them fell sick from exhaustion and hunger. One of them injured himself to be released from active duty."

This NVA soldier's 200-mile journey took him two months to complete. That was a long and treacherous supply line for the North Vietnamese Army.

-    -   -   o   -   -   -

We Delta Dogs continued north with twelve men fewer than we had when we left Charlie Brown, due to heat-stroke and combat losses. Later, Sgt. Kepler from the Second Platoon had heat stroke and we had to evacuate him also. It was another hot, grueling day, but we continued moving forward. By this time the company strength was down to seventy-five of us conducting the search and destroy mission.

We loggered on a mountain ridge that evening. On Saturday, 17 May, we moved south again. We were transferred back to our own infantry battalion, the Third of the First. We swept south in the hot, tropical heat. The day's sweep was uneventful, and we loggered at 1630 hours for our evening meal.

As we finished supper, my men reported enemy movement in the rice bowl to the north of us. From where we sat, I could see them with my binoculars. They appeared to be North Vietnamese soldiers and were moving in a column, without any signs of weapons. The line of soldiers dressed in North

Vietnamese Army uniforms snaked out of a pass from the west side of the rice bowl. The enemy soldiers followed an irrigation ditch towards the east end of the rice bowl where the village of Xuan Thanh was located.

To be sure that they were not friendly troops, I called battalion and asked if we had any US troops operating in the rice bowl near the coordinates I had coded and sent to them. Battalion reported no US troops were in that area. I asked them to check with the South Vietnamese Liaison Officer to see if any South Vietnamese Army soldiers were operating there. After a short time, they reported back that no South Vietnamese soldiers were operating south of Duc Pho.

The situation was no friendlies in the area; Lt. Faust, my Artillery Forward Observer, was still convalescing from the stomach infection he'd gotten while eating in Thach By; and his RTO Midge was also in the rear area being treated for heat stroke. I switched my radio over to the Artillery Forward Observer radio frequency and requested an artillery strike. I gave the coded coordinates. I pinpointed the location of their exit point at the mountain pass on the west and the coordinates in the east where the lead enemy soldier was at that time. I gave the direction in which they were heading. I informed the radio operator I would give him the word to fire when the last man exited the mountains or when the first man arrived at the village that appeared to be their destination.

The soldier at the other end of the radio rogered my plan. He relayed the information to his fire support coordinator at the base and stayed on the radio with me as we waited for the opportunity to catch as many enemy soldiers in the open as possible. As the lead man approached the village of Xuan Thanh, where Cato had been wounded, I gave the artilleryman the coordinates where I thought he would enter the village. The last man had not exited the mountain range.

The radio operator at the other end informed me no other targets of opportunity for his artillery battalion had been identified, so I might get the entire 105-Howitzer battalion to fire this mission. Then, he later radioed that a 155-Howitzer battery was also available to fire this mission. He said all batteries were preparing to use Fire-cracker rounds.

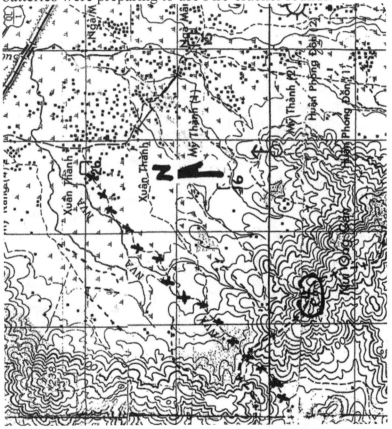

NVA Battalion moving across the rice bowl.

Fire-cracker rounds are artillery projectiles that opened several hundred feet above ground and spewed out hundreds of grenade-size projectiles. When the grenade-size projectiles reached a couple hundred feet from the ground, they exploded. Each explosion peppered the ground below it as if several hundred grenades had exploded over the target's head. The coordinates I gave him covered a rectangle of almost 2,000 meters by 3,000 meters. The artillerymen were about to rain shrapnel down on the two square mile area.

There was no way to tell from where I was, but I thought the enemy in the valley might have been the NVA outfit we fought on 12 May when we lost Rozow. It looked as if the enemy soldiers were heading to the village for a supply run of rice and fish, their main food staple.

When the first man reached the edge of the village, I gave the order to fire. A minute later it looked like strings of fire-crackers exploding over the two-mile area of the rice paddy fields. We didn't hear the explosions in the air of the main projectiles, but we heard the explosions of the thousands of individual projectiles. We saw the massive area of puffs of smoke as the final explosions occurred and the cascade of dust and dirt spewed into the air as the shrapnel peppered the field.

A minute later, a second set of Fire-crackers exploded in unison. Then, a few minutes later a third volley peppered the valley below us. We watched the barrage as if we were witnessing a Fourth of July fireworks show. The large area covered by all the explosions was a spectacular sight, we were spellbound by the massiveness of the artillery strike.

As the sun set, we waited for darkness. Watching the valley floor, I estimated the North Vietnamese soldiers had been about three to five meters apart as they followed each other across the rice paddy field. Their path was about 4,000 meters long, and that meant we must have caught an entire battalion in the artillery barrage. Since the artillery strike did not hit the village, nor was fired into the mountain pass to the west, it appeared that only those who had made it to the village or had not yet left the mountain pass were spared.

We started our movement to another location for our night logger position. I received calls from battalion requesting our coordinates and with that came the usual complaints about being the last company in the brigade to report our night location coordinates.

It seemed no matter how successful we were at engaging the enemy, battalion was only concerned with our following their lock-step orders. The two square mile carnage we had just directed had killed and wounded hundreds of North Vietnamese Army soldiers. We Delta Dogs had killed and wounded more enemy than our entire battalion had killed and wounded in the past three months. These spectacular results were not recognized by our battalion operations center.

The Third Battalion of the First Infantry operations officer, Capt. Walters, and our battalion commander, LTC Elliott, did nothing to celebrate the battalion's most successful enemy engagement. Hundreds of enemy dead and wounded, with no friendly casualties was virtually ignored.

I somewhat expected that Capt. Walters and LTC Elliott would suppress the success of the Delta Dogs enemy engagement. However we grunts had the satisfaction of knowing how successful we were as jungle warriors. The Delta Dogs and the artillery batteries which fired the Fire-cracker barrages, plus the few at our battalion operations center who were on duty at the time knew of our overwhelming success.

That night it was difficult for me to fall asleep. My pride and satisfaction would not stop running around in my head. As for the men, they knew nothing of my on-going battle with battalion regarding the nightly logger report.

The next day was Sunday, 17 May, and I was ordered to move my company north to a blocking position. An intelligence report which battalion had received said a North Vietnamese regiment was moving south and would be passing our assigned blocking position the next day. We were ordered to move north about 10,000 meters (six miles) as quickly as possible so we would be in the blocking position before nightfall.

We didn't have to sweep and look for enemy positions during our move north, so I ordered my men to move in a column formation. Since we were fully supplied with rations and ammunition, the only hazards we had to look for were spike-holes, booby-traps, possible ambush sites and streams to resupply ourselves with water. We moved down the mountain into the valley west of the ridgeline on the side of the rice bowl and up the valley just south of the battlefield where we had been ambushed on 29 March.

It was a grueling and fast march, but it was easier than cutting through the jungle. We arrived at our blocking position well before 1700 hours. I deployed the men along the steep ridge to give us good visibility to the north end of the valley that ran along both sides of us. The vegetation around us provided good cover, so we dug in. Men took turns carrying canteens down the steep slope behind us to get water from a stream in the valley.

We spent the night and the next day in the same location. Normally, I didn't like to eat, sleep, and then eat again in the same place. However, the plus side was not having to move all day and all night. The mission gave us a chance to rest and time to cool off. I was pleased we had no heat casualties or booby-trap injuries from the long move north nor from the restful hours of the blocking mission.

The next day, Tuesday, 20 May, our easy assignment ended. We were ordered to move down into the valley and

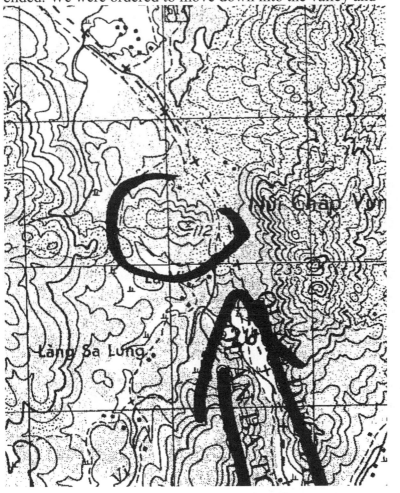

D Company takes a blocking position on the ridgeline.

sweep south. But that too turned out to be another easy day. In the afternoon the Chaplain flew out with our recovered heat casualties and held both a religious service and then a memorial service for Rozow.

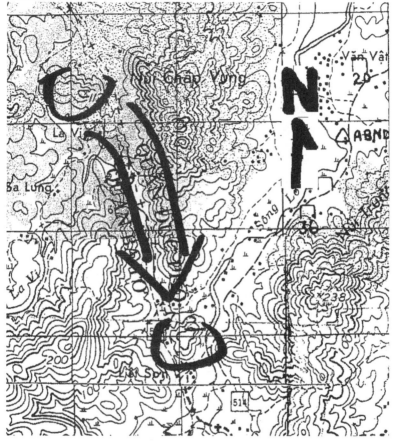

Delta Dogs logger on a hill after memorial services.

I usually didn't attend the Protestant services, but it was different when it was a memorial service for one of our men. Some men were positioned around the riverbed where the services were held to assure we had adequate security.

After the services, the Chaplain was picked up by the chopper, and we stayed in the valley using the stream to bath and shave. Some of the men took a dip in the two-yard wide shallow stream, which ran through the valley. During the rainy season this rocky river bed would be a 30-foot wide raging river. Since this was the dry summer season in this part of Vietnam, the river was shallow and cluttered with boulders, rocks, and vegetation.

After awhile, we moved south a short distance and stopped for the evening meal. When it was dark, we moved to a small hill in the middle of the valley. The rocky, almost empty river bed ran around both sides of the hill we occupied. I didn't send out twiggies, because the wide, rocky river bed didn't provide any cover or concealment. Instead, each platoon sent out a pair of men to the bottom of the hill, a short distance in front of their night position. If an enemy approached our position, the men in the listening posts would warn us before the enemy reached our main location on top of the small hill. The listening posts checked in each hour, just as they would have if they were twiggies. Throughout the night, they depressed their send buttons on their radios to let us know they were awake and everything was all right with a short buzz of static.

As usual, I prepared a shallow depression to roll into if needed. I took off my rucksack and helmet, blew up my air mattress, and I placed my rifle next to the depression and took off my boots. I covered my body with a poncho liner and spread my olive-drab handkerchief over my face to keep the mosquitoes off. I had already applied insect repellent on my neck, hands and face. The rice paddies were a breeding ground for mosquitoes. They took flight at night in search of blood. The poncho liner and handkerchief were added precautions to protect me from the pesky little bloodsuckers that saturated the area. I could hear hordes of mosquitoes buzzing around me as I tried to fall asleep. It was too hot to cover myself with a poncho liner and a handkerchief, but I did as I felt the heat was less an irritant than the mosquitoes.

Around one in the morning, Joe woke me and placed the radio handset next to my ear, without saying a word. I listened to the hushed voice reporting, "They are all around me; they just keep coming."

"Over here too. They are all over the place," another soldier reported, in a low voice.

One whisper after another let those of us who could hear the transmissions know the NVA regiment was passing through our position. Each man in the company was silently awakened, just in case we were discovered and had to fight.

I slipped on my boots, put on my helmet and slid into the slight depression in the ground. *Why in hell didn't I dig a deeper hole?* I listened to the brush and branches rustle on both sides of our location. I could hear the NVA soldiers slip, stumble, and fall on the rocks and boulders in the river bed on both sides of us. Occasionally, I could hear some curse in Vietnamese when they fell and crashed onto the debris in the river bed.

The moon was only twelve-percent illuminated, so it was very dark. The 75 of us tried to breathe quietly and lay still in hopes the NVA soldiers wouldn't realize we were in the valley with them.

We also hoped one of them wouldn't bump into one of us by chance in the dark. Seventy-five against nearly 4,000 was not the kind of match-up we wanted. For the next three hours we heard the enemy infiltrate past our position.

Our combat philosophy was one of overpowering the enemy with firepower superiority. Combat doctrine did not account for our situation. We could handle the known danger which we encountered during a battle, however this time we were facing a much larger enemy force. The possibility of being discovered cloaked us with a fear that completely inundated us that night.

An hour after we heard the last of the NVA soldier pass our position, I called for an artillery strike in the valley south of us. After requesting the artillery barrage, I radioed battalion and reported we had come in contact with a large enemy force to the south of us. We stayed at the ready while the rounds hit the enemy's location. We were ready in case they headed back towards us in order to get out of the impact area.

When the artillery stopped firing, battalion ordered us to sweep north in the valley and perform a search and destroy mission. Apparently battalion must have thought we had bumped into the advanced forces of the NVA regiment and that the main force was moving in the area north of our position.

Battalion didn't ask for my assessment of the situation, and I didn't volunteer it. Moving north was okay with me. I had no confidence in our battalion's leadership. I believed that if we moved south and made contact with the NVA regiment, I would not receive any more support from my battalion commander and operations officer than I had in the other two battles the Delta Company men had fought. I knew exactly what to expect - no water, no ammo, no food, and no sound tactical deployment of additional troops. That scenario was not appealing to me. I now understood why Company B hadn't moved several days earlier. I could also understand why E Troop hadn't swept when ordered to do so. It was also clear why Company C had refused to move when we were shifted to the other infantry battalion. I believe we all felt we would lose men needlessly because of the incompetence of our battalion commander and the operations officer. None of the units were apparently willing to take unnecessary risk with such leadership.

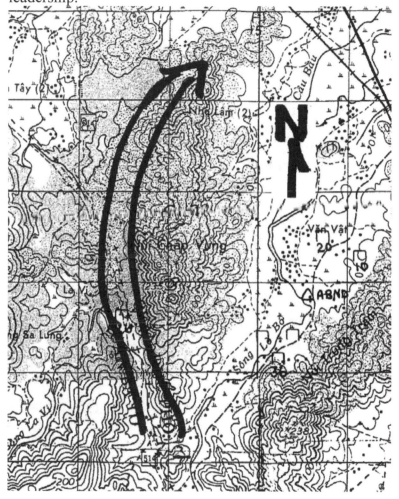

D Company moves north and is resupplied.

I ordered the company to pack their gear, and we moved north in the early morning light for about 500 meters before we stopped for our morning meal. We formed in a tactical logger defensive position to eat. After completing our meal, we spread out and continued sweeping the valley to the north. We completed the sweep around 1500 hours and loggered on the west slope of a low sloping side of a mountain where we were resupplied by a helicopter. Along with the water and rations, three new men came out to join us. They were Pfc.'s Randy Leiphart, Denver Lewis, and Richard Lehman. I assigned them to their platoons, and we settled in to eat an early evening meal, since we had been resupplied in an area, which could be defended easily.

As we were finishing our meal, we received orders to move 2,000 meters south of our position before nightfall. At 1800, an hour before sunset, our lead element bumped into some NVA soldiers who were heading north on the same path we were using. The NVA troops behind their point man spread out and engaged us in a firefight. We dispersed and returned fire.

Since this appeared to be a chance encounter, I was not surprised when they broke off the engagement and retreated. However, I couldn't help wonder if their retreat was a ruse to draw us into an ambush like the one we had encountered on 29 March. I reported the enemy contact to battalion, and they ordered us to pursue the enemy. With a feeling of deja vu, I ordered the company to move very slowly to the south.

As we edged cautiously along the dikes of the muddy rice paddies in the narrow valley, we all kept our eyes peeled to catch sight of anything unusual. The mountains surrounding the valley were covered with trees and thick shrubbery. As we proceeded south I saw one of the new men lying curled up in the corner of the dry rice paddy.

"Soldier, is this your first firefight?" I asked.

He looked up from his fetal position and answered, "Yes, Sir."

"Well, it's over now. Why don't you get up and join us? If you don't, you're going to be left here all by yourself. We're the last of the friendly troops you are going to find in this valley. The only ones behind us are the NVA."

He quickly jumped up, climbed out of the rice paddy and onto the dike. I smiled to myself, realizing the first firefight always seemed to be the scariest. He followed us for a short distance, than I ordered the company to stop and take up defensive positions. The new man joined his platoon.

The war was a kind of coming-out ritual for boys, quickly forging them into men. They learned the concepts of loyalty, discipline, the many survival techniques with enthusiasm, and eventually became military professionals at a young age. Most of all, they learned to care for their fellow infantryman, even to the point of offering up their life in order to save a comrade's life.

It had been over an hour since the firefight. We had only moved 100 meters south, and it was starting to get dark. The moon was up, and we only had 19 percent illumination. The moon was scheduled to set at 2324 hours, which would leave us with a moonless night in about four hours. I ordered the platoon leaders to join me. I didn't want to continue heading towards the enemy during the night and I didn't want to logger here in the valley. It was too close to where we had engaged the enemy. I showed them on the map where I wanted to head up the side of the mountain on our east side. We could then logger on the mountain ridge or continue south on the ridge before loggering for the night, depending on the time it took us to climb the side of the mountain.

As the sun set, we cut our way into the jungle growth, heading up the wall of the mountain to the east of us. In order to move as fast as we could, I told the company to change to a single column formation. In this formation we could rotate the point men frequently to minimize his fatigue from cutting through the dense jungle.

Machete cutting was a skill not easily learned. In Panama I watched a soldier cut himself twice in a row before he even discovered that his machete blade was being deflected to his hand when he tried to cut the resilient and flexible jungle vines.

As we snaked up the side of the steep mountain, it turned darker with each step because the thick canopy shaded what little moonlight there was. Soon it was almost pitch black. I could barely make out the silhouette of the RTO walking in front of me. The 78 men bunched closer to the man in front so as not to get lost in the dark, dense jungle.

The steep ground seemed more like a path once we no longer had the low vegetation. Suddenly we were in a small valley instead of the steep mountain slope pictured on the map.

The man in front of me held his hand out toward me. It hit me in my chest, and I stopped. He took a step forward then reached back for my hand. In the dark he guided my hand until I touched a tripwire strung across the path. He let go and moved a few steps forward. I reached back and touched the chest of the man behind me.

I carefully stepped over the tripwire in the dark. Once on the other side of the wire, I reached back and silently took the hand of the man behind me. I moved his hand down until he could touch the tripwire. I let go of his hand and moved a couple steps up the path. I stood with my rifle ready to fire in case the enemy detected us. While the next man moved over the wire and then cautioned the man behind him, I peered around the path and saw the outline of the tops of foxholes and

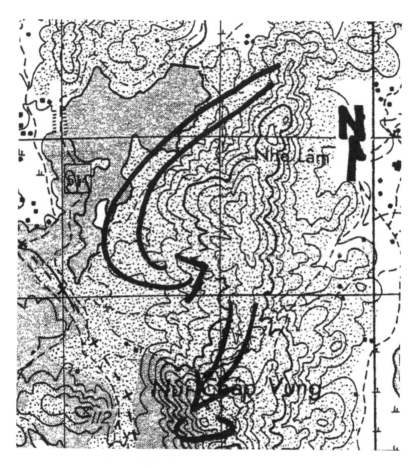

The Delta Dogs move through a NVA base-camp.

bunkers. We each took a couple steps in the dark and waited before stepping forward until we had all crossed the tripwire.

We had stumbled into an enemy base-camp. I didn't know if anyone was home or if they were all out on patrol for the night. To be prudent, all radios were turned off, no one spoke, and we all moved as quietly as we could. Seventy-eight of us stepped over the tripwire successfully and slowly edged our way up the 100-meter long path through the silent, dark enemy base-camp.

I thought of the new men who had just joined the company a few hours earlier. One had appeared to be so frightened when the shooting started earlier. I could only imagine how the not-yet twenty-one year-old-boy we found in the rice paddy earlier must have been feeling stepping over a tripwire and creeping through an enemy base-camp in a pitch black night on his first day in the field as a Delta Dog.

Stepping over the tripwire was not like playing jump rope. It was an ordeal in itself because we had more to worry about than our legs tripping the wire. We had to be sure our baggy pants, rucksack, the machete we all carried on our cartridge belts, and our rifle didn't hit the wire as we balanced ourselves on one foot while doing a high kick to get the other leg over the wire. We did that while being weighed down with all our ammunition and gear.

I was perspiring profusely, not only because of the over one-hundred-degree night, but from the tension generated while tiptoeing through the enemy's position in the darkness.

The move up the mountainside would normally have taken an hour or two at the most. Moving across the tripwire and each man trying to step only in the footprints of the man in front of him took much longer. I was convinced that the enemy was not in the base-camp but they probably left some guards, so we had to move stealthily. Sweat streamed down the grime on my face as we slowly moved through the night.

Some time after midnight we were on the ridgeline above the enemy base-camp. I ordered the company to continue moving south until we were about 1,000 meters away from the hidden valley. The company loggered for the short night's sleep. We were up before morning nautical twilight, when it started to get light. I told the men to eat breakfast in-place, without moving to a different location. I wanted to remain where we had loggered so I would have good visibility of the area surrounding the enemy base-camp.

I waited until I thought all the enemy had returned to their base-camp before reporting to battalion what we had found and requested an air strike.

A couple hours later an air traffic controller flew over us in a small fixed-wing aircraft. I popped smoke to identify our position and gave him the coordinates of the enemy base-camp. I also informed him I would observe the first bomb drop and let him know if they had to adjust the target area. Soon two Marine Phantom II jets from the Marine Air Group 52 stationed at Chu Lai flew over our area. The air traffic controller gave them directions, and the jets made a pass over the hidden valley. Each jet dropped a pair of 250-pound bombs on their second pass. I confirmed they were right on target, so they made another pass and dropped their second load of bombs on the enemy base-camp.

After the jets left the area I realized just how tired I was from the long night's trek and the little sleep I had. In spite of that, I felt pretty good about making it through the enemy base-camp without being detected and then calling in a good air strike.

There never seemed to be much time to rest on one's laurels. We were immediately ordered to move 8,000 meters south (5 miles). After the extra long day before and two stressful nights, another 8,000 meter move through the thick jungle was quite a task for us.

While moving south on Thursday, 22 May, we were faced with another hot, tiring day of cutting our way through the jungle, searching for the enemy, and trying not to succumb to either heat stroke or exhaustion.

We arrived at our new position early and loggered quickly

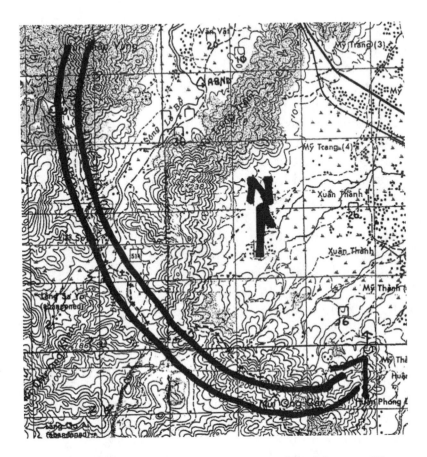

D Company moves 8,000 meters to a blocking position.

in order to get some much needed rest. It had been an extra hot day, and the night didn't cool down much. Just about everyone in the company had trouble sleeping because of the heat, even though we were dog-tired.

The following morning, Friday, 23 May, was as hot as the day before. Three additional men suffered from heatstroke. Pfc. Jerry Musteen from the First Platoon, Pfc. Winston McFarlane from the Second Platoon and another infantryman were medevac'ed to the rear. Later, Spc.4 Harworth Askew had a foot infection. I had the radio operator call for another dust-off so he could be treated. Three men, including Lt. Faust and Midge Anderson who had been in the rear were brought back out to join us.

Since our mission was to maintain a blocking position while stretched out over a 100-meter front, we didn't move Friday. We stayed on the barren ridge with no trees and little shrubbery to provide shade. I wished we had received orders to move somewhere instead of having to stay exposed to the relentless sun.

At 1455 hours, I received orders to move northeast down into the valley's farmland to assist a platoon of Company B and a cavalry platoon of E Troop. The combined infantry and cavalry units were in contact with a larger enemy force. After scurrying down the side of the low mountain, I told my men to top off their canteens with water from the stream we crossed. During the next two hours, we advanced tactically by leaps and bounds for 3,000 meters north.

When we got close to the point of contact, we slowed our advance and started moving by leap-frogging in the empty plowed field. This allowed the stationary men to provide covering fire for the men who were advancing. Near 1800 hours, while still in the open plowed field, we engaged the enemy in the firefight. They were dug in and camouflaged in the hedgerows alongside the large field. We were in the plowed open field when the firing started. We all hit the ground and returned fire while lying flat in the barren field.

We tried to gain fire superiority to keep the enemy from returning fire while the rifle squads leap-frogged each other to move to a more defensible position.

We suffered one casualty during the initial contact. As we fought our way forward, the enemy started firing from a new

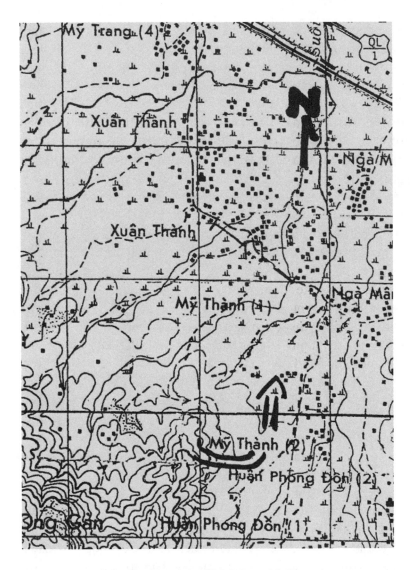

Battleground of 23 May 1969.

location on our left side and we took another casualty. The
two casualties were Spc.4 Frederick Givan who was wounded

in his armpit and Spc.4 David Robbins who was shot in the head. The enemy was now firing at us from both the north and west.

We fought our way forward until we reached some dikes that we could use for cover. We got to the foxhole of one enemy soldier we had killed, and captured his assault rifle. We continued the attack and suffered another casualty. Spc.4 Charles Karpiak, from the Weapons Platoon, was hit in the leg and arm.

Midge Anderson jumped down from the top of the dike and grabbed Karpiak to help him up the four-foot-high vegetation-covered dike wall. Vaughn Vandermeer was on the top of the dike, exposed to the enemy gunfire as he pulled the injured man up.

After getting the man over the dike and out of the line of fire, Vandermeer pulled the wounded man's pants down to look at his leg wound. It was such a bloody and gruesome sight, both Midge and Jimmy Cumbee, my two RTO's, looked away with sickened expressions on their faces. Vandermeer, my medic, quickly bandaged him to slow the bleeding and called for some of the wounded man's buddies to take him to a secured area to the east and south of us so he could be medevac'ed to the rear for treatment.

Pfc. Raymond Jackson was firing at the enemy while still lying in the flat open field. He shouted in pain when he was wounded in the foot. Without a moment's hesitation and with complete disregard for his own safety, Midge once again jumped off the dike into the open field to help Jackson up the steep bank of the dike. Vandermeer and Cumbee exposed themselves to enemy fire as they pulled Jackson up. As Midge was pushing Jackson up, he was hit in the side. Joe and Cumbee jumped down and pushed Midge up as bullets hit all around them. Roger Faust and I faced the enemy gunfire as we grabbed Midge and helped get him out of the flat open farmland and into a safe place behind the dike. Joe, Roger, Jimmy, and I huddled around Midge while Vandermeer was attending Jackson.

The bullet had passed through both his lungs. He couldn't speak, and his lungs quickly filled with his own blood. We could do nothing to save the 19 year-old boy's life. We just held our hands on him to let him know we were there.

I told him, "Midge, we are here with you, buddy."

There was nothing glorious, nothing poetic, and nothing heroic about dying. He only gurgled his blood as he fought to breathe. Within moments of being shot, he was gone.

I knew the kind of man one is could not be concluded until after he has taken his last breath. While becoming a professional soldier, Midge served fearlessly under harsh conditions in close combat with a tenacious enemy. He took his last breath after saving the lives of two men. Midge Anderson was a man who at 19 gave his life for his brethren. To me, he was quite a man and had the courage that true heroes are made of. Midge became a man among men during his short 19 years.

I once heard that drowning was a quick, easy way to die. When I almost drowned as a kid, it wasn't painful. It had just seemed like the lights went out. Then they came back on again when I was resuscitated. The only suffering I felt was after I was revived, and I gagged to clear the water out of my lungs and breathing passages. I've always wanted to believe Midge died quickly and relatively painlessly.

The Weapons Platoon moved the wounded Given, Jackson, Karpiak, and Robbins, along with Midge's body and the body of Spc.4 Thomas Odea, who had also been killed in the battle, to the southeast for evacuation. Meanwhile, Roger, Joe, Jimmy, and I fired our assault rifles into the hedgerow just to the west of us when ever we saw a flash or a puff of smoke from the enemy's rifle fire. I fired more rounds that day than in any battle I had ever fought in my life.

It was 2100 hours and rapidly getting dark when I received orders to consolidate my company with the Company B platoon and the Cavalry platoon for an assault of the enemy's position at the north end of the battlefield. Delta Company moved into the farm field. The two platoons, one from Company B and one from Troop E, infantry and cavalry, joined us. My men flanked the three armored personnel carriers. The battalion chopper was in the air to the rear of us. The artillery forward observer in the chopper was directing artillery strikes beyond the brush barrier to the north, about 500 meters from us.

We started moving towards the enemy's position in the northern hedgerow and the deep irrigation ditch at the north edge of the farm field. The field looked to be about 200 meters wide and over 300 meters long. The land was as flat as a football field, with stubs of already harvested crop evenly dotting the dry ground. The area was lined with hedgerows like the one we had just fought through south of us. The enemy was entrenched within the foliage on both sides. It was a sure bet they also occupied the hedgerow to the north of us that connected the two, which ran on each side of us. The closest hedgerow was no more than 30 meters on the side.

With the armored personnel carriers beside us, I felt like a walking target at the end of the level, flat, open field.

As it approached 2200 hours, we moved forward firing our assault rifles while the personnel carriers fired their 30-caliber and 50-caliber machine-guns. The enemy didn't return any gunfire, and I wondered if they had already withdrawn or were waiting for us to move too far into the killing zone to withdraw.

It was almost completely dark as we moved forward. After moving about 50 meters in the dark, the tracked vehicles stopped and their engines shut down. I called the Cavalry platoon sergeant and asked why their engines stopped.

He said one of his vehicles had broken down, and they couldn't get the engine started.

"We can't leave a single vehicle alone on the battlefield. I have to provide security for the disabled vehicle with the other two tracks," he reported.

I called battalion and let them know what was happening. They informed me the platoon from Company B would stay with the cavalry and provide security for them. Company D was to continue to advance without the other two platoons.

It was nearly 2300 hours and we Delta Dogs had had little sleep three nights in a row. My men and I were physically exhausted and emotionally drained. Continuing in the dark, with the less than a quarter-moon for illumination which would set within an hour, meant our mission would be a slow and difficult ordeal for us.

I gave the order to advance forward, hoping the enemy would think we had stayed with the tracked vehicles. As we moved forward slowly, I doubted the track vehicle couldn't start. I had been a cavalryman for fifteen years, five as a noncommissioned officer and ten as an officer. I knew armored personnel carriers had two engines, one for each set of tracks. If one engine failed, then we would still hear the other one running. When both stopped at the same time, someone had turned their engines off. I could have jumped on the personnel carrier and thrown the ON switch, then pushed the two START switches and started the engines for them. If the battery was low, then I would have jumped up on top of the personnel carrier and pulled the lawnmower-type cord and started the auxiliary engine, which we called 'Little Joe.' Then

'Little Joe' would provide the electricity to start the two vehicle's engines. I could have started the disabled personnel carrier even with dead batteries.

Even though I felt the cavalrymen were faking it, I let it slide. Our mission was to move across an open field and engage the enemy if they were still there. Battalion was using my company like chess pawns, expendable elements. If the NVA soldiers had pulled out, then we were expected to fumble around in the dark and find any dead North Vietnamese soldiers left behind so battalion could get credit for the kills. Neither objective was based on military needs, and the risks far outweighed any tactical value. I knew well if we came under enemy fire, we were on our own. Battalion would not support us. I'm sure the cavalrymen knew it too. Consequently, I felt if the other two platoons could get out of going on such a useless mission, then more power to them. Plus, the large armored vehicles were too big and noisy a target to be near. During the 29 March battle when we were ambushed, we suffered as many causalities during the half-hour we were aboard the armored vehicle carriers as we had received all day long. I felt we could move more stealthily without the rumbling large vehicles giving away our location.

About midnight we heard some brush rustling to the west of us and after calling for artillery illumination, we observed about 50 enemy soldiers withdrawing to the west of us. I ordered the company to turn around so we were facing them. We opened fire on them, and Lt. Faust called in artillery to fire on their position. The battalion chopper was gone. The bunker commandos, which is what we called those who slept in the rear, were already back at Bronco fast asleep. We had no aerial support, which I felt would have been a hindrance more than help for us based on past experiences.

After the engagement, I ordered the platoon leaders to reorganize their men to continue the move north. The platoon leaders reported they couldn't keep their men awake long enough to get them moving again. Lying in the prone position, while engaging the enemy, made it too easy for them to fall asleep when the firing stopped. When they woke one man, he was asleep again by the time they woke the next man. In the meantime, the night shift battalion duty officer and duty NCO were calling me requesting our status and inquiring if we had reached our objective yet.

We had been up for 20 hours and were completely exhausted. It was almost 0200 hours. I stood in the dark, feeling frustrated and overwhelmed. I was losing control of my men due to their exhaustion and I was physically and emotionally drained. One of my best friends, Midge, had been killed. I had spent every waking and sleeping hour next to Midge, Joe, Roger, and Jimmy. I needed sleep. All of us needed sleep. I just wanted to get this mission over. I had hit my limit of endurance, and was at my weakest point.

I reached down towards Joe, who was sitting on the ground. I grabbed his shoulder and looked into his face, illuminated only by the stars. I told him, "Joe, radio the platoon leaders and tell them I am moving to the objective. If they want to join me, then get moving. If they don't, it's okay."

I let go of him, turned north, slung my assault rifle off my shoulder, and held it in front of me at the ready position. I stepped forward into the darkness and slowly moved north.

Joe quickly got on the radio. "Delta One, Two, Three and Four. The old man is moving to the objective by himself. Get your men moving now so we can join him. Out."

Joe nudged Cumbee awake and then Vandermeer. The three of them got up and followed me. The platoon leaders and

Lt. Faust followed my RTO's. The squad leaders followed the platoon leaders. The team leaders followed the rest of us. The riflemen followed, knowing if any men remained they would be alone on the killing field.

Every man followed me. I knew these men, and I knew they would. They always followed me. They were my warriors. I knew they would not fail me, and they knew I would not fail them. We were brothers in arms - - we were combat infantrymen. We were Delta Dogs. Yes, even Willie stood up and walked into the jaws of death with me that dark, hot and scary night.

We moved forward in a battle formation we'd never used before. We were not side-by-side and we were not in a column. I was at the point of a 'V' that was filled in by Delta Dogs. We trudged on as a wedge until I was about 10 feet away from the north hedgerow and irrigation ditch.

I stopped, and fell asleep. I was out before I hit the ground. The clanging of my steel helmet didn't wake me. I slept where I crashed, exhausted. My men dropped one after another. The volume of the radios had already been turned down to prevent the enemy from detecting us. No twiggies were positioned. No listening posts were established. No sleeping in shifts was used. No clicking of a radio send button was performed. No one was watching for the enemy. No one was awake. Worst of all for a cavalryman, I had fallen to sleep with my boots on.

- - - o - - -

THE DELTA DOGS TRUDGED ON
Across the plain of death staggered the seventy.
Half a field, half a field, the grunts trudged on.

"Forward Delta Dogs!" their commander shouted.
"Move to the enemy's position," battalion had said.
The brave and fearless seventy trudged on.

Forward Delta dogs, was there a man not moving?
Not that any knew, even though it was dark that night.
Battalion had blundered, so Delta Dogs would win or die.
Into the plain of death the seventy trudged on.

Enemy trenches on the right, enemy trenches on the left.
Enemy trenches in the front. What waits for each grunt?
Asleep, yet awake, nearing their four in the morning fate.
Boldly the infantrymen moved on, into the jaws of death.
Into the mouth of Hell, the seventy trudged on.

Each rifle at the ready, each weapon held steady.
Determined all the while, while no one else seemed to care.
Moving in the lingering smoke, exhausted but spirit not broke.
If the enemy was there, they would feel their ire.
Even tired from the long fight, they followed their leader.
The brave seventy trudged on.

They dropped one by one, when the killingfield end was found
Asleep before they hit the ground, not hearing the sound.
Reaching their objective, that day's task was complete.
Too tired to care, no time to remove their boots from their
feet.
Death didn't seem worse than the pain they had known,
When they walked to the end of the kill-zone.
The seventy no longer trudged on.

When if ever can their glory fade,
Even though no one else knew?
Honor the price of their suffering and pain,
These Delta Dogs, so heroic these few.
Father, husband, brother or son.
Each one a brave son-of-a-gun.
They did not hesitate, not even one.
These noble Seventy who trudged on.

-   -   -   o   -   -   -

A shocking roar startled me awake. I held my hand over my head to shield my eyes against the hurtful sunlight. I looked around to figure out where the sound was coming from. Whump, whump, whump, the helicopter blades resonated down onto the ground. The noise awakened everybody. Each man rose and looked up, as if we were a field of sunflowers seeking the sun. Cumbee increased the volume on his radio, as the men were looking around, trying to recognize their surroundings.

"Delta Six, this is Hotel Six. Over," the radio blared.

I grabbed the handset and answered, "Hotel Six, this is Delta Six. Over."

"Delta Six, what kind of formation is that? Where is your security? Why haven't you answered any of our calls all night? What are you doing there? Over."

I didn't know which question to answer, so I responded, "This is Delta Six. We reached the objective and found no enemy or enemy dead. Over."

LTC Elliott barked, "This is Hotel Six. Move your unit to . . . . . ," then he transmitted the coded coordinates of the location to which we were to move.

415

"This is Delta six. Wilco. Out," I answered.

I ordered the men to check the irrigation ditch just to be sure what I had reported was accurate. After we moved north of the hedgerow and ditch, we stopped for breakfast. Then, we moved towards the map coordinates given me. We were sweeping and searching as we moved as scrimmagers.

Well, he finally got me at my weakest point. He drove us until he got the results he wanted. I wonder if he intends to ruin my so-called military career like he had threatened. Instead, he could be benevolent, I mused. He could let it slide. I guess I'll have to wait to see what his true nature is. I don't care one way or the other.

On Sunday, 25 May, we swept across the valley while heading to our assigned position. When we arrived at the foot of the hill, we moved into a column formation and climbed to our assembly point. At 1300 hours we were snaking up the hill and into our defensive perimeter. We ate lunch after our perimeter was established.

One of my men spotted an NVA soldier in a ravine about 1,000 meters to the north of us. As I looked through my binoculars I observed a couple of NVA soldiers popping their heads out from behind the brush, which screened them from our view. I directed Lt. Faust to observe their location and call an artillery strike.

I had already notified the battalion operations center that we had arrived at our assigned location. It appeared the battalion commander and his operations officer were out to lunch, in more ways than one. The battalion operations center informed me to stand by for further orders. My battalion radio frequency RTO, Jimmy Cumbee, was standing next to me while I verified the artillery rounds were falling in the correct location. We were standing shoulder-to-shoulder in the hot sun with our helmets off while waiting for the call from battalion.

As we watched, the artillery rounds smashed into the enemy's position. One round resulted in a larger explosion then the rest. It appeared the secondary explosion was from the artillery round hitting an enemy ammunition supply point.

Cumbee uttered, "Sir. I've been hit."

I lowered my binoculars to look at him and saw the half-a-dime size shrapnel fragment sticking out of his forehead. I yelled, "Vandermeer; Cumbee has been hit. Get over here."

I reached into my pocket and pulled out my handkerchief. I dabbed the slow trickle of blood that was edging down Cumbee's forehead.

Vandermeer sat Cumbee down and looked at the small piece of steel sticking out of his forehead. He asked him, "How do you feel?"

Cumbee answered, "I've got a terrible headache, and I can't see well. Everything looks blurry."

I tried to reassure him by saying, "You're a lucky guy, Cumbee. You've got a going-home wound. Just think, Cumbee, you're going home."

Twenty-year-old Spc.4 Jimmy Cumbee forced a smile in response to the idea that he was going home. In less than ten minutes the medevac chopper had landed and flown Cumbee back to LZ Bronco for emergency medical care.

After Cumbee had been evacuated, I got a radio call from battalion. LTC Elliott said, "Delta Six. This is Hotel Six. I am relieving you of your command. Turn your company over to your most senior officer in the field. Board a helicopter I'm sending out for you to return to LZ Bronco. Over."

I answered, "This is Delta Six. Wilco. Out."

My immediate thought was, *All right. I can get a shower and a cold drink.* It had been three weeks since I had a shower and change of clothes. I called 24-year old Lt. Miller and said, "Lieutenant, I am relinquishing my command to you. I am returning to LZ Bronco. You will command Company D until a new company commander is assigned."

I handed him my roster and turned to Joe. "Joe, Lieutenant Miller is now your company commander. You are his RTO."

Joe, Vandermeer, Lt. Miller, and Lt. Faust had expressions of disbelief on their faces. I had not shared with them my ongoing battle with the battalion commander and his operations officer. I turned, grabbed my equipment and moved away from the group. I sat down on my helmet and waited for the battalion chopper.

I thought to myself, *Well, you think you are hurting my career, huh? The joke is on you. The military is not my career. Being assigned as a bunker commando who will have ice-cream, cold milk, and ice-cold sodas and beer available twenty-four hours a day is not punishment. What you are giving me is a gift from Heaven.*

The command and control chopper picked me up and returned me to LZ Bronco. I was sleep deprived, physically exhausted, and thirsty when I reported to the office of LTC Elliott, as instructed. He informed me, "For four hours on 12 May you were not able to get your unit to move. Your failure caused battalion to change our tactics. On 24 May your company received sporadic small arms fire. In spite of my orders to move, you stayed in the same position. That is why I am relieving you of your command. Report to the transit officer's quarters and wait for reassignment."

I saluted him and said, "Thank you, Sir." I believe only a grunt would know the joy of being taken out of harm's way, and assured of the ability to shower, change into clean clothes, to be have access to cold drinks, and to be in an air-conditioned bunker. I was pleased with the change of assignment and couldn't wait to shower and get some sleep.

I became a member of Colonel Treadwell's staff as the Eleventh Light Infantry Brigade's Assistant Intelligence Officer.

Two days after Cumbee was evacuated, he died in the Army hospital. The Georgia boy went home, but not the way we all had hoped he would.

Lt. Miller and his RTO were riding on top of an armored personnel carrier four days after he took command of the company when they both were wounded in action. An NVA self-propelled rocket hit the personnel carrier, causing their wounds. The next day Lt. Miller died in the Chu Lai base-camp hospital. Five days after turning the Delta Dogs over to Lt. Miller, he was dead.

LTC Elliott received his promotion, but it would be his last before he was forced to retire. A year later I got my promotion to Major and six months after being promoted, I retired after twenty-two and a half years of military service. Lt. Faust, Lt. Hodgkinson, Sgt. Zartuche and Spc.4 Dodson all returned home safely to civilian life.

-    -   -   o   -   -   -

This is a list of those Delta Dog's heroes who were identified in this chapter.

Lieutenant James G. Miller, from Newark, OH
* * Killed in hostile action.

Sergeant Gerald D. Gerlach, from Mount Vernon, SD
* * wounded by booby-trap.

Specialist Fourth Class Mark H. Ambler, from Homer, MI

Specialist Fourth Class Millard (Midge) R. Anderson, from Wooster, OH * * killed in hostile action.

Specialist Fourth Class Harworth W. Askew, Elsinore, CA

Specialist Fourth Class Jimmy D. Cumbee, from Twin City, GA * * Killed in hostile action.

Specialist Fourth Class Joe W. Dodson, from Mayfield, KY

Specialist Fourth Class Frederick Givan * * wounded in the arm by enemy gunfire.

Specialist Fourth Class Andrew Garcia

Specialist Fourth Class Charles Karpiak, from Conklin, NY
* * wounded in the arm and leg by enemy gunfire.

Specialist Fourth Class Thomas P. Odea, from Tucker, GA
* * Killed in action.

Specialist Fourth Class David P. Robbins, from Gary, IN
* * wounded by enemy gunfire.

Specialist Fourth Class David J. Spear, from Beaver Creek, OR * * wounded by booby-trap.

Private First Class Paul D. Brophy, from Bordentoen, NJ
* * wounded by booby-trap.

Private First Class Herbert T. Aue, from Lone Pine, CA

Private First Class Denver L. Lewis, from Tulsa, OK * * wounded by enemy gunfire.

Private First Class Raymond Jackson, from Los Angeles, CA
* * wounded by enemy gunfire.

Private First Class Randy L. Leiphart, from Wrightsville, PA

Private First Class Richard G. Lehman, from E. Greenwich, RI

Chapter Thirteen

GOING HOME

When LTC Elliott relieved me of my command, I felt relief. I was free from trudging great distances in the hot, humid, blistering sun. I no longer had to take each step cautiously to avoid spike-pits, spider-holes, bobby-traps, or possible enemy ambush locations. I could remove the clothes I had worn for 24 hours a day for as long as three weeks. I could take a shower for the first time in three weeks. I would now be assigned as a bunker commando, operating in the shade of the bunkers with fans, swamp-coolers or air conditioners keeping me cool. Chairs, tables, and beds were now available to me, plus out-houses.

During my duty shift, I could have ice tea, lemonade, cold sodas, and ice water. At meals I could have all the cool drinks that were available during duty hours, plus ice coffee and cold milk. Instead of hard-tack crackers and jelly or hard cookies and applesauce, I could have a real freshly prepared breakfast. I was now able to sit at a table in the mess hall during my meals. It turned out that it wasn't a mess hall after all; the colonel's mess was more like a fine restaurant or a state-side officer's club where meals were ordered and served by waiters.

Off hours could be spent sleeping in cool bunkers, watching television, playing Ping-Pong, shooting pool, or playing poker, while drinking cold beers or mixed drinks. In addition, during the day or in the evening, I could play oriental chess with my Vietnamese counterparts or occidental chess with the American officers. There were so many simple pleasures that became available to me. As an example, I could use a washcloth for the first time and not have to use the same towel for three to four weeks at a time.

When I was told that I was officially relieved of my duties as an infantry company commander and would be reassigned, I was in a state of euphoria. It was ecstatic. I replied to LTC Elliott with, "Thank you, Sir." It was the only good thing he ever did for me.

After leaving Delta Company and the Third Battalion, First Infantry, I served as the assistant S-2 from June to December 1969 on Colonel Treadwell's Eleventh Light Infantry Brigade staff. While performing my Infantry Company Commander and Brigade Staff duties, I discovered a large number of army officers on the battalion and brigade staffs were jacks-of-all-trades and masters of none. Front line army officers served the first half of their Vietnam tour as an infantry platoon leader or an infantry company commander. Those officers who were not seriously wounded were assigned staff position for the second half of their tour. Lt. Evans was the platoon leader of the Second Infantry Platoon in Delta Company before being assigned as the company administrative officer. Capt. Boots Blanks was the C Company commander before he was assigned as the maintenance officer for the Third Battalion, First Infantry.

When I joined the brigade headquarters staff, I believe I brought with me more experience than any other staff officer there. I had over twenty-years of Army and Army National Guard experience. I had served as part of the occupation forces in Japan in 1950 and as a paratrooper in the Eighty-Second Airborne Division at Fort Bragg, North Carolina in 1954. After attaining the enlisted rank of Sergeant First Class as a tank commander and reconnaissance platoon sergeant, I attended the Army Infantry Officer Candidate School at Fort Benning, Georgia in 1955.

In 1957 I completed the Armor Officer's Basic Course at Fort Knox, Kentucky and in 1965 completed the Armor Officer's Career Course. I also successfully completed the Nuclear Weapons Employment Officer training course. In the California Army National Guard, I had served as a Reconnaissance Platoon Leader, Reconnaissance Troop Executive Officer, and Troop Commander. In the 160th Infantry Brigade, I served as the Headquarters Company Commander, Brigade Assistant Operations Officer (assistant S-3), and the Brigade Chemical Officer.

I joined the First Squadron, Eighteenth Armored Cavalry two years before their call to active duty and I successfully passed two US Army Readiness Training Tests as the Squadron Intelligence Officer (S-2). These readiness tests were conducted in 1966 and 1967 at Fort Irwin, California, the home of the US Army desert training center. After the 1/18 Cavalry's activation into the regular army, as the S-2, I successfully passed the US Army's Readiness Training Test at Fort Lewis, Washington, in 1968.

The squadron's Administrative Officer (S-1), the Operations Officer (S-3) and the Squadron Executive Officer didn't do as well. They were all replaced. The other officers who performed well during the test and I maintained our assignments.

What I brought to the 11th Brigade Intelligence Section in Vietnam was a thorough knowledge of an infantry unit's tactics, an understanding of the enemy's tactics and detailed knowledge for the successful operation of an intelligence section. I reorganized the brigade intelligence section so we could better provide accurate and timely enemy assessments.

In addition to daily overseeing of the brigade intelligence section activities, I had several other interesting duties. One was the responsibility for all the Kit Carson Scouts who were assigned to each infantry company in the brigade.

Another duty I had was performing the task of the liaison officer from the brigade to the US Army Military Intelligence unit stationed at LZ Bronco. I was also the liaison officer between the brigade and the South Vietnamese Army Intelligence Unit stationed in Duc Pho, adjacent to LZ Bronco.

My ability to expertly play both Occidental chess and Oriental chess (called Co Tuong in Vietnam) enhanced our relations with the South Vietnamese soldiers and facilitated the interaction between our two cultures.

My second six-month administrative position as the assistant intelligence officer gave me an opportunity to review the enemy reports that were mentioned in the prior chapters.

During my assignment in the brigade intelligence section, through the analysis of US and Vietnamese intelligence reports, I was able to plot the location of the North Vietnamese Army Division Headquarters that was operating south of LZ Bronco.

I initiated the B-52 bombing of the enemy's division headquarters, but the target area was changed to the center of the valley floor. Some things never changed.

When the bomb assessment infantry companies were heliported into the bombed area, they found that the target of my initial assessment would have been more effective. The enemy division headquarters location was discovered to be on the side of the mountain where I had identified it when requesting the B-52 strike. The enemy had run into the jungle after the bombs were dropped. This turned out to be a lost opportunity to cause heavy damage to the enemy, an opportunity wasted by not bombing the location I had targeted.

As a result of my performance, the brigade commander, who took command after Colonel Treadwell, asked that I extend my tour in Vietnam and remain in his intelligence section when my yearlong tour was over. If I had been a full time army officer, it would have been a good career move to accept his offer, but I was anxious to return to civilian life and I declined his offer. I never regretted that decision.

In spite of all the difficulties we grunts had with the enemy soldiers, with our own command officers, and with the anti-soldiers activities in the United States, I believe we were successful in Vietnam. Over two million North Vietnamese soldiers and two million Viet Cong died in the war compared to just over 58,000 US military members. When the peace accord was signed between the North and South Vietnamese governments, our US forces returned home. The success of the United States effort in Vietnam was a turning point for communism. Because of the success of our commitment in Vietnam, the ASEAN (Association of Southeast Asian Nations) countries of the Philippines, Indonesia, Malaysia, Singapore, and Thailand stayed free. With America's commitment to fight communism, the Indonesians threw the Soviets out in 1966. The fall of South Vietnam happened later when the South Vietnamese military lost their fight with the North Vietnamese communist forces.

-   -   -   o   -   -   -

In 1969 I felt I had been in three concurrent wars. The first, against the Viet Cong and North Vietnamese soldiers. The second war was the combination of Army politics, inadequate command and staff personnel, and officers who put their individual career advancement above the welfare of their men. The third war I faced was the one I came home to. I didn't recognize the extent of the damage the war-of-the-words had done until after my return. The American people had changed and so had the fabric of the nation. No longer were men treated with respect after returning from war. It appeared the enemy had fared much better here in the States than on the battlefield.

The only clothes I had to wear when I arrived at Fort Lewis, Washington, in December were the lightweight summer army uniform I brought back with me from Vietnam. As a result, I wore my summer army-green Class A dress uniform on the trip from Fort Lewis, Washington, to Los Angeles. Traveling in military uniform was not unusual, but for some reason not generally preferred by servicemen. I didn't understand why, but soon found out.

I was proud to wear this great country's army uniform. I had performed my duty unlike many who did everything they could to avoid the draft. Some hid their cowardliness under the ruse of being against the war.

For the commercial flight from the Seattle-Tacoma airport to Los Angeles, I sat in a seat next to the window, wearing my uniform with my paratrooper's badge, Combat Infantryman's Badge, and 14 ribbons on my Captain's uniform jacket. I happened to be seated next to a little, white-haired old woman who at one point asked if I had been in Vietnam. I said yes.

Then, she asked, "Why did you go over there to kill those innocent men, women and children?"

I was shocked at her question. I stared at her in disbelief for a few seconds, and then responded, "Because you and the rest of the people in this country sent me."

After that, I looked out the window for the rest of the flight home. She mumbled something further to me, but I tuned her out and only thought of the joy of spending Christmas with my family. However, I never wore my ribbons in public again, only my combat infantryman's badge and my paratrooper wings. Those who knew what those two badges symbolized, knew where I had been and what I had done to earn them. I was very disappointed in my fellow countrymen. The fifth column was very effective in the United States during the 1960's and 1970's.

By contrast, I was a 22-year-old Private First Class paratrooper from the 82nd Airborne Division when I was returning home in 1954. I was hopping a free military airplane ride from Fort Bragg, North Carolina, to Los Angeles, California. Willing to take any flight available, I caught a flight to Washington, DC where more westbound flights could be caught. A late night hop to Detroit, Michigan was available, so I took it.

My mother and father had divorced in 1940, and then my dad went into the Army. He returned to Detroit, remarried, and I had two half-sisters and a half-brother whom I had never seen. The flight to Detroit gave me the opportunity to visit my father, his second wife and my siblings.

The military transport arrived in Detroit at two in the morning. I needed to get to Nor-Wayne, a community just west of Detroit. I had not been to Detroit since I was eight years old, and I didn't know my way around. At three AM, I was at the bus depot searching for a bus going to Wayne or Nor-Wayne, where my father lived.

I found a bus going to Wayne. I stood there in my paratrooper's Class A brown uniform with my duffel bag on the floor next to the collection box. I wore the uniform because it was required when hitchhiking by air on military aircrafts. My cloth parachute's badge was sewn on my envelope-type army hat, and my shiny silver parachutist's badge was pinned on my chest above my ribbons for Japan Occupation, National Defense, and Good Conduct.

I reached into my pocket for the bus fare and asked the bus driver how much it would cost to get to Nor-Wayne. The driver responded, "Your money isn't any good here."

I was surprised. I didn't understand why my money wasn't good.

"Keep your money in your pocket. You ride free," the gray-haired man said.

I had experienced this friendly, patriotic, warm reception before in several states when on military leave. Due to a private's low pay, I had hitchhiked across the United States from Georgia, North Carolina and several times down the California coast to my home in Los Angeles. Each time, I reveled in the genuine friendliness that Americans had for their servicemen. Back then it was not uncommon. It seemed they knew how little we were paid and how much we were sacrificing. Friendly Americans made me proud to be in the United States Army in those days.

The bus was almost empty at three in the morning and I sat near the front entrance by the driver, so I could ask when to get off.

"Are you from Michigan?" The driver asked.

"No, I'm from Los Angeles. I'm pulling a surprise visit on my dad and family. They've written me and invited me to drop by whenever I was up this way, when I had a chance to catch a flight up here, I took it."

428

"It's too early to wake them up. Why don't you come home with me? I'll have my wife cook us some breakfast. She's up already. After breakfast, around seven or seven thirty, I'll drive you to your dad's house. They should be up by then, don't you think?"

The offer sounded good to me, and I accepted. I didn't know how to get to my dad's house in Nor-Wayne. I figured the bus driver would have better luck at finding the house than I would on foot. After the driver checked in and parked the bus, he drove us to his house in Wayne. His wife was waiting for him with some warm coffee. Breakfast was ready to start. She just fried some extra eggs, ham and potatoes so all three of us could have breakfast together. During the meal, he told his wife I had just flown in from Fort Bragg, North Carolina, and was going to surprise my dad when the sun came up.

We talked about my family, the driver's kids and grandkids and the weather in Michigan compared to sunny California. We didn't talk about the military at all. At six-thirty, I thanked his wife for a great breakfast, and we said good-bye. Then the bus driver drove me to my dad's house. I thanked him as I left his car. He waited at the curb until my stepmother answered the door and gave me a big hug. I turned and waved good-bye to my Good Samaritan, and he returned a wave before he drove off. That is how I was treated as an American soldier in the 1950's.

- - - o - - -

For the reader to better understand how this war-of-words was fought, I will review a little military history. First I would like to point out that in the war-of-words, a key element is to disguise the true reasons for the battle. The communist dictators professed they were for the people instead of being

429

interested only in their own rewards. Supporters of Hitler proclaimed they were for peace. Those who wanted communism to continue oppressing millions of Koreans, Vietnamese and Chinese peasants claimed we should make love, not war. Those who supported the Islamic religious extremists and the subjugation of women proclaimed they wanted our troops brought home, instead of saying they wanted us to give up what progress we had made. They wanted our servicemen, who gave their lives for liberty, to have died for nothing. Double-speak was the main weapon in the fifth columnist's arsenal.

The Fifth Column is the name military historians gave those who either purposely or unintentionally undermined the support of their country's troops in order to help the enemy win the battle. In ancient times, when the armies went to war, they formed for battle in four columns. The first column consisted of the sword and shield bearing recruits and conscripts from the defeated armies. After several battles, those who proved that they were good enough fighters to survive were placed in the second column.

The second column's duty was to kill any in the first column who turned and tried to run, and to fight any enemy who cut their way through the first column. After more battles, the good fighters in the second column were moved back to the third column. The best and most experienced fighters were located in the fourth column.

One might think that the best fighters should be in the first column where they could do the most damage. The reason for having the best fighters in the back rank was to weaken the enemy before they engaged the best fighters. When the enemy had fought their way through each column, stronger fighters met them. By the time they had fought through the third column, the enemy soldiers were truly challenged when they met the strongest, most experienced fighters.

The biggest threat to the fourth set of men was an end-run by the enemy. That maneuver would cause the fourth column to be attacked first. During both World Wars, the traitors, spies, and enemy sympathizers who worked to defeat our army by undermining their support and supply system were called fifth columnists. Their objective was to divide and conquer by attacking the war effort from within the army's home country, stabbing our military in the back.

When I returned from Vietnam I found we veterans were facing the fifth columnists that worked hard to undermine the American public, turning our people against the war and our military personnel.

The fifth columnists were not effective during World War Two. Japanese and Nazi supporters were quickly squelched when Japan bombed Pearl Harbor. Those who said they were for peace or against the war were quickly blacklisted, ostracized, and branded as traitors during WW II.

It was different during the Korean War. Those who pressured our politicians for peace and picketed against the war were very successful in causing the loss of thousands upon thousands of American, South Korean, and allied soldiers lives. Their anti-war campaign resulted in our president guaranteeing England we would not let Chiang Kai-shek invade China if the Chinese army invaded Korea. The Englishman Philby and his buddies leaked this information to the Russians. The Russians gave the guaranty to China, and the Chinese used every fighting force in their country to fight our forces in Korea.

The losses and ordeals our men suffered at 'The Frozen Chosen' in that Korean battle can be directly credited to the

American anti-war effort. Chiang Kai-shek could have walked across China unopposed if our country hadn't held him back.

Holding him back allowed the Chinese to overpower our men in Korea, causing an enormous number of American servicemen's deaths and injuries.

During the Vietnam War, the fifth columnists were very effective once again. They not only pressured our government to stop the South Vietnamese army from marching north to defeat the North Vietnamese communists, they turned the heartland of America against their own servicemen. We told the South Vietnamese people to stand up and fight the communists, and we would stand and fight along side them. When the fight got rough, we ran home and left them alone. The 60's peaceniks in the US caused the expulsion of over five million South Vietnamese, many of who died of exposure and starvation when they were kicked out of their homes and businesses. They were sent out to the countryside to perish.

The Desert Storm War was over so quickly the anti-war people had so little time to prepare. Little anti-military activity was shown in the 1990's quick victory.

Operation Enduring Freedom had little resistance at first. However, once the fifth columnists got organized and mustered resistance in the United States, they found plenty of politicians who would turn against our own fighting men and women in order to gain a few more votes. Fathers and Mothers grabbed the spotlight and protested after their sons, who voluntarily joined the military, were killed in hostile action. They did not ask the hard question, "Why did my son choose to live by the sword and die by the sword?" Instead they asked, why did my elected officials kill my son? The misinformation continued.

-   -   -   o   -   -   -

How effective the fifth-columnists were in 1969 through 1973 may be illustrated by what happened to me and one of my buddies. In December 1969 I flew back to the United States with a fellow Captain whom I had known for fifteen years. We had both served in the reconnaissance squadron and again in the cavalry squadron together. We were both activated with the Burbank, California Army National Guard cavalry squadron and flew to Vietnam together ten months later. We both served in the same sector of Vietnam, but in different units. We returned on the same flight from Vietnam. I visited and saw him a number of times during the first year after our return. He committed suicide just over a year after coming back from Vietnam. His death had quite an impact on me.

-    -   -   o   -   -   -

I'm trying to emphasize what we Vietnam Veterans faced when we returned home. I felt that we were treated very poorly by the public. For me, it started with the little old woman on my flight back home to Los Angeles.

I had worked for a defense company for almost eight years before being called to active duty in 1968. After being gone for almost two years, I was a little behind times at work. In the computer industry in the late sixties, technology changed about every seven months and being gone for almost two years meant I was three technologies behind those who had not been called to active military service.

In California, labor regulations were enacted so a Vietnam veteran could not be terminated for one year after his return. This was enacted to provide a returnee, like myself, an opportunity to catch up with the next technology that was emerging.

I was an electronic test supervisor before shipping out, and my assistant took my place when I left. Upon my return, I was not given my old position. Instead, I was provided a desk away from the testing area, given a non-descriptive task, and within months of my return I was laid off. The war-industry supply company I worked for found a loophole. Because I had been part of management, they said I wasn't protected by the labor regulation.

Sometimes I would wake up in the middle of the night in a cold sweat, not knowing where I was. If a car door slammed or my son knocked something to the floor, I would jump out of bed and press myself to my bedroom floor as tightly as I could, waiting for shrapnel to fly over me. During the day I was edgy due to lack of sleep and the uneasiness, which I felt in a world that was not the same as the one I knew before I went to war. My condition was called Post-traumatic Stress Syndrome, which I didn't know I had at the time. My wife and I had difficulty adjusting to one another and within a short time divorced.

The nervousness due to my Post-Traumatic Stress Syndrome, the loss of my job, a divorce, being insulted by my fellow countrymen and co-workers, and being a bachelor father to my nine-year-old son led me to think I easily could end my misery, as my friend did.

According to the Disabled American Veterans report published in 1980, over 58,000 Vietnam Veterans ended their own lives. More veterans committed suicide after returning home from Vietnam than the near 56,000 who at that time were reported killed in the entire Vietnam War. Both numbers increased after the 1980 numbers were reported.

I now believe the circumstances which prevented me from just giving up was my son living with me, my brother who brought me money and bags of groceries, my neighbors who lent me money and who baby-sat for me when necessary, and the GI Bill that paid me for going back to college. I truly believe those were the rudders, which kept my life heading in the right direction.

-    -   -   o   -   -   -

After 35 years of not watching movies about Vietnam I am finally able to put my war experiences behind me. For the first time I feel free to contact my war buddies and to write to the families of those who have fallen, were wounded, or were emotionally scarred as a result of their Vietnam experience. These memoirs attempt to right the wrong that was done to the Delta Dogs who served their country so bravely as infantrymen in Vietnam. I propose Los Angeles name a building after Raymond Jackson. Boston, name a building after William C. Gould, Junior. Caldwell, Idaho, name a Fourth of July or a Memorial Day parade after James Bradley Claybough. Wooster, Ohio, name a playground or park after Millard 'Midge' Anderson. Philomath and Corvalis, name a gymnasium or library after David Ira Styles. Twin City, Georgia, name a park or playground after Jimmy Cumbee. Alma, Arkansas, could you name a town hall or school auditorium after William Roger Wilson, your only town member to die in the Vietnam war. Tucker, Georgia, please name a bus depot or bridge after Thomas P. Odea. Milwaukee, name an expressway or stadium after Alfredo 'Touce' Zartuche. Sacramento, name a concert hall or hospital building after Robert 'Rocky' Cole. Columbia, Kentucky, Ronnie

Janes' church have a picnic, carnival, or bazaar to honor their preacher as a war hero.

I believe it is time to look in the back of these memoirs and identify the men who came from or moved to your city, town, parish, county, and state. It is time to publicly recognize these brave men for all they suffered for their country. Call and write your city, county, state and federal elected officials and demand these men be honored in some way. Write to your congressman and the US Army and request they re-evaluate the awards that should have been given these brave young men. Midge Anderson, Touce Zartuche, Mike Gould, and many of the other Delta Dogs need to be recognized. If you and I don't do something to recognize these valiant veterans of the Vietnam War, we have lost our honor.

Major George A. Durgin
US Army, Retired
Combat Infantryman
Jungle Warrior
Paratrooper
Cavalryman
Delta Dog

APPENDIX A

GLOSSARY

GLOSSARY

NOTE: A number of definitions were taken from CASSELL'S DICTIONARY OF SLANG, by Jonathon Green, Cassell & Co., London, England, 1998 and BLAKISTON'S GOULD MEDICAL DICTIONARY, McGraw Hill Book Co., New York, 1984.

Artillery Net - The radio frequency that the infantry company's forward observer used to communicate with the supporting artillery unit in the base-camp.

Base-Camp - The home base of solders operating in the boonies.

Battalion Net - The radio frequency that the infantry companies used to communicate with the battalion commander and the battalion operations center located in the base-camp or in the Command & Control helicopter.

Boondocks - Rough country, jungle, isolated or wild region. It means out in the bush, in the field, or anywhere troops operate that is not a fire-base, base-camp, or village that is occupied by civilians, or friendly forces.

Boonies - Another word for the boondocks or outside the villages and base-camps.

Bug-out - To flee an area. To leave stealthily. To leave as quickly as possible.

Charlie - A North Vietnamese soldier or a Viet Cong insurgent.

Chopper - Slick, gun-ship, hook, medevac or Command & Control helicopter.

Chow	-	Food in an institutional setting, such as in an army mess hall.
Chow down	-	A soldier eats quickly in the mess hall or in the field.
Chu Lai	-	The large base-camp for the Americal Division, Marine jets, helicopters, army hospital and many other military units that provided support for the 20,00 soldiers of the Infantry Division.
Company Net	-	The radio frequency that the infantry company's platoons used to communicate with the company commander and with the company orderly room personnel in the base-camp.
Dink	-	A Vietnamese person who has not been identified as an enemy or friendly person. This word was derived from dinky, as the Vietnamese were small in stature compared to the American soldier.
Dust Off	-	Medevac or a medical evacuation by helicopter.
Fire Base	-	The base-camp that provides supporting fires for the soldiers in the field.
Gook	-	The derogatory term for enemy North Vietnamese soldiers or Viet Cong when the type of enemy is not identifiable.
Grunt	-	A combat infantryman. The Vietnam era successor to the Doughboy of WW II.
Heat Exhaustion	-	A heat exposure syndrome characterized by weakness, vertigo, headaches, nausea, and peripheral vascular collapse, usually precipitated by physical exertion in a hot environment.

Heat Stroke	-	A heat exposure syndrome characterized by hyperpyrexia and prostration due to diminution or cessation of sweating, occurring most commonly in persons with underlying disease.
Hook	-	CH47 Chinook Medium Lift Helicopter that can hold about thirty infantrymen.
Hootch	-	Any form of shelter from a peasant's thatched roofed hut, to a bunker, or a building.
Horn	-	Slang for the field radio used to communicate with other soldiers in the field or soldiers in the rear base-camp.
Huey	-	UHID helicopter configured to haul combat soldiers (Slicks), to provide air fire support (Gun Ships), medical evacuation (medevac), or configured for command personnel (Command & Control choppers).
Hump	-	Patrolling by foot with a heavy pack, weapon and supplies.
Kit Carson Scout	-	A former Viet Cong or North Vietnamese soldier who now worked for the South Vietnamese Army as an interpreter for one of the American Army ground forces, such as our infantry company.
Logger	-	A defensive position, much like the wagon trains of the old west. The elements circle up to provide a defensive position for all sides.
LZ	-	Landing Zone. This could also be a rear base with a landing location for helicopters and sometimes fixed-wing aircraft. Could be the landing site for an assault, pick-up, or medical evacuation.

LZ Bronco	-	The one mile diameter base-camp located outside the village Duc Pho, which was the 11th Infantry Brigade's home-base, with landing facilities for both fixed-wing aircraft and helicopters.
Married	-	Married-up, Joined. Joined together.
Mess	-	A meal eaten in the mess hall or in the field.
Mess Kit	-	Mess Gear. Eating utensils, a metal cup and dish to cook and eat food out of.
Mess Hall	-	An army kitchen where food is prepared and eaten.
Muster	-	A military assembly where roll call is taken.
NCO	-	A non-com. A non-commissioned Officer. A rank of corporal or any sergeant rank.
NVA	-	North Vietnamese Army soldiers.
Officer	-	A commissioned officer. A military rank bestowed by an act of congress.
Orderly Room	-	The infantry company's office where the executive officer, first sergeant, and company clerk operate. A desk is available for the company commander when he is in the rear conducting administrative tasks.
Red Ball	-	Highway Number One. The main north-south highway in Vietnam.
Red-leg	-	An artillery soldier. Red is the branch color of the artillery. Blue the infantry. Yellow the cavalry. "She wore a yellow ribbon for her cavalryman."
Roger	-	Rogered or responded affirmatively to receiving a message.
RVN	-	Republic Of South Vietnam soldiers.
RVA	-	Republic Of South Vietnam Army.

RTO	- Radio telephone operator who operates the radio on one of the radio net frequencies, battalion, company, platoon, artillery or medical evacuation.
Saddle Up	- The act of putting on the soldier's helmet and back pack, picking up his weapons, and getting ready to move out on a mission.
Scrimmagers	- Military formation for a miner battle where both sides face each other similar to two football teams before the snap of the ball.
SOI	- Signal Operation Instructions. The secret document that provided the daily challenge and pass-word, plus the daily number-to -letter conversion table for verbally communicating numbers (times and location coordinates).
Sun Stroke	- A form of heat stroke occurring on exposure to the sun, characterized by extreme pyrexia, prostration, convulsion, coma.
Sweep	- Moving forward in an assault formation where the soldiers are side by side to assure the enemy does not infiltrate between the infantry elements.
The World	- Back home in the United States.
Point-man	- The soldier who was the front man or first man in a movement forward. The point-man observes for booby-traps, trip-wires, spike-holes, possible ambush sites, and for signs of enemy soldiers.
Wilco	- Will comply.

APPENDEX B

DELTA DOGS ROSTER

DELTA DOGS ROSTER

Sgt. David E. Curry	
Liberty Lake, WA	Unknown
Sgt. Robert Duesterhoeft	
New Holstein, WI	Redwood City, CA
Sgt. Juan Espinoza	
Unknown	Unknown
Sgt. Gerald D. Gerlach	
Mount Vernon, SD	Horace, ND
Sgt. Lawrence C. Goodrich, II	
Lowell, MA	Unknown
Sgt. Larry E. Kepler	
Bassett, NB	Unknown
Sgt. Michael E. Meier	
Unknown	Loveland, OH
Sgt. Robert C. Reed	
Lathrup Village,MI	Unknown
Sgt. Ronald Scribner	
Unknown	Unknown
Sgt. Charles Shaheen	
Altoona, PA	Unknown
Sgt. David Shea	Richmond, VA
Richmond, VA	
Sgt. William Smallwood	
Wichita, KS	Wichita, KS
Sgt. Omer (Lee) Taylor	
Muncie, IN	Muncie, IN
Sgt. Elwood P. Wampler	
Jonestown, PA	Jonestown, PA
Sgt. John L. Wheelan	
Unknown	Hampton Hill, IL
Sgt. Alfredo R. Zartuche	
Milwaukee, WI	Dalton, WI
Spc-4 Richard Anastasio	

Belmont, MA	Unknown
Spc-4 Mark H. Ambler	
Homer, MI	Tekonsha, MI
Spc-4 Millard R. Anderson	
Wooster, OH	Killed in action.
Spc-4 Harworth W. Askew	
Elsinore, CA	Carson, CA
Spc-4 JamesC. Baillie	
Revere, MA	Unknown
Spc-4 David A. Banks	
Brookfield, MA	Unknown
Spc-4 Dana B. Barnes	
Sebring, OH	Beloit, OH
Spc-4 Michael R. Belardi	
Long Island, NY	Unknown
Spc-4 Larry M. Busbee	
Unknown	San Antonio, TX
Spc-4 George Cato	
Unknown	Unknown
Spc-4 Michael J. Chance	
Ambler, PA	Unknown
Spc-4 Michael D. Chappel	
Unknown	Unknown
Spc-4 Michael Chiprean	
Clearwater, FL	Unknown
Spc-4 Robert O. Cole	
Sacramento, CA	Killed in action.
Spc-4 Gregory Collins	
Levittown, NY	Unknown
Spc-4 Thomas W. Connelly	
St. Petersburg, FL	Unknown
Spc-4 Paul J. Coyne	
Brooklyn, NY	Unknown

Spc-4 Marcelo Cruz	
Tuscon, AZ	Unknown
Spc-4 Jimmy D. Cumbee	
Twin City, GA	Killed in action.
Spc-4 Joe W. Dodson	
Mayfield, KY	Mayfield, KY
Spc-4 William M. Donaldson	
Los Angeles, CA	Compton, CA
Spc-4 James R. Doursisseau	
Palmettl, LA	Omaha, NE
Spc-4 Richard J. Feola	
Rome, NY	Muncie, IN
Spc-4 William Ferrell	
Wylliesburg, VA	Wylliesburg, VA
Spc-4 Michael Flanagan	
Hibbing, MN	Lawrenceville, NJ
Spc-4 Charles R. Freeman	
Atlanta, GA	Unknown
Spc-4 Michael B. Fusillo	
Canastota, NY	Unknown
Spc-4 Andrew Garcia	
Unknown	Unknown
Spc-4 David L. Giles	
St. Paul, MN	Maplewood, MN
Spc-4 Fredrick Givan	
Unknown	Unknown
Spc-4 William C. Gould	
Boston, MA	Killed in action.
Spc-4 Earl Gray, Jr.	
Lemoyen, LA	Unknown
Spc-4 Gordon A. Gray	
Kearns, UT	Unknown

Spc-4 Terry G. Gum
Mount Vernon, MD   Unknown
Spc-4 Ronald W. Isenhour
Fort Myers, FL   St James, FL
Spc-4 Gregory Jackson
Houston, TX   Houston, TX
Spc-4 Ronnie Janes
Columbia, KY   Columbia, KY
Spc-4 Michael S. Jarmus
Englishtown, NJ   Brick, NJ
Spc-4 William N. Jasper
Marthasville, MO   Unknown
Spc-4 Floyd Johnson
New Orleans, LA   Kenner, LA
Spc-4 Steven M. Jones
Fort Wayne, IN   Unknown
Spc-4 Charles Karpiak
Conklin, NY   Unknown
Spc-4 Jerry D. Koontz
Mocksville, NC   Unknown
Spc-4 Roger L. Leath
Galax, VA   Unknown
Spc-4 Daniel A. Lecher
Cascade, WI   Kewaskum, WI
Spc-4 Royce W. Lloyd
Bristol, CT   Bristol, CT
Spc-4 Jesse T. Logan
Birmingham, AL   Unknown
Spc-4 Robert Lombardo
New Haven, CT   North Haven, CT
Spc-4 Willie E. Mathews
Monticello, AR   Monticello, AR

Spc-4 Wayne H. McBurnett
Atlanta, GA   Oliver Springs, TN
Spc-4 James D. McConnell
Rosebush, MI   Rosebush, MI
Spc-4 Steve C. McCoy
Cloverport, KY   Cloverport, KY
Spc-4 Timothy L. Nolan
Unknown   Kansas City, MO
Spc-4 Thomas P. Odea
Tucker, GA   Killed in action.
Spc-4 Daniel S. Payton
Louisville, KY   Unknown
Spc-4 Donald J. Prochaska
David City, NB   David City, NB
Spc-4 William H. Pyatt
Santa Ana, CA   Unknown
Spc-4 William Rawlings
Eunice, NM   Eunice, NM
Spc-4 Jose I. Rivera
New York, NY   Unknown
Spc-4 Juan Resto Rivera
Rio Piedros, Puerto Rico   Unknown
Spc-4 David P. Robbins
Gary, IN   Michigan City, IN
Spc-4 Wesley Rochelle
Bristol, CT   Bristol, CT
Spc-4 Marcos Rodriguez
Bueon 15, Puerto Rico   Unknown
Spc-4 Harvey F. Rosenblum
Bronx, NY   Unknown
Spc-4 Isaiah Saunders, Jr.
St. Mary's County, MD   Unknown

Spc-4 Robert R. Sedimeyer
Redford, MI   Unknown
Spc-4 John P. Sell
Hartford, WI   Hartford, WI
Spc-4 Lee L. Smith
Warsaw, NY   Averill Park, NY
Spc-4 Stephen M. Smith
New Orleans, LA   Unknown
Spc-4 Thomas Smith
Unknown   Nacogdoches, TX
Spc-4 John F. Speachlcy
Pearl River, NY   Unknown
Spc-4 Davc J. Spear
Unknown   Beaver Creek, OR
Spc-4 Reginald E. Steele
Charlotte, NC   Charlotte, NC
Spc-4 Richard Sterling
Plainfield, NJ   Unknown
Spc-4 Jimmy M. Stoner
Tuckerman, AR   Diaz, AR
Spc-4 David I. Styles
Blodgett, OR   Killed in action
Spc-4 Frederick Tafuro
Wantagh, NY   Unknown
Spc-4 Robert J. Taormina
West New York, NJ   Ciffside Park, NJ
Spc-4 Samuel Taylor
Clarksville, TX   Unknown
Spc-4 Diego Tenorio
Unknown   Unknown

Spc-4 Gantt Thomas
Opeloussas, LA   Unknown
Spc-4 Larry L. Thomas
Unknown   Unknown
Spc-4 Michael G. Urell
Unknown   Mill Valley, CA
Spc-4 Vaughn S. Vander Meer
Grand Rapids, MI   Phoenix, AZ
Spc-4 Ramon Vasquez
Puerto Nueno, Puerto Rico   Killed in action.
Spc-4 Christopher Vavak
Robertsville, MO   Deceased.
Spc-4 Frederick A. Verry
Jamestown, NY   Killed in action.
Spc-4 Jerry L. Vickers
Arcadia, CA   Deceased.
Spc-4 David G. Warn
Dairien, WI   Unknown
Spc-4 James A. Warner
Trappe,MD   Unknown
Spc-4 Michael L. Wilkins
Poirtland, OR   Killed in action.
Pfc. William E. Abernathie
Tulsua, OK   Parsons, KS
Pfc. Ronald L. Albert
Joliet, IL   Unknown
Pfc. Edwin C. Allen
Tampa, FL   Unknown
Pfc. Walter F. Attinger
National City, CA   Deceased.
Pfc. Herberet T. Aue
Lone Pine, CA   Unknown

Pfc. Gerald Bloom	
Unknown	Unknown
Pfc. Coker B. Bonaparte	
Darlington, SC	Richmond, VA
Pfc. Andrew L. Bracy	
Mobile, AL	Unknown
Pfc. Roger E. Bradley	
Elkhart, IN	Unknown
Pfc. Paul D. Brophy	
Bordentoen, NJ	Yardley, PA
Pfc. Daniel M. Butler	
Unknown	Unknown
Pfc. Jack Calamia	
Glendale, NY	Unknown
Pfc. Alan J. Cap	
Niagara Falls, NY	Niagara Falls, NY
Pfc. Layfette L. Chiles	
Newark, NJ	Unknown
Pfc. Lloyd L. Chisley	
Monroe, LA	Unknown
Pfc. Bill A. Cousins	
Huntsville, AR	Unknown
Pfc. Samual Cucciniello	
Staten Island, NY	Unknown
Pfc. John D. Davenport	
Dallas, TX	Unknown
Pfc. Charlie R. Dennis	
Abbeville, MS	Unknown
Pfc. William C. Elliott, Jr.	
Baldwin, Long Island, NY	Winchester, OR
Pfc. Billy R. Franks	
Unknown	Unknown

Pfc. Freddie Frederick
Coffeeville, KS   Unknown
Pfc. Gerald L. Gable
Unknown   Unknown
Pfc. Henry M. Green
Leachville, AR   Unknown
Pfc. John M. Gillmore
Unknown   Unknown
Pfc. Steven Hill
Unknown   Unknown
Pfc. James W. Hodge
Unknown   Keyport, NJ
Pfc. Bruce E. Holland
Unknown   Unknown
Pfc. Franklin C. Horlback
Charleston, SC   Unknown
Pfc. Leonard R. Hunter
Columbus, OH   Unknown
Pfc. Raymond Jackson
Los Angeles, CA   Unknown
Pfc. Bernard Kelly
South Orange, NJ   Unknown
Pfc. Richard G. Lehman
East Grenwich, RI   Unknown
Pfc. Randy L. Lephart
Wrightsville, PA   Unknown
Pfc. Denver L. Lewis
Tulsa, OK   Unknown
Pfc. John T. Lynch
Queens, NY   Unknown
Pfc. Vaughn C. McClendon
St. Louis, MO   Unknown

Pfc. Richard McConnell
Marietta, SC   Easley, SC
Pfc. Winston McFarlane
Gamboacz, Panama   Unknown
Pfc. David R. Millard
Princeton, NC   Unknown
Pfc. Robert P. Murphy
Cortland, OH   Ponchatoula, LA
Pfc. Jerry M. Musteen
Springdale, TX   Unknown
Pfc. David C. Nelson
Queens, NY   Unknown
Pfc. Edward L. Newton, Jr.
East Fultonham, OH   Zanesville, OH
Pfc. Carl L. Paradis
Unknown   Unknown
Pfc. William B. Parker
Lorain, OH   Metamora, MI
Pfc. Dale A. Pierce
Unknown   Unknown
Pfc. Moses F. Pigrum
Memphis, TN   Unknown
Pfc. Michael Pridgen
Littleton, NC   Unknown
Pfc. George Schwartz
Unknown   Unknown
Pfc. John E. Ritter
East Boston, MA   Stroudsburg, PA
Pfc. John Rozow
South Bend, IN   Killed in action.
Pfc. James E. Singletary
Bronx, NY   Unknown

Pfc. James A. Skaparas	
Braintree, MA	Unknown
Pfc. Tom Solapari	
Unknown	Unknown
Pfc. Eric C. Sykes	
Dayton, OH	Dayton, OH
Pfc. Gary E. Thompson	
Charlotte, NC	Unknown
Pfc. Ronald Van Duzer	
Wadsworth, OH	Killed in action.
Pfc. John E. Vanhook	
Memphis, TN	Unknown
Pfc. John T. Watkins	
Unknown	Unknown
Pfc. Charles Weaver	
West Springfield, MA	W. Springfield, MA
Pfc. Matthew White, Jr.	
Bane, SC	Unknown
Pfc. Roger Wilson	
Unknown	Unknown
Pfc. William A. Wordell	
Lakesville, MA	Unknown

DISCUSSION TOPICS

1. What would you have said to Midge Anderson when he received his 'Dear John' letter?

2. What would you have said to Midge Anderson when he was drowning in his own blood?

3. Would you have let the prostitutes inside the perimeter on Charlie Brown?

4. What would you have said to the young man who wanted to give his pay and death benefits to a prostitute?

5. Would you have done anything different when no one volunteered to recover Jack Rozow's body in front of the enemy's 60-caliber machinegun?

6. Who was your biggest hero? Your next biggest?

7. Who was your biggest villain? Your next biggest?

8. How would you have felt crossing the inlet from the South China Sea into the Song Tra Cau lake if you were hydrophobic?

9. What scène in the book emotionally moved you the most?

10. If you were the company commander of the Delta Dogs, what is one thing would you have done differently?

MANAGEMENT DISCUSSION TOPICS

1. Because a person is assigned to a leadership job, is that person a leader?

2. Can an organization succeed with poor leadership and good lower level leaders?

3. Is one-way communications an effective leadership tool?

4. If your subordinates believe in your leadership, will these employees stand up when you need them?

5. Could you be misinformed, not informed, and lied to if you are not a trusted leader?

6. Is a person performing the lowest level task sometimes more knowledgeable about that task?

7. Are those whom perform well at lower level good candidates for a promotion?

8. Will those whom you support and promote from within your organization be loyal and support you?

9. Is it true that there are heroes everywhere; they just need the opportunity to show themselves?

10. Are there many lessons which can be learned from an organization unlike yours?

Publisher:

GMD Distribution Co.
4464 La Quinta Place
Oceanside, CA 92057-5055

QUICK ORDER FORM

Please send me the following The Delta Dogs book(s).

Print

Name

Street address   Apt. #

City   State   Zip

BOOK	QUANTITY	COST EACH	TOTAL
PAPERBACK		$14.95	
HARD COVER		$22.95	
		SHIPPING & HANDLING	$4.00
SALES TAX		7.75%	
		TOTAL ENCLOSED	

Mail Quick Order Form, plus check or money order to:

GMD Distribution Co.
4464 La Quinta Place Dept. B
Oceanside, CA92057-5055

Over 1,000 North Vietnamese communist soldiers surrounded 60 American combat infantrymen. Twenty of the 60 U.S. soldiers were killed or wounded that one day. That was one of ten battles the Delta Dogs infantry company fought during the 1969 Tet Offensive in Vietnam. The book **THE DELTA DOGS** is a copy of the infantry company commander's daily journal from the 70 days of the Tet offensive.

The book **TEN DELTA DOGS** covers 10 of the 180 Delta Dogs that at one time or another participated in the 1969 Tet Offensive while in D Company, 1st Battalion, 3rd Infantry, 11th Light Infantry Brigade, 23rd Americal Division. This book covers before they were drafted, basic training, some different experiences during the Tet Offensive, and what it was like for each of these 10 men upon returning home.

Join these young heroes as they are ambushed, who overrun a North Vietnamese prison camp, who cautiously pass through an enemy base-camp in the darkness of the night. Run five miles with them, with 100 pounds on your back in the 120 degree heat in an effort to save other infantrymen's lives. Get a glimpse into the daily ordeals of these young soldiers. This is a war story like no other, a unique love story, and a tragic story of some of your neighbors, your friends and for some your family members. Your eyes will be moistened, your heart will ache, you will be disgusted, and you might even find some humor. But most of all, you may understand why this is the time to honor those who gave so much only to receive so little from their fellow countrymen when they returned home.

They all had different backgrounds, different personalities, and some different experiences after returning from the hot part of the cold war against communism while in Vietnam.

QUICK ORDER FORM

Please send me the following Ten Delta Dogs book(s).

Print

_____

Name

_____

Street address   Apt. #

_____

City   State   Zip

BOOK	QTY	COST EACH	TOTAL
THE DELTA DOGS PAPERBACK		$14.95	
TEN DELTA DOGS PAPERBACK		$14.95	
THE DELTA DOGS HARD COVER		$22.95	
TEN DELTA DOGS HARD COVER		$22.95	
SHIPPING & HANDLING		$4.00 per item	
SALES TAX		7.75%	
TOTAL ENCLOSED			

GMD Distribution Co.
4464 La Quinta Place   Dept. B
Oceanside, CA92057-5055

**Another book written by the author
Major George A. Durgin
US Army, Retired
CQE, CMQ/OE, PE**

- - - o - - -

The Reliability Disc SlideRule Instruction Manual and Reliability Tutorial

The reliability disc can be used to quickly determine one-shot or attribute data reliability by placing the number of failures in the appropriate confidence level window and then reading the reliability aligned with the total tests number.

Variable data or continuous operation Mean Time Between Failures can be determined by placing the number of failures in the appropriate confidence level window and reading the MTBF value aligned with the total tests number. Aligning the MTBF found with the required hours or cycles and reading the reliability value in the reliability window can determine the continuous operation reliability in time or cycles (MCBF).

The Reliability Disc Slide Rule is easy to use and carry to design, test, qualification, validation, and verification activities. The instruction manual gives many worked examples of the above stated and other uses, such as determining sample sizes, additional cycles or time to be run when a failure occurs resulting in addition testing being required, and for standard deviation conversion to percent of the normal distribution.

For thirty years many Aerospace, Military-industrial, Nuclear, and Medical Device Industry companies have used the Reliability Disc Slide Rule successfully. The convenient six-inch disc can be tucked into a day-planner, appointment book, notepad holder, or pocket. The plastic reliability disc can be carried in the Instruction Manual disc pocket or hand carried into board meetings, during compliance visits, into the manufacturing area, in the clean room, and to other meetings.

GMD DISTRIBUTION COMPANY
4464 La Quinta Place
Oceanside, California 92057
(760) 722-3883
gdurginsr@sbcglobal.net

QUICK ORDER FORM

Please send the following Reliability Disc Slide Rule items.

NAME *Print*

ADDRESS   **CITY**

STATE   **ZIP**

ITEM	COST FOR EACH ITEM	QUANTITY	GRAND TOTAL
Disc with Manual	$49.95 Each		
Disc without Manual	$40.00 Each		
Shipping & Handling	$4.00 For Each Item		
SALES TAX	7.75%	——	
	TOTAL ENCLOSED	——	

Mail Quick Order Form, plus check or money order to:

GMD Distribution Co.
4464 La Quinta Place Dept. DD-2
Oceanside, CA92057-5055

Another book written by the author
Major George A. Durgin
US Army, Retired
CQE, CMQ/OE, PE

- - - o - - -

The Reliability Disc SlideRule Instruction Manual and Reliability Tutorial

The reliability disc can be used to quickly determine one-shot or attribute data reliability by placing the number of failures in the appropriate confidence level window and then reading the reliability aligned with the total tests number.

Variable data or continuous operation Mean Time Between Failures can be determined by placing the number of failures in the appropriate confidence level window and reading the MTBF value aligned with the total tests number. Aligning the MTBF found with the required hours or cycles and reading the reliability value in the reliability window can determine the continuous operation reliability in time or cycles (MCBF).

The Reliability Disc Slide Rule is easy to use and carry to design, test, qualification, validation, and verification activities. The instruction manual gives many worked examples of the above stated and other uses, such as determining sample sizes, additional cycles or time to be run when a failure occurs resulting in addition testing being required, and for standard deviation conversion to percent of the normal distribution.

For thirty years many Aerospace, Military-industrial, Nuclear, and Medical Device Industry companies have used the Reliability Disc Slide Rule successfully. The convenient six-inch disc can be tucked into a day-planner, appointment book, notepad holder, or pocket. The plastic reliability disc can be carried in the Instruction Manual disc pocket or hand carried into board meetings, during compliance visits, into the manufacturing area, in the clean room, and to other meetings.

GMD DISTRIBUTION COMPANY
4464 La Quinta Place
Oceanside, California 92057
(760) 722-3883
gdurginsr@sbcglobal.net

QUICK ORDER FORM

Please send the following Reliability Disc Slide Rule items.

NAME *Print*

ADDRESS **CITY**

STATE **ZIP**

ITEM	COST FOR EACH ITEM	QUANTITY	GRAND TOTAL
Disc with Manual	$49.95 Each		
Disc without Manual	$40.00 Each		
Shipping & Handling	$4.00 For Each Item		
SALES TAX	7.75%	——	
	TOTAL ENCLOSED	——	

Mail Quick Order Form, plus check or money order to:

GMD Distribution Co.
4464 La Quinta Place Dept. DD-2
Oceanside, CA 92057-5055

Specialist Fourth Class Marcos Rodriquez from Puerto Rico who lost a leg, with Specialist Fourth Class Michael Jarmus in the center, and on the right, Specialist Fourth Class Ramon Vasquez from Puerto Rico who was killed in action two months later in Vietnam.

THE DELTA DOGS CASUALTIES

Millard "Midge" Anderson   Wooster, Ohio
18 years old   **Killed In Action**
Jim Claybaugh   Caldwell & Boise, Idaho
25 years old   **Killed In Action**
Robert "Rocky" Cole   Sacramento, California
20 years old   **Killed In Action**
Jimmy Cumbee   Twin City & Atlanta, Georgia
20 years old   **Killed In Action**
William "Bo" Gould   Kingston & Boston, Massachusetts
22 years old   **Killed In Action**
James "Greg" Miller   Newark, Ohio
24 years old   **Killed In Action**
Tom O'Dea   Tucker, Georgia
21 years old   **Killed In Action**
John "Jack" Rozow   South Bend, Indiana
20 years old   **Killed In Action**
Dave Styles   Blodgett, Oregon
20 years old   **Killed In Action**
Ron VanDuzer   Wadsworth, Ohio
20 years old   **Killed In Action**
Ramon Vasquez   Puerto Nueno, Puerto Rico
21 years old   **Killed In Action**
Fred Verry   Jamestown, New York
20 years old   **Killed In Action**
Mike Wilkins   Portland, Oregon
22 years old   **Killed In Action**
Bill Wilson   Alma, Arkansas
22 years old   **Killed In Action**

Richard Anastasio   Belmont, Massachusetts
                            Wounded in action
Paul Brophy   Bordentoen, N J & Yardly, PA
20 years old   **Wounded in action**
Dan Butler

                            Wounded in action

George Cato

Wounded in action

Mike Chappel

Wounded in action   Fort Petersburg, Florida

Tom Connelly
21 years old   **Wounded in action**   Liberty Lake, Washington

David Curry
20 years old   **Wounded in action**   Mayfield, Kentucky

Joe Dodson
25 years old   **Wounded in action**   Los Angeles, California

Bill Donaldson
20 years old   **Wounded in action**   Reseda & Oceanside, California

George Durgin
37 years old   **Wounded in action**

Juan Espinoza
21 years old   **Wounded in action**   Wylliesburg, Virginia

Bill Ferrell
20 years old   **Wounded in action**   Coffeeville, Kansas

Freddie Frederick
20 years old   **Wounded in action**

Andy Garcia

Wounded in action   Mount Vernon, South Dakota

Gerald Gerlach
23 years old   **Wounded in action**

John Gilmore

Wounded in action

Fred Given

Wounded in action   Greenback, Tennessee

Guy Gourley   **Wounded in action**

Steve Hill

Wounded in action   Houston, Texas

Greg Jackson   **Wounded in action**   Los Angeles, California

Raymond Jackson
23 years old   **Wounded in action**   English Town & Brick, New Jersey

Mike Jarmus
24 years old   **Wounded in action**

Charley Karpiak
22 years old   **Wounded in action**

Denver Lewis   Tulsa, Oklahoma
19 years old   **Wounded in action**
Bob Lombardo   North Haven, Connecticut
                                    Wounded in action 5 times
Carl Paradis

                                    Wounded in action
Dave Robbins   Gary, Indiana
20 years old   **Wounded in action**
William Rawlings   Eunice, New Mexico
20 years old   **Wounded in action**
Juan Rivera   Rìo Piedros, Puerto Rico
20 years old   **Wounded in action**
Marcos Rodriguez   Bueon 15, Puerto Rico
                                    Wounded in action
Jim Smith

                                    Wounded in action
Tom Smith   Nacogdoches, Texas
                                    Wounded in action
Dave Spear   Beaver Creek, Oregon
24 years old   **Wounded in action**
Eric Sykes   Dayton, Ohio
20 years old   **Wounded in action**

Charley Weaver   West Springfield, Massachutes
21 years old   **Wounded in action**
Roger Wilson

                                    Wounded in action